Thomas Mann's
Doctor Faustus

GUNILLA BERGSTEN

——

Thomas Mann's Doctor Faustus

The Sources and Structure of the Novel

——

TRANSLATED FROM THE GERMAN
BY KRISHNA WINSTON

The University of Chicago Press
CHICAGO AND LONDON

Translated from the German, *Thomas Manns Doktor Faustus:
Untersuchungen zu den Quellen und zur Struktur des Romans*
Published 1963 AB Svenska Bokförlaget, Stockholm C, Sweden

Library of Congress Catalog Card Number: 69-14483

THE UNIVERSITY OF CHICAGO PRESS, CHICAGO 60637
THE UNIVERSITY OF CHICAGO PRESS, LTD., LONDON W.C. 1

Contents

Foreword

Thomas Mann's *Doctor Faustus* is a book of paradoxes, and one of them is that this the most German of all Mann's novels was written in the United States at a time when that country was engaged in war with the writer's own fatherland. At the same time attempting to convince his fellow countrymen of their crime and guilt and to explain to the rest of the world the causes of National Socialism, Mann embarked upon a search for origins that led him deep down into the past of the German people. That the fictional account of this search should attract attention in America is natural, and in H. T. Lowe-Porter's translation *Doctor Faustus* was immediately recognized as one of the greatest novels of our century. To translate a dissertation on the sources and structure of that novel seems, however, a different matter. But that is not a decision for me to criticize. I can only say that I am surprised and happy.

I am particularly happy to have had such an expert translator. Miss Krishna Winston's conscientious work commends itself. In order to demonstrate how closely Mann sometimes copied his sources in *Doctor Faustus*, I have arranged the text of the sources and that of the novel in parallel columns. The already existing translations of the novel and of the sources, which have been used in the present edition, occasionally fail to bring out the verbal correspondence between the German texts used by Mann and his own work. That some of Mann's *Tiefsinnigkeiten* lose their luster when rendered into English is, of course, inevitable.

Since I completed my dissertation in 1963, there have appeared some new material and a number of critical studies relating to *Doctor Faustus*. It has proved impossible, however, to include these new findings in the present book without extensive rewriting, but I wish to draw the reader's attention to the expanded bibliography.

In the preface to the German edition of this book I expressed my gratitude to a number of people, teachers and others, who had forwarded my work by means of help, advice, and encouragement. Here I wish to add one name to that list, the eminent Thomas Mann scholar, Professor Klaus W. Jonas.

G.B.

Uppsala, December 1967

Introduction

Probably few books in world literature have been provided with as much commentary by their authors as Thomas Mann's *Doctor Faustus*. In its thoroughness, Mann's *The Story of a Novel: the Genesis of Doctor Faustus*, composed with the help of diaries and similar documents, may well be unique. It shows us Thomas Mann's intellectual and emotional world at the beginning of the 1940's when *Doctor Faustus* was in the writing, and it sheds light on Mann's work methods and his daily life. We are told what he was reading and what music he listened to, and we gain insight into matters which, although not directly related to the novel, preoccupied Mann during this period — lectures and addresses, travels and social encounters, and the problems with his health that take on a special significance. Mann intended the *Story of a Novel* to furnish an adequate commentary, yet despite all the valuable information it offers, the reader's curiosity is more aroused than satisfied.

When we inquire in what way this detailed record fails us, we soon discover that Mann often uses relatively inessential particulars in order to conceal the more profound import of *Doctor Faustus*.[1] In the course of our study we shall frequently have to draw upon material from sources used but not mentioned by Thomas Mann; in fact, a considerable amount of such material can be traced. But first certain points of the genesis as recorded by Thomas Mann require augmentation. For example, whereas Mann begins his account with the period just prior to the writing of *Doctor Faustus*, it is important for us to see what the previous few years had meant to Mann, how exile had affected him and his work. Mann does mention these matters in *The Story of a Novel*, but he reveals far more in other contexts, and we have in addition the testimony of many persons who were close to him while he was in America.

1. H. Petriconi considers *The Story of a Novel* "a highly literary work" deserving of an interpretation in its own right. See *Das Reich des Untergangs: Bemerkungen über ein mythologisches Thema*, p. 163.

1

Thomas Mann's view of the political and intellectual evolution of Germany is also of central importance for our understanding of the novel. *The Story of a Novel* says almost nothing on this subject, but the newspaper articles and the addresses written before or contemporaneously with the novel bristle with programmatic statements. Mann's letters also contain material that must be taken into consideration. When I wrote this study, only the first volume (1889–1936) was available, but these letters give a good indication of how the ideas later incorporated into *Doctor Faustus* were taking shape.

When on May 23, 1943, a Sunday morning, Thomas Mann began writing his novel *Doctor Faustus,* he had spent a scant two months in preparation.[2] For two years he had been living in the house with a view over the Pacific[3] which he had built outside Los Angeles. Ten years had passed since he had left his home on the banks of the Isar in Munich, the city where he had lived and worked for almost four decades. To understand his state of mind when he began *Doctor Faustus,* we should familiarize ourselves with the changing outward circumstances of Mann's life during these ten years. After leading a dignified and to all appearances untroubled life, Mann was forced at fifty-seven to pull up his roots and start on an uncertain and sometimes unstable existence filled with the refugee's constant worries over passports and residence permits — a provisional existence lived out in hotels and marked by frequent changes of location.[4] In the meantime his native country deprived him of his citizenship, all his property, and his honorary doctorate from the University of Bonn. His works were banned and burned.[5]

Toward the end of the winter of 1933 Mann had left Munich on a lecture tour to Amsterdam, Brussels, and Paris.[6] He was never to see his house again. The last letter before his depar-

2. *The Story of a Novel,* tr. R. and C. Winston, p. 30.

3. Mann to K. Kerényi, *Gespräch in Briefen,* p. 100. Cf. Mann, *Altes und Neues* (hereafter cited as *AN*), p. 687.

4. E.g., *Briefe* 1:329, 356.

5. On December 2, 1936 Mann was deprived of his citizenship. On December 19 his honorary doctorate from Bonn was cancelled; this was the occasion for his famous letter of reply, published along with the University's notification under the title *Ein Briefwechsel* (Zurich, 1937) and in English as *An Exchange of Letters* (New York, 1937). See W. A. Berendsohn, "Thomas Mann und das Dritte Reich," p. 246. Cf. also *Briefe* 1:430–32.

6. *Briefe* 1:326, 517.

ture, on February 11, for the Netherlands, is dated January 21.[7] The next letter preserved is written on March 13 from Arosa, where Mann wished to relax for a few weeks with his family after the tiring lecture tour.[8] Thus, when the National Socialists won the elections and dictatorship was instituted after the Reichstag fire on February 27, Mann was in Switzerland. He decided to remain there, for at home he had become the butt of ugly attacks in the press and on the radio as a result of some ideas, in his recent speech on Wagner,[9] that were distasteful to the new rulers. Among other things, he had protested against the subsuming of Wagner's German patriotism under the new ideology, calling it a gross abuse of "the innocence of the artist."[10]

After a short stay in the South of France, Mann in the fall of 1933 rented a furnished house in Küssnacht, on Lake Zurich, and did not give it up until the summer of 1939.[11] By then he had already made preparations for emigrating to the United States. When he visited the United States in April, 1937, he was received with open arms,[12] but the actual move did not come until a year later, in September, 1938, when he received an appointment from Princeton University.[13] In the summer of 1939 he returned to Europe for a short visit. When the war broke out, he was in Stockholm, and from there, as Viktor Mann reports, he undertook "an adventuresome flight . . . to London and a dangerous crossing to his new country."[14] He remained in Princeton until he moved to California in the early summer of 1941,[15] where he took up permanent residence. The German colony around Los Angeles, in which he lived, included such well-known artists as Franz Werfel, Arnold Schönberg and

7. *Ibid.*, p. 327.

8. *Briefe* 1:328.

9. *Ibid.*, pp. 328, 518. Cf. B. Richter, Thomas Manns *Stellung zu Deutschlands Weg in die Katastrophe*, pp. 15ff.

10. "Sufferings and Greatness of Richard Wagner," *Essays of Three Decades*, p. 346.

11. *Briefe* 1:520. The letters are dated from Arosa, Lugano, and Bandol (Var), reflecting the unsettled life the family led during the spring months of 1933 before it found a temporary summer place in Sanary-sur-Mer. Mann was drawn, however, to return to German-speaking territory (*ibid.*, p. 334).

12. See "Famous German Champion: Dr. and Mrs. Mann Arrive in New York City on April 12," *Life*, April 16, 1937.

13. *Gespräch in Briefen*, p. 80 (letter of July 13, 1938). Cf. Klaus Mann, *The Turning Point: Thirty-Five Years in this Century*, p. 319.

14. Viktor Mann, *Wir waren fünf: Bildnis der Familie Mann*, p. 567.

15. *Gespräch in Briefen*, p. 100 (letter of September 7, 1941).

Bruno Walter. These moves were accompanied by two changes in citizenship; after being stateless for a time, Mann received Czechoslovakian citizenship,[16] which he exchanged, on June 23, 1944 for American citizenship.[17]

That Mann was able, at fifty-seven, to bear the difficulties of travel, of repeated moves, and of the whole emotional upheaval after 1933 must be credited largely to the fact that he persistently went on writing. Even after he had been thrust out of his accustomed Munich milieu, the *Joseph* novels lent an inner continuity to his externally fragmented life; the legendary atmosphere of the world of the Old Testament offered him a refuge from the tumultuous events of the present. Mann worked on the great tetralogy — with several rather long interruptions — from 1926 to 1943. The novel *The Beloved Returns*, finished in 1939 in Princeton, formed a sort of intermezzo.[18] Mann himself often voiced his gratitude to the *Joseph* novels for sustaining him during these trying years.[19] But by the spring of 1943 the external conditions of Mann's existence were fairly settled; he had had a home of his own again for some time. However, the inner continuity provided by the *Joseph* novels was now gone, and with it a significant link to the old days in Munich. Mann now had a strong sense of that restlessness and uneasiness that affect many artists when they have finished one work and not yet embarked upon a new one. Mann suffered the more because the precarious state of his health gave him reason to wonder whether, at sixty-eight, he still had the vital energy to begin something new. Mann was also deeply depressed by the grim developments in Germany.[20]. But exile, illness, and advanced age could not break his will to live and his creative power. He drew strength from the conviction that he had a mission: to warn and exhort his misguided people and to argue the case of the "good" Germany before the American people. Nonetheless, his firmness in political matters could not eliminate his painful inner conflict.

16. *Briefe* 1:430.
17. S. J. Kunitz, *Twentieth Century Authors*, First Supplement, p. 637.
18. *AN*, p. 684.
19. See Mann's introduction to *Joseph and his Brothers*, and the letter to Rudolf Kayser, November 1, 1933: "Burying ourselves in an innocent and serene creation of the spirit is the only thing that can help us over all the horror." (*Briefe* 1:336)
20. See *Story of a Novel*, e.g., p. 23. Cf. letter to Erika Mann, December 23, 1926: "I am very glad I am writing again. I really only feel like myself and know something about myself when I am doing something. The intervals are gruesome" (*Briefe* 1:261).

In his relation to Germany, Mann was torn by irreconcilable emotions. With all his soul he hated and despised the Germany which had forced him to flee, which banned his works and daily shocked and terrified the world with its atrocities. In the radio addresses to Germany which Mann gave from 1940 on, the "letters into the night," [21] he does not hesitate to bring out the strongest invectives in his arsenal. He characterizes the Hitler regime as a "scourge of God," [22] an "infernal evil," as "downright diabolical." [23] He openly expresses his resentment that the National Socialist regime has deprived him of his German citizenship and renamed the family house in Lübeck, the "Buddenbrook House," which represented for Mann the tradition in which his work was rooted; it was now called the "Wullenweber House." [24] Mann's second home, the villa on the Isar, before being destroyed in the summer of 1944, was turned into a home for women who were expected to produce children for the Führer.[25]

By contrast, America, for Thomas Mann, was a haven of freedom, democracy, and tolerance. There he had finally found a refuge and a new home under the blue skies of California. Many of Mann's statements reveal that he greatly appreciated and admired the country which provided him with a home and a sense of well-being.[26]

Yet his situation was by no means easy or unambiguous. Again and again in this period Mann gives vent to feelings of alienation. The country which had given asylum to him and to his fellow countrymen could never truly become his own. While he hurled verbal thunderbolts against the Germany which had become "completely foreign" to him,[27] while his family began to take root in the new soil — three of his children were fighting on the American side — he still felt himself bound heart and soul to another Germany, the one that had formed

21. "Warum ich nicht nach Deutschland zurückgehe," p. 359.
22. *Listen, Germany!* (*Deutsche Hörer!*), p. 68.
23. *Deutsche Hörer! 55 Radiosendungen nach Deutschland*, p. 47.
24. *Listen, Germany!* p. 86.
25. See Erika Mann, "Letter to My Father," *The Stature of Thomas Mann*, ed. C. Neider, p. 57. Cf. V. Mann, *Wir waren fünf*, p. 568.
26. E.g., *Gespräch in Briefen*, pp. 81, 83, 90–91; Erika & Klaus Mann, *Escape to Life*, p. 89. The speech delivered by Mann on his American tour in the winter of 1937–38, "The Coming Victory of Democracy" (see Mann, *Order of the Day*), contains several passages showing that he considered America the homeland of democracy.
27. "Frankfurter Ansprache im Goethejahr" (1949), *AN*, p. 416. This rather exaggerated statement is of a rather late date, but earlier ones indicate that the feeling had been present. See *Briefe* 1:357.

the basis of his entire earlier life and of his cultural tradition.[28] He could never be anything more than a guest in America, for this young country would never comprehend a spokesman of the old Europe. Despite his words of praise for America, he felt repelled by "a certain primitiveness, lack of sensibility, simplicity,"[29] and he confessed that he feared having to be buried in American soil.[30]

It involves great physical and mental strain for someone rather advanced in years to establish a new mode of existence. To a person of Mann's pedantic habits and highly developed sense of tradition, such a radical change of milieu must have been almost shattering. We have numerous descriptions of his absolutely regular work pattern, of his study, the "magician's" workshop, which was forbidden territory during the earlier part of the day but was open to the family and friends in the evening, when they were allowed to hear the results of the morning's labors. Mann's children have given lively accounts of this attractive room. His personality was reflected in the rigid orderliness of the desk, in the cherished objects, some exotic, some less so, in the books that filled the shelves and were stacked on the chairs and tables, in the red velvet carpet and the subtle scent of cigar smoke and eau de cologne.[31] These surroundings were the prerequisites for Mann's creative work, and all during the years of turmoil he tried to reproduce them as faithfully as possible.[32]

Far removed from his home, Mann felt a deep inner bond with the German cultural tradition, a bond which neither war nor exile had been able to destroy. We see this in the words he wrote shortly after the end of the war, when it seemed possible to return to Germany:

> But once I am back, I have a feeling that anxiety and alienation, those products of a mere twelve years, will not be able to resist a power of attraction which has older memories, thousand-year memories, on its side.[33]

Mann's vivid sense that he was the representative of an old cultural heritage intensified as he came to feel that he was

28. *AN*, p. 417.
29. *Gespräch in Briefen*, p. 90–91 (letter of August 2, 1939).
30. *Letters to Paul Amann*, p. 121 (letter of June 3, 1951).
31. See Erika Mann, "Letter to My Father," p. 55; E. & K. Mann, "Portrait of our Father," p. 59; Monika Mann, *Vergangenes und Gegenwärtiges: Erinnerungen*, p. 40.
32. See *Gespräch in Briefen*, p. 81 (letter of September 9, 1938).
33. "Warum ich nicht nach Deutschland zurückgehe," p. 365.

living in a land without tradition and without history. Lübeck remained his spiritual background, to paraphrase one critic.[34] Only when we know this background does Mann's classic statement upon moving to America fully make sense: "Where *I* am, there is German culture." [35] Many of his fellow refugees recall that Mann's house in Los Angeles was a center of emotional strength and a meeting place for the exiled German artists.[36] And Mann's preeminence was not restricted to the artistic and intellectual spheres. His personality was so authoritative and "representative" that at the beginning of the 1940's certain circles conceived of making him the head of a German government in exile, a position which, however, he declined.[37]

While Mann was helping construct a little Germany in America, he also proclaimed his solidarity with the suffering German people. It would be an exaggeration to suggest that he felt guilty for having escaped the immediate horrors of war; but certainly he tried to demonstrate that the sufferings of exile were equal to those of war. Although he admits in his writings that the Germans who stayed at home had to suffer things he had avoided, he adds: "but you never knew the coronary spasms of exile, the uprooting, the nervous shocks of homelessness." [38] What made exile so difficult for Thomas Mann and at the same time gave him natural precedence among the other emi-

34. R. Schneider, "Kurzer Nachruf auf Thomas Mann," p. 527.
35. Heinrich Mann, *Ein Zeitalter wird besichtigt*, p. 208. In a letter to René Schickele dated April 2, 1934, Mann writes that he feels himself a stranger in the new world dominated by National Socialism. "We are aliens in it," he says, "and ultimately can do nothing but resign ourselves. I at any rate have long since begun to regard myself as historical, a leftover from a different cultural era, which I as an individual will carry on to its end, although in reality it is dead and buried" (*Briefe* 1:357). Mann frequently expresses his conviction that he is a typical representative of Germany. Shortly after the uproar occasioned by his Wagner lecture in 1933 he writes, "I am much too good a German, far too closely linked with the cultural traditions and the language of my country for the thought of an exile lasting years, if not a lifetime, not to have a grave, a fateful significance to me" (*Briefe* 1:329). In a letter dated December, 1933 he writes, "At bottom I am aware that my books are not written for Prague and New York but for Germans" (*Briefe* 1:340).
36. See H. Kesten, "Words and Deeds," *The Stature of Thomas Mann*, p. 30: "In exile he performs the functions of a German shepherd or an emigrated German Pope." See also F. Kaufman, "An Address," *ibid.*, p. 52; D. Thompson, "To Thomas Mann," *ibid.*, p. 101; and F. Gumpert, "Für Thomas Mann," pp. 137–38.
37. *Story of a Novel*, pp. 59–60.
38. "Warum ich nicht nach Deutschland zurückgehe," p. 359. According to Monika Mann, *Vergangenes und Gegenwärtiges*, p. 88, Mann experienced the "loss of his homeland as his own doom."

grés was his relation to the German language. As a master of that language he soon became the spokesman for the German intellectual world in America, but at the same time he felt he was working in a vacuum. He himself never became fluent in English,[39] but around him grandchildren were growing up with English as their mother tongue. He was out of touch with the people that understood his work, and the American public, for all its goodwill and openmindedness, could never really understand Mann's books on their own terms.[40]

Mann was not alone in this difficult situation. Several of the refugees have described the sense of paralysis that overtook German writers when they were robbed of the public which alone made their work meaningful, and were forced to live and work in an unfamiliar part of the world with an unfamiliar language. Hans Mayer offers an excellent summary of the difficulties they encountered:

Many of them experienced a homelessless which was bound to affect them more deeply than any other emigrés. German dramatists without the German theater? The poets . . . writing German poems in the midst of a people that understood only the language of Baudelaire or Shakespeare? The literature of the emigrés was destined only to be inadequately translated or to be pushed into a drawer for the future. Most German literature was now without a public; the literature of the homeless became a literature without a home.[41]

This exceptional situation of the writers and poets becomes more striking when one compares it with the situation of other German artists in exile. Bruno Walter, who was Mann's friend and neighbor in Munich and, like Mann, spent the war years in America, explains in his memoirs that the move did not cause him any hardship for the reason that, in contrast to the writers and actors, he could speak his own language, music, anywhere.[42]

The language problem of the emigré writers was not, however, entirely to their disadvantage. Mann speaks, for instance,

39. See M. Childs, "Thomas Mann, Germany's Foremost Literary Exile Speaks Now for Freedom and Democracy in America," *Life,* April 17, 1939, and K. Oliver, "Two Unpublished Letters of TM," *Monatshefte,* 51 (1959): 325.

40. E. Koch-Emmery, "Thomas Mann in English Translation," pp. 275 ff. demonstrates by comparing original passages with their English translations that Mann's unique qualities as an artist suffer greatly in the process of translation.

41. S. Hermlin and H. Mayer, *Ansichten über einige neue Schriftsteller und Bücher,* p. 22.

42. B. Walter, *Theme and Variations: An Autobiography,* p. 341.

of the "active fidelity to the German language, that true homeland which can never be lost, which I took with me into exile and from which no despot can expel me. It has never entered my mind to emigrate as a writer."[43] Aware that he was too old to change his language, Mann deepened the Germanic qualities of his language more than ever[44] — this was a sort of protest against his banishment. For *Doctor Faustus* he drew on the old German chapbooks and Luther's pithy language. He could claim with justified pride that he had enriched the German language.[45] In this way he transformed the difficulties into an asset, and the only major work that he wrote entirely outside of Germany proved to be the most German of all.

43. *AN*, p. 417.

44. See Mann's statement about the Joseph novels in a letter written in 1936: "The whole, once done, will at least be a memorable curiosity, if nothing more — for one thing, because it is astonishing that anything of the sort could have been carried out in these times, but also because a so characteristically and incomparably German work had to be written in exile" (*Briefe* 1:427).

45. "I shall never cease to consider myself a German writer, and even during the years when my books had to struggle along in English, I remained true to the German language, not simply because I was too old to adjust to a new language but because I was also aware that my work occupies a modest place of its own in the history of the German language" ("Warum ich nicht nach Deutschland zurückgehe," p. 363). See L. Feuchtwanger, "Thomas Mann im Exil," pp. 139–40.

1

The Sources for Doctor Faustus

THE MONTAGE TECHNIQUE

When Mann began writing *Doctor Faustus* in May, 1943, he had already collected a considerable amount of material, which he describes in *The Story of a Novel* as follows:

A sizable pile of notes had accumulated, testifying to the complexity of the plan. I found I had some two hundred half-quarto sheets: a wild medley of disordered, boxed-in notes from many fields — linguistic, geographic, politico-social, theological, medical, biological, historical and musical.[1]

Unfortunately, I have not had access to these papers, if indeed they still exist in their original form. Speculation cannot fully establish the contents of these valuable papers, but there are certain clues which will enable us to reconstruct roughly what the "pile" contained.

Several avenues of approach are open to us. We can, for example, study the specialized literature in the fields suggested by the book titles Mann mentions in *The Story of a Novel*; we can examine how and to what extent Mann used these works in *Doctor Faustus*. Mann scholars have taken this course and found it helpful, but so far no one has undertaken an exhaustive and methodical survey of the available material. I was fortunate in having access to Thomas Mann's own library, now at the Thomas Mann Archives in Zurich.[2] Many of the books named in *The Story of a Novel* are shelved there, and they often contain significant underlinings or notes in the margin which may suggest, or confirm, their use in *Doctor Faustus*. As a matter of fact, one soon discovers that the novel contains many allusions or word-for-word quotations from these books.

But the "sizable pile" must have contained much more than

1. *The Story of a Novel*, p. 27.
2. The Archives, inaugurated in February, 1961, are administered by the Swiss Federal Institute of Technology in Zurich. A precise description can be found in W. A. Berendsohn's article "Thomas Mann's Hinterlassenschaft," pp. 215 ff.

Mann's excerpts from his reading. It probably included some of the letters, notes, newspaper clippings, and other jottings which were given to the Archives by Mann's heirs and have not yet been sorted or catalogued. The available folder of papers relevant to *Doctor Faustus* contains a great deal of material which no scholar could have arrived at by study of the novel alone; some of it gives us quite a new perspective on the content and structure of the novel.

Thus the references in *The Story of a Novel* and the accessible notes and excerpts provide some essential clues to Mann's method of work. But the guidelines set by Mann himself are often misleading or incomplete. To fill the gaps in the list of sources in *The Story of a Novel* and other documents, one must have a sound memory and simple good luck. The secondary literature on *Doctor Faustus* gives ample evidence that readers often stumble upon interesting "finds" in books that seem totally irrelevant to the novel. A sentence here and there strikes one as familiar, and closer investigation turns up yet another literal quotation in *Doctor Faustus*. Quite a few of my own contributions on Mann's sources were discovered in just this way, and considering the length and richness of the novel, it is probable that many additions are still to be made. Certainly much new material will come to light when Mann's diaries are released for study. They are under seal at the Zurich Archives until twenty years after Mann's death.

It is well-nigh impossible to give a comprehensive survey of the work already done on the sources of *Doctor Faustus*. But the actual relationship of *Doctor Faustus* to its sources has hardly been discussed; most scholars content themselves with passing remarks on the subject. Many of the critics' observations are of such a general nature that they turn up in almost every analysis of *Doctor Faustus*. As my footnotes will indicate, certain scholars deserve particular attention for their general findings. Among them are Hans Mayer, whose *Thomas Mann, Werk und Entwicklung* (1960) lays the foundation for any analysis of *Doctor Faustus*, and Jonas Lesser with his book *Thomas Mann in der Epoche seiner Vollendung* (1952). Two unpublished dissertations, by Karl Heim and Hans Olschewski, have much to offer.

It is not surprising that most scholars have taken over the term Mann himself uses for his particular method of utilizing

11

source materials: "montage technique." In *The Story of a Novel* he discusses this method as something new in his literary practice.[3] After dealing with the large body of source material, I shall examine the function of the montage technique. But first it is necessary to define more sharply Mann's concept of montage. It is clear from *The Story of a Novel* that montage entails weaving in "factual, historical, personal, and even literary data,"[4] that is, "borrowing" anything, from real or fictional personal biographies to literary allusions and verbatim quotations. For this broad and rather vaguely used word "montage" Mann sometimes substitutes the word "quotation"; the two terms are often used interchangeably. Thus Mann occasionally calls a literal quotation "montage" but uses the word "quotation" for allusions to the life of a historical figure or to a literary motif.[5] But the fact that the distinction between the two concepts is blurred does not have any practical significance; both express the same artistic procedure.

When we try to order the heterogeneous material of the novel systematically and distinguish among the different types of montage, we find two major groups. The first group of material can be designated as "reality"; Mann calls it "factual, personal data"; to this group belong the real persons, authentic milieus and actual events used in the novel. The second main group contains quotations in the conventional sense of the word, that is, literal or almost literal repetitions of material which has already been written up. Within this group we can discern two categories: the "open" quotations, which the reader is supposed to recognize, and the "hidden" quotations, which have been woven so skillfully into the text that the uninitiated reader does not notice them. These hidden quotations can in turn be divided into several types. One large subgroup is comprised of material from fields with which the educated person would be familiar; this Mann took from newspaper articles, reference works, and the relevant specialized literature; another group includes material linked with a specific person. An example would be a word-for-word quotation from a biography of Nietzsche. To this group belong the self-quotations which Mann scattered throughout the novel, probably not expecting

3. P. 32.
4. *Ibid.*
5. *Ibid.*, p. 33.

that a number of readers would recognize them.[6] We can now set up the following outline:

I. Reality. Material not previously put in words (authentic milieus, real persons and events).
II. Quotations.
    A) "open" quotations (e.g., well-known Shakespeare passages in English, sections from the Doctor Faustus chapbook in archaic language).
    B) "hidden" quotations (e.g., from general reference works, newspaper articles, studies of a particular person or subject, or from Mann's own works).

As regards the concepts "montage" and "quotation," it proves most convenient to follow the general practice of Mann scholarship and use the word "montage" in its broadest sense. In the following pages the term will cover everything included in the above outline. When we want to emphasize that we are dealing with a word-for-word borrowing, we will call it a quotation. If a passage from the novel deviates from the exact wording of the text it is taken from, we will refer to it as a paraphrase, in accordance with the usual meaning of the term.

This schematic outline of Mann's varieties of montage provides welcome clarity, but as a principle for organizing the following discussion of the source materials it is less useful. The numerous borderline cases could only be decided arbitrarily; an obvious example would be the fluid boundary between

6. Doctor Faustus (hereafter cited as *DF*) contains several passages that occur verbatim in Mann's letters and speeches for the year 1943–47. It is often impossible to decide if the passages in question were written originally for the novel and then proved useful for other contexts or vice versa. Many indications point to the first alternative. Zeitblom's reflections on the outcome of the war, for instance, turn up in English in the address "What is German?" p. 80. According to *The Story of a Novel* (pp. 50–51, 53), Mann had reached chap. 8 when he interrupted his work to write the speech that contains the quotation from chap. 5. One cannot, however, exclude the possibility of a later addition to *DF*. It is probably quite natural that Mann's utterances on the contemporary political situation should be so similar within and outside the novel, but one could also infer a particular intention from the similarity. By putting his own words from other contexts in Zeitblom's mouth, Mann stresses his own identity with Zeitblom and the confessional nature of the novel. Hans Mayer (*Thomas Mann*, pp. 327 ff.) alludes to this question; J. Lesser (*Thomas Mann in der Epoche seiner Vollendung*, pp. 426 ff.) sees *DF* as Mann's final reckoning with his previous political positions, and proves that the Winfried discussions contain a quotation from the *Betrachtungen eines Unpolitischen*.

open and hidden quotations, where the reader's own knowledge, interests, and even nationality affect the classification.

It might be possible to discuss the source materials for *Doctor Faustus* according to the order in which they appear in the novel — page by page and chapter by chapter. This arrangement would be quite natural if we were preparing an annotated edition of the novel, but for our purposes it seems too mechanical. Rather we shall divide the material into a number of major groupings according to content or subject — topography, personal histories and music history. Such a system has disadvantages. It may prove difficult to assign a given document to one field rather than another, especially when it recurs in different contexts. Still, this system has the advantage of allowing us to separate important elements from the less important.

Before we begin, a few words are in order about the usefulness of *The Story of a Novel* as a guide in searching out sources. When reading this little "novel on a novel" one would do well to remember its author's famous irony. It contains quite a few digressions in a serious, almost pedantic style which actually say nothing significant about *Doctor Faustus*. Mann could confidently expect that hordes of literary scholars and critics would seize upon this "key" which he himself had provided, and he seems to have enjoyed making them rack their brains a bit while also giving valuable pointers and references.

The tension in *Doctor Faustus* between irony and deep earnestness is reflected in the style, which oscillates between parody and pathos; it dictates the choice of the heterogeneous source materials. From one source Mann takes a spicy expression, a piquant detail, or a burlesque anecdote, from another a profound formulation, a suggestive symbol, or a poignant episode.

SETTINGS

The settings in the novel are often unmistakably related to reality. Mann concentrates on places with which he was familiar, although he sometimes lends them fictitious names. Kaisersaschern, the city in which Adrian Leverkühn and Zeitblom spend their childhood, is, as many readers have observed, a symbol of the typical German Protestant city with a medieval heritage. It has traits borrowed from Naumburg, Nuremberg

14

and Aix-la-Chapelle.[7] But above all Kaisersaschern is a portrait of Mann's own birthplace, Lübeck. In the address "Germany and the Germans," which Mann wrote while working on *Doctor Faustus,* he describes the archaic mood of Lübeck in much the same terms as he uses in the novel for Kaisersaschern.

Germany and the Germans:
No, in the atmosphere itself something had clung of the state of mind of, let's say, the hysteria of the dying Middle Ages, something of latent spiritual epidemic. It's a strange thing to say about a sensibly sober, modern, commercial city, but it was conceivable that a Children's Crusade might suddenly erupt here, a St. Vitus Dance, an outbreak of fanaticism coupled with mystic processions of the people, or the like — in short an anciently neurotic substratum was perceptible, an arcane spiritual state that was outwardly evidenced by the many "characters" to be found in such a city.[8]

Doctor Faustus:
But something still hung on the air from the spiritual constitution of the men of the last decades of the fifteenth century: a morbid excitement, a metaphysical epidemic latent since the last years of the Middle Ages. This was a practical, rational modern town. . . . Rash it may be to say so, but here one could imagine strange things: as for instance a movement for a children's crusade might break out; a St. Vitus's dance . . . miracles of the Cross, fantastic and mystical folk-movements — things like these, one felt, might easily come to pass. [36]*

The "characters" which Mann goes on to describe in "Germany and the Germans" also turn up in Zeitblom's picture of Kaisersaschern; again the wording is almost identical. Such details in the novel as street names are taken from Lübeck; for instance, Adrian's uncle lives on the Parochialstrasse, which really exists in Lübeck.

7. The following scholars pick out Lübeck and Naumburg as the two foremost components of Kaisersaschern: Mayer (*Thomas Mann*, pp. 332 ff.), and E. Heller (*The Ironic German: A Study of Thomas Mann*, p. 276). R. Faesi (*Thomas Mann*, p. 145), and F. Kaufmann ("Dr. Fausti Weheklag," pp. 17–18) also finds traits of Nuremberg and Aix-la-Chapelle.

8. "Germany and the Germans," *Thomas Mann's Addresses at the Library of Congress*, p. 50. Other literal correspondences on pp. 50 and 49 will be found to *DF*, pp. 37, 38 and 179. Erika Mann calls Kaisersachern "the town of 'Buddenbrooks' (for Lübeck is the place, although he called it Kaisersaschern)" (*The Last Year of Thomas Mann*, tr. R. Graves, p. 59). See H. Ewers, "Lübeck im Kunstwerk Thomas Manns," *Der Wagen: ein lübeckisches Jahrbuch*, pp. 123–32.

* Translator's note: The page numbers following this and all subsequent excerpts from or allusions to *Doctor Faustus* refer to the translation by H. T. Lowe-Porter, which has been used throughout this book with the kind permission of the publisher, Alfred A. Knopf, Inc.

This veracity also obtains in the descriptions of other cities and places which Adrian visits in the course of his life: Mann describes the Church of Saint Moritz and the Hansastrasse in Halle, Auerbach's Inn and the Peterstrasse in Leipzig, the Herrengasse in Vienna, the Via Torre Argentina in Rome, and the Mythenstrasse in Zurich. Parts of the description of Palestrina can be found in Mann's autobiographical *A Sketch of My Life*.[9] Most of the novel takes place in Munich and its surroundings, where Adrian settles after the student years in Halle and Leipzig and the trip to Italy; here Mann's thorough knowledge of the milieu stands him in good stead. Although he wrote the book on the other side of the Atlantic and ten years after leaving Munich, the details have the ring of truth. Thomas Mann makes liberal use of Munich street names, many of which are in some way connected with his own life.[10] Thus the Rodde family, for instance, live on the Rambergstrasse, where Mann's own mother lived, and Zeitblom rents a room on the Hohernzollernstrasse "in Schwabing . . . not far behind the Siegestor" (332), that is, in the area where Thomas Mann had his bachelor lodgings.[11]

The description of the Schweigestill farm and its surroundings is likewise largely taken from a real place; Mann introduces certain changes to bring out the symbolic implications of Pfeiffering, as he also does with Kaisersaschern. But to this day one can follow Zeitblom's directions and go to the Starnberg Station in Munich and take the Oberammergau train, the line which "is for most of the distance the same as the Garmisch-Partenkirchen line" (427); after an hour and ten minutes one arrives in Polling, the Pfeiffering of the novel (204). The portrayal of the farm is based on actual conditions; the deep window niches in the walls, the "ecclesiastical arms" (204), the chestnut trees (325): these features are present on the old Schweighart farm in Polling. Viktor Mann, Thomas Mann's younger brother, has confirmed the accuracy of most of Zeitblom's information. Viktor spent several years in his youth as an agricultural trainee with the Schweigharts, and in his biography of the Mann family, *Wir waren fünf*, he gives a

9. 1930; tr. H. T. Lowe-Porter (1960), p. 12. See Lesser, *Thomas Mann*, p. 465. K. Kerényi gives an exact account of the correspondences between Leverkühn's and Mann's visits to Palestrina in the article "Thomas Mann und der Teufel in Palestrina."

10. See for instance Mayer, *Thomas Mann*, pp. 338–39.

11. *Sketch of My Life*, p. 15.

16

detailed account of the history of the old monastery and of the Schweighart family. His book corroborates such particulars as Frau Schweigestill's remark that Pfeiffering is overrun with artists (206).[12] The pond in Pfeiffering (25) also really exists, although it is not in Polling. When describing the summer vacations of his childhood in Bad Tölz, Thomas Mann's son Klaus mentions "our summer pond." It actually was called the "Klammer pond."[13]

Why did Mann change the name Polling to Pfeiffering? It could hardly have been that he wished to shield the real model; one can recognize the place from the description at once. Nor was it for the same reason as with Kaisersaschern, where the fictitious name covers several real cities. The explanation lies in the name — Pfeiffering — which Mann found in the old Faust chapbook.[14] Since Adrian Leverkühn is a modern Doctor Faustus, many of the places he visits are connected with the Faust legend. The Faust figure has its roots in the Middle Ages; accordingly Kaisersaschern has typically medieval features, and it is fitting that the place where Adrian creates his Faustian works should be related to the legend. The similarity between the names Pfeiffering and Polling may also have affected Mann's choice.

During his seventeen years in Pfeiffering Adrian travels very little, but on one occasion he takes an excursion with friends to several well-known villages in Upper Bavaria. At Adrian's express desire the little company goes to Oberammergau and then on to Kloster Ettal via Linderhof, the castle of Ludwig II. When describing these places, Mann again makes use of his exact knowledge of the locale. Thus he mentions Oberammergau's "quaint peasant houses with their rich ornament of carven balconies and ridge-poles" (428), and gives a particularly thoroughgoing description of the Rococo castle Linderhof (430). This visit is the occasion for the argument between Rudi Schwerdtfeger and Zeitblom over the supposed insanity and the dethronement of King Ludwig. Zeitblom defends Ludwig and becomes so aroused that he delivers an inpassioned speech on the narrow-minded, philistine brutality of the king's doctors. The royal mode of existence, he contends, is based on different assumptions from that of the average man; it can all

12. Viktor Mann, *Wir waren fünf*, pp. 191 ff.
13. K. Mann, *The Turning Point*, p. 43.
14. J. Scheible, *Das Kloster*, 5:180.

too easily be mistaken for madness. The source for this episode can be found not only in the thought familiar to us from *Royal Highness* and *Frederick and the Grand Coalition* but also in a novella by Mann's son Klaus, *Vergittertes Fenster: Novelle um den Tod des Königs Ludwig II von Bayern* (1937) ["The Barred Window: The Death of King Ludwig II of Bavaria"]. The content of Zeitblom's portrayal is identical with that of the novella, and there are even some similarities in the wording. In the novella Ludwig II is upset, like Zeitblom, over the indifference of the doctors: "They didn't even take the trouble to examine me." [15] Thomas Mann has borrowed the observation that the doorknobs have been removed, and the novella's title has been slipped into Zeitblom's long reply (431).[16]

In the past, novels have certainly contained realism of detail in their milieu descriptions, but when we consider the conditions under which Mann wrote *Doctor Faustus*, we can discover a particular motivation for his adopting such a method. Exiled and far from home, he must have taken a melancholy pleasure in bringing back to life the places, houses and environments where he had once led a rich, free life. Thus it is not surprising that he returns to the Lübeck of his childhood or that he re-creates from memory the Munich of his manhood. Polling, too, had possessed a magic all its own for him. Viktor Mann writes: "When, after years of separation, I first saw Thomas again in July, 1947 by the Lake of Zurich, he quickly brought the conversation around to Polling. 'You will find the Schweigharts in my *Doctor Faustus*,' he said. And then thoughtfully, 'Polling had atmosphere. Remember, the old parlor?' " [17]

The different milieus in which Leverkühn spends his life thus have a solid basis in reality, even if it is sometimes disguised. As we shall see, the same is true of many of the characters in the novel. Hans Mayer makes an important point about the disguise. He differentiates between three degrees of identity in the descriptions of places and persons.[18] First, there is clear and unambiguous identity: the Munich of the novel is the real Munich, and the Bruno Walter of the novel who directs Leverkühn's *Cosmic Symphony* is the real Bruno Wal-

15. *Vergittertes Fenster*, p. 52. See *DF*, p. 431.
16. *Vergittertes Fenster*, p. 14.
17. *Wir waren fünf*, p. 182.
18. *Thomas Mann*, pp. 323–24.

ter.[19] The second degree is the lightly disguised identity between, for example, the Pfeiffering of the novel and the Polling of reality, between Jeanette Scheurl in the novel and the writer Annette Kolb. Details and dates coincide, and all that has been changed are the names. Finally there are more complicated, symbolic forms of identity in which persons or places of the novel are a composite of various real models. To this category belong Kaisersaschern and, among the characters, Adrian Leverkühn himself.

CHARACTERS — THOMAS MANN'S FAMILY

Among the characters that appear slightly disguised and with fictitious names in *Doctor Faustus* are several who in life were very close to the author. With unusual candor Mann portrays personalities and tragedies taken from his own family. Perhaps the most truthful and ruthless portraits are those of Ines and Clarissa Rodde, in reality Mann's sisters Julia and Carla.[20] In his *A Sketch of My Life* Mann recounts the life and fate of his sister Carla in details which reappear, often verbatim, in the picture of Clarissa Rodde. He mentions her ambitions to be an actress despite her lack of the prerequisites of success; the "macabre aestheticism" expressed by the skull on her writing desk; her attractiveness to men; and the projected marriage with the "young son of an Alsacian industrialist."[21]

Klaus Mann speaks of his aunt's "sensual charms and slightly provoking manner," of her "saucy hats" and her cigarette smoking;[22] those details, too, occur in the portrayal of Clarissa. A comparison of the following quotations will indicate how closely the Clarissa of the novel adheres to her model:

A Sketch of My Life:	*Doctor Faustus:*
Then she took her cyanide, enough to kill a whole company of soldiers. The deed was done almost in the presence of our	Clarissa received the registered letter in Pfeiffering, where after the close of the Pforzheim theater season she was spending

19. See E. Heller: "We know by now the model 'in real life' for almost every character in the book (and the time may not be too far off when innocent researchers will set about discovering the true identity of true identities — 'I know who Schildknapp is, but who is Bruno Walter?')" (*The Ironic German*, p. 276). But Heller does not take the trouble to name all the models he claims to have identified.

20. Among others, Lesser (*Thomas Mann*, p. 466) and Mayer (*Thomas Mann*, p. 339) have pointed out this identity.

21. *Sketch of My Life*, p. 39.

22. *The Turning Point*, p. xiii.

poor mother, at her country home in Polling, near Weilheim in Upper Bavaria, whither she, the once admired *grande dame*, had withdrawn. . . . My sister was on a visit to her, and the betrothed had made his appearance. Coming from an interview with him, the unhappy creature hurried past her mother, locked herself into her room, and the last that was heard from her was the sound of the gargling with which she tried to cool the burning of her corroded throat. She had time, after that, to lie down on the couch. Dark spots on the hands and face showed that death by suffocation — after a brief delay — must have ensued very suddenly. A note in French was found: *Je t'aime. Une fois je t'ai trompé, mais je t'aime.* My wife and I were roused by a telephone call, the veiled language of which did not do much to hide the truth, and in the dawn I drove to Polling, to my mother's arms, to receive her moans upon my breast.[23]

a few weeks with her mother in the cottage under the chestnut trees. It was early afternoon. The Frau Senator saw her daughter hurrying back from a walk she had taken alone, after the midday meal. They met on the little open place in front of the house and Clarissa brushed past her mother with a blank, dazed look and fugitive smile, into her own room, where with a swift and violent movement she turned the key in the door. Next door the old lady presently heard her daughter at the wash-hand-stand, gargling her throat — we know now that it was to cool the frightful corrosive action of the acid. . . . The same only too convincing sight met my eyes when I hurried over from Freising, having been informed by our landlady on the telephone. I took the wailing mother in my arms, a distressed and consolatory family friend. . . . Dark blue spots of congested blood on Clarissa's lovely hands and on her face indicated death by quick suffocation, the abrupt paralysis of the organs of breathing by a dose of cyanide large enough to kill a regiment. . . . There was a hasty pencilled note to her betrothed, with the words: *"Je t'aime. Une fois je t'ai trompé, mais je t'aime."* [384–85]

Clarissa's mother, the widow of Senator Rodde, bears some outward resemblance to Thomas's own mother, Julia Mann. Just as Frau Mann had withdrawn from the social life of Munich to rural tranquility in Polling, Frau Rodde moves to Pfeiffering (325). Before that she lives with her daughters, just like Frau Mann, on the Rambergstrasse.[24] A letter from

23. *Sketch of My Life*, pp. 39–40.
24. V. Mann, *Wir waren fünf*, pp. 26 ff.

Thomas Mann to his brother Viktor indicates, however, that the similarities are purely external: "You could not be more right about Frau Rodde. She is related to Mama only through the daughters and, at the most, through her position as an uprooted North German patrician in Munich." [25]

There are many correspondences between Ines Rodde, who marries Helmut Institoris, and Mann's sister Julia Löhr. To be sure, Julia lived after her marriage on the Habsburger Platz,[26] not on the Prinzregentenstrasse like Ines (325), but she also had three daughters, the two youngest of whom were twins. The description of her "immaculate eight-roomed apartment" (328) coincides with Viktor Mann's picture of the Löhr apartment: "Not a speck of dust dulled the gleam; the children and servants always looked freshly starched and ironed, and I had the feeling that one could only enter the rooms, the kitchen included, in patent leather shoes." [27] Julia's cold beauty, her shy, reserved manner, her sense of tradition and her longing for a secure position in the bourgeois world are described by both Viktor and Klaus Mann.[28] The characterization of Ines Rodde is very similar (197). Like Ines (197), Julia wrote "reflective poems," [29] and Ines' appearance unquestionably borrows traits from Julia Mann.[30] The fate of his sister likewise provided Mann with the raw material for Ines Rodde's tragic end. Without going into particulars, Viktor Mann states that Julia committed suicide when she found that her life was becoming a dead end. Klaus Mann gives the full details of the death of his aunt, and his words are perfectly applicable to Ines Rodde: ". . . she hanged herself. She had always been very bourgeois and proper, mincing and affected, with dull eyes and pursed mouth, but secretly dissolute; she had an unfortunate penchant for narcotics and good-looking gentlemen of the upper middle class." [31]

Yet another of the important characters in *Doctor Faustus* is modeled on a member of Mann's family, but the portrait has been surrounded with an aura of unreality appropriate to the character's symbolic function. This is Nepomuk Schneidewein,

25. *Ibid.*, p. 595.
26. *Ibid.*, p. 288.
27. *Ibid.*, p. 289.
28. *Ibid.*, pp. 121, 454. K. Mann, *The Turning Point*, p. 25.
29. V. Mann, *Wir waren fünf*, p. 38.
30. See the picture of Julia in *Wir waren fünf*, opposite p. 288.
31. K. Mann, *Der Wendepunkt: ein Lebensbericht*, p. 282. [This passage is missing from the English version.]

Adrian Leverkühn's angelic little nephew; he is modeled on Mann's grandson Frido. It would be superfluous to prove the identity by referring to individual traits; Mann himself confesses the identity in his letters and in *The Story of a Novel*, where he says, for instance, of the child's peculiar manner of speech:

> I described the frail little boy in all his elfin charm. I took the tenderness of my own heart and transformed it into something no longer entirely rational, endowing the child with a loveliness which was somehow divine, so that people felt him as a visitor from some high and faraway realm, an epiphany. I had the little messenger make his strange pronunciamentos, patterning these on the voice and the accents of the angelic little chap which rang clearly in my own ear. At least one of those curious phrases, the "Well, you are glad I did come, yes?" was actually spoken at one time. The whole act of transformation and transcendence that I was undertaking is comprised in the beautiful, transparent double meaning which this "come" assumes, as if of its own accord.[32]

Despite the "act of transcendence" performed on the boy Frido, the similarities were so striking that Mann was worried about the reaction of his daughter-in-law, Frido's mother, to the terrible section that describes Echo's illness and death.[33]

Echo is primarily a symbolic character with many characteristics absent from Mann's grandson. But Mann did not invent these characteristics at random. It has already been pointed out that Echo has some of the traits of Shakespeare's Ariel, of Euphorion in Goethe's *Faust*, and of the "divine child" of myth, a subject treated by Mann's friend, the religious historian and mythologist Karl Kerényi.[34] Thus Mann borrows

32. *Story of a Novel*, pp. 217–18.
33. *Ibid.*, p. 220.
34. Interpretations of the figure of Nepomuk vary greatly. Lesser (*Thomas Mann*, p. 449) finds references in the figure to Goethe's Euphorion and Goethe's and Shakespeare's Ariel, while Mayer (*Thomas Mann*, p. 344) emphasizes that Echo represents a retraction of the Euphorion figure. F. Kaufmann even sees in Echo a parallel to Christ ("Dr. Fausti Weheklag," p. 23). P. M. Pickard considers possible similarities to Johannes Nepomuk, the patron saint of Bohemia ("Thomas Mann's *Doctor Faustus*," p. 100). J. Plöger sees Echo primarily as the archetypal child, like Hanno and Tadzio ("Das Hermesmotiv in der Dichtung Thomas Manns," p. 158). A. Dornheim interprets Echo as "the divine child" ("Goethe's 'Mignon' und Thomas Mann's 'Echo'," pp. 315 ff.). H. Olschewski criticizes this interpretation and cites instead Ovid's tale of Echo and Narcissus ("*Doktor Faustus* von Thomas Mann: Struktur und Problematik eines modernen Romans," pp. 113 ff.). Olschewski also refuses to accept the interpretation that Echo personifies everything good, noble, angelic (*ibid.*, p. 117). It should be mentioned as a curious sidelight that Ariel was a demon referred to as the "Great Prince"

additional material to heighten reality; he supplements his own experience and his family history with material from literary, mythological, and other sources. The grandson's personal idiom gives Mann an excuse for a short digression on linguistic history.* Echo's evening prayers are taken, as Mann himself points out, from a thirteenth-century text, Freidank's *Bescheidenheit*.[35] In his description of Echo's illness, Mann reveals an amazing degree of medical expertise; he indicates its source in *The Story of a Novel*: "A letter to Dr. Rosenthal asking for information on the course of meningitis was dispatched at the end of February."[36] The material which Mann blends with such consummate artistry to produce the figure of Echo thus comes from the most disparate sources.

CHARACTERS — MANN'S FRIENDS AND ACQUAINTANCES

Mann does not restrict himself to using members of his own family in the drama of Adrian Leverkühn's life; friends and acquaintances also receive roles of varying importance. We have already seen that Polling, the home of the Schweighart family, finds its way into the novel, and it comes as no surprise that the occupants of the farm are also included. Viktor Mann's account indicates that Frau Schweigestill *is* Frau Schweighart.[37] He describes her as a stately woman "with smooth, dark hair"; Frau Schweigestill has "brown hair, only touched with grey, drawn smoothly away from the parting" (206). Viktor Mann calls Frau Schweighart "the very epitome of a mother," and the motherliness of Frau Schweigestill is much stressed; she is even called

---

or the "Prince of Hell"; he is pictured as completely black and spitting fire in an illustration to one of the Scheible editions of Faust (*Doktor Johannes Faust's Magia naturalis et innaturalis* . . . , p. 91 ff., plate 33.).
* Translator's note: P. 712 in the 1947 Stockholm edition. On p. 469 of the Lowe-Porter edition, the translator has substituted "a figure of speech" for Zeitblom's explanation of a medieval word used by Echo.
   35. *Story of a Novel*, p. 218. But the real source for Echo's prayers is the collection *Sprichwörter des Mittelalters* by Samuel Singer, mentioned simply in the *Story* as "purely philological matter which fed and stimulated my linguistic imagination" (213). This is pointed out by J. F. White ("Echo's Prayers in Thomas Mann's *Doktor Faustus*"), who also establishes correspondences between Singer's commentaries and Zeitblom's. White discovered one of Echo's prayers in Valentin Schumann's *Nachtbüchlein*. This latter is part of the volume *Vierhundert Schwänke des sechzehnten Jahrhunderts*, ed. F. Bobertag, which Mann also used for other purposes (*Story*, p. 63) and from which he took, as White remarks, the name Heini Klöpfgeissel.
   36. P. 217.
   37. V. Mann, *Wir waren fünf*, p. 183 ff.

"Mother Schweigestill." The description of the mistress of Pfeiffering corresponds exactly to its real model, even to dialect expressions like "Gellen's ja?" (206).[38]

The master of Pfeiffering and his son do not play an important part in *Doctor Faustus*, but they, too, reveal Mann's determination to remain true to reality. Herr Schweigestill even takes the name of Max from his model, and both are taciturn, reflective pipe smokers (455).[39] The son at Pfeiffering, Gereon, has some of the characteristics of the eldest Schweighart boy, Oskar. According to Viktor Mann, Oskar Schweighart devoted himself enthusiastically to rationalizing farming and "waged a respectful but passionate battle with his father over the first mowing machine."[40] Gereon is portrayed as "a young man very progressive in agricultural matters, always thinking about new machinery," (26) "a young farmer rather disobliging and curt but obviously knowing his business" (225). Viktor Mann picks out the same traits in Oskar Schweighart: "For all his industriousness and sobriety, Oskar was never a grumbler or a wet blanket; still, he remained reserved."[41] Even the dog at Polling turns up in *Doctor Faustus*. Viktor Mann comments: "Pfeiffering, from Mother 'Schweigestill' to the crazy baroness and the demonic dog 'Kaschperl,' whom I had known as 'Luxl,' were important features of my youth, and it all came back to me, with both pleasure and pain, as I read the book."[42]

Some of Mann's friends from the two decades spent in Munich after 1910 serve as models for Adrian's acquaintances. Bruno Walter, the Manns' neighbor, appears undisguised.[43] Of the slightly disguised members of Adrian's circle we have already mentioned Jeanette Scheurl — in reality Annette Kolb, the Franco-German writer with a strong interest in music. Klaus Mann speaks of her "long, well-bred face" and her "highly individual idiom, a mixture of Bavarian and Parisian."[44] In

38. *Ibid.*, p. 261.
39. *Ibid.*, p. 184.
40. *Ibid.*, p. 188.
41. *Ibid.*, p. 187.
42. *Ibid.*, p. 596. The "crazy Baroness" appears in *DF* as the Baroness of Handschuchsheim (207). See V. Mann, *Wir waren fünf*, p. 200.
43. One of Adrian Leverkühn's Zurich acquaintances taken from real life is Frau Lilly Reiff, who maintained "a highly respected and hospitable house in Zurich" (*Briefwechsel Thomas Mann / Robert Faesi*, ed. R. Faesi, p. 48).
44. K. Mann, *Der Wendepunkt*, p. 324. [Not included in the English version.]

Thomas Mann's version this becomes: "She was aristocratically ugly . . . with a face like a sheep, where the high-born and the low-born met, just as in her speech her French was mingled with Bavarian dialect" (201). Mann emphasizes Jeanette's love for Mozart; during a visit to Adrian in Pfeiffering she sits at the piano in the Schweigestills' "peasant parlor" wearing her eternal black hat, and plays Mozart (260). Klaus and Erika Mann give the same picture of Annette Kolb.[45] Mann changes Jeanette to the daughter of a deceased Bavarian administrative official, whereas Annette Kolb's father was a Bavarian landscape architect attached to the Botanical Gardens, but Madame Scheurl lives near the Botanical Gardens (201). Mann completes the portrait with a few facts from Annette Kolb's life: we hear that Jeanette is "a writer on Schubert" (201); in 1947 Annette Kolb published her biography of Franz Schubert.[46]

Another character that Mann transports from reality into the novel is Adrian Leverkühn's friend Rüdiger Schildknapp. The accuracy of the portrait makes it easy for the initiated to recognize the model, in spite of the invented name. Nowhere does Mann borrow so drastically from reality as here, and it cannot have been entirely flattering to the original. The identity was at once noticed and pointed out, although the name was concealed for reasons of discretion. Later on, however, Mann himself spoke out, when in 1954 he sent a birthday salute to the poet and translator Hans Reisiger, a friend since 1906.[47] In the salute Mann describes him much as in the novel, and states in conclusion that Reisiger has forgiven Mann for turning him into "a humoristically engaging fantastical figure who, however, totally lacks a sense of responsibility toward life" in Mann's "novel about Germany's descent to hell."[48] It might seem as if Mann had come dangerously close to the dubious manner of the roman à clef, but he testifies that he had an entirely different intention. In a passage he later deleted from *The Story of a Novel*, he says of the portrait of Schildknapp, "Its frankness is radical," and he quotes a few words of a dedication written into a copy of *Doctor Faustus* for an old friend in Germany: "It would be a pity if this book, which has cost *me* so much of my

---

45. E. & K. Mann, *Escape to Life*, pp. 65–66.
46. *Franz Schubert: sein Leben.*
47. "Hans Reisiger zum siebzigsten Geburtstag," (1954), in *Nachlese: Prosa 1951–1955*, p. 204.
48. *Ibid.*, p. 208.

life-blood, were also to wound my fellow men!"[49] The earnestness of such a statement shows that the montage technique in *Doctor Faustus* is far more than a whim or novelistic experimentation for the sake of artistic effect.

In most cases, however, Mann seems to have had few compunctions about mixing real persons with the fictitious ones in his novel, and presenting even sharper caricatures than the one of Reisiger. A case in point is the impresario Saul Fitelberg, whose visit to Adrian takes up an entire chapter in the novel (XXXVII). In *The Story of a Novel* Mann writes of Fitelberg's model: "I need only recall the general lineaments of an old friend of mine in New York, formerly active in Paris as a literary and theatrical agent (though, it is true, he had nothing to do with music). He could supply the face for my man of the world."[50] The real name behind the initials S.C.* is not important. Identifying the real model does not fully explain who Fitelberg is. "The face" is taken from a real person, but, like so many other characters in *Doctor Faustus*, Fitelberg has a symbolic function: he is one of the novel's incarnations of the tempter.[51]

Another representative of the international musical scene is Dr. Edelmann, the director of the "Universal Editions" music publishing house in Vienna. He visits Adrian in his retreat in Pfeiffering to "offer . . . his service as editor and publisher" (390). This is appropriate because in actuality the Universal Editions published several works of Schönberg and other modern composers. And it is one of the real directors of the firm, Dr. Hans Heinsheimer, who appears here as Dr. Edelmann.[52]

49. MS of the *Story*, p. 68. The figure of Schwerdtfeger has been seen as a similar vilification: "To make things worse, the vain fiddler Rudi Schwerdtfeger is based on a venerable poet who more than made up for the unsound leanings of his youth by a terrible fate and who now receives from Mann a posthumous portrait that is so heartless and venemous that one cannot read it without feeling ashamed for such a biographer (W. Milch, "Thomas Mann's 'Doktor Faustus.' "

50. Pp. 201–2.

* Translator's note: Given only in the German text.

51. Fitelberg's role as a devil has been mentioned by Mayer (*Thomas Mann*, p. 369) among others.

52. This was pointed out by J. Krey ("Die gesellschaftliche Bedeutung der Musik im Werk von Thomas Mann"). The similarity emerges clearly from George Antheil's *Bad Boy of Music*, pp. 205 ff. A section of this book was published in *Omnibook*, from which Mann tore out a few pages which are now in the Zurich Archives. One cannot determine the date of publication from the underlined fragments.

The foundation in reality is different for Wendell Kretsch-mar,* the organist of the Kaisersaschern cathedral and Adrian Leverkühn's music teacher. It has been suggested that he possesses features of the music historian Hermann Kretschmar. Richard Engländer points out some of the similarities in his method of musical analysis and the manner of his lectures; Engländer sees Wendell Kretschmar's stammering as an intentional exaggeration of Hermann Kretzschmar's manner of speech; he did not stammer, but sometimes had difficulty making himself understood: he spoke Saxon dialect, and when excited he had trouble producing comprehensible sounds. According to Engländer, Wendell Kretschmar's familiarity with English is a rarity for a German of that period (it is under his influence that Adrian studies English [71]). Hermann Kretzschmar, too, knew English very well and was, in fact, married to an Englishwoman.[53]

THE KRIDWISS CIRCLE

The foregoing examples have shown that Mann "documents" relatively unimportant secondary characters by basing them on real persons or on figures from art and literature. In general he separates them from their original context and incorporates them so smoothly into the novel that they almost always seem created specifically for this work. But in a few cases Mann goes a step further and transplants figures from history or contemporary reality into the novel along with their authentic social settings and connotations.

* Translator's note: This name is spelled "Kretzschmar" in the original. Mann's spelling underlines the reference to Nietzsche. The spelling used here is that of the Lowe-Porter edition.

53. R. Engländer, "Thomas Manns Faustroman," pp. 133–34. Engländer added further material to this article in his lectures in the fall of 1961, "Thomas Manns Faustusroman som musikalisk spegelbild." According to H. Bürgin, Kretschmar is "a reminiscence of Lübeck, copied from the Kapellmeister Hans Wetzler who emigrated to America" ("Thomas Mann und die Musik," p. 313). The idea of giving Adrian Leverkühn a private music teacher received support from Bruno Walter or was perhaps even suggested by him. Walter writes a letter dated May 31, 1943 in reply to a question of Mann's: "Just so much for today: the interpreting musician needs a conservatory education; one could, however, conceive of a composer without regular schooling in the different 'subjects,' but not without *instruction from a revered teacher*." The words in italics were underlined by Thomas Mann. This letter is quoted with the kind permission of the now deceased Dr. Walter.

The circle of artists and scholars around the graphic arts expert Kridwiss (362–70) is one such group of characters that evokes an entire milieu in real life. Zeitblom gives lengthy introductions for the ten or so intellectuals who gather for the "round table sessions." Here we meet the private scholar and "polyhistor" Dr. Chaim Breisacher (279 and 363), who is of Jewish descent and has an uncanny sense for all the undercurrents of the times. Scholars from different fields take part in the discussions: the paleozoologist Dr. Egon Unruhe, the literary historian Professor Georg Vogler, the art historian and Dürer-expert Professor Gilgen Holzschuher. Then there are a few vivid personalities with a more general devotion to questions of culture: a manufacturer, Bullinger, and "two members of the grand-ducal house of Hessen-Nassau," (263) who are studying in Munich. Finally there is the poet Daniel zur Höhe, who appears in priestly robes and comports himself with the arrogance of a seer.

Earlier in the novel Zeitblom describes similar gatherings, where people meet in a salon — at the Roddes' or the Schlaginhaufens' — to play music and discuss cultural topics (279–84). Adrian occasionally takes part in these gatherings, whereas he is never present at the meetings of the Kridwiss circle. These occur in 1919, the year in which Adrian experiences an upsurge of creative activity. The ideas occupying Adrian at this time and finding their expression in his apocalyptic oratorio are intimately connected with the topics discussed in the Kridwiss circle. Just as the different salons are based largely on the real literary and cultural salons which Mann visited early in the century,[54] these ideas represent what was prevalent in German cultural circles of the period. Since we are dealing here with an extremely significant example of Mann's borrowing from reality, a summary of the circle's opinions seems appropriate.

The discussions provide the members of the circle with a welcome opportunity for voicing their disaffection, directed primarily against the so-called evolution of culture. They see history as a process of decay, and violently reject the notion of progress (280). The conventional values of the bourgeois tradition, "culture, enlightenment, humanity" (365), are subjected to merciless criticism; in their place is proclaimed a new scale of values, which culminates in "violence, authority, the dictatorship of belief" (368). Zeitblom notes with resignation

54. *Sketch of My Life*, p. 33.

that history moves in circles and has now returned to medieval conditions. These intellectuals believe that individual freedom must be restricted and the masses must be nourished on "mythic fictions" (366) that will direct their political activity. They advocate theories of racial hygiene that call for liquidating all diseased and unfit elements of the race. It is obvious that these are ideas which were to come to fruition in the National Socialist movement; they grew out of the general cultural exhaustion which found its expression in Spengler's *Decline of the West* (1918–22), a book widely read and highly thought of in Germany.[55] It has been pointed out that Spengler's ideas are most vividly reflected in the statements of Breisacher.[56]

Many of the real figures who represented pre-Nazi ideas in Munich appear under fictitious names in Mann's novel. Sixtus Kridwiss bears a strong resemblance to the president of the Bavarian Academy of Fine Arts, Emil Preetorius, who, like Kridwiss, was "an expert in the graphic arts and fine editions, collector of east-Asiatic colored wood-carvings and ceramics" (362). Before 1933 he belonged to the circle of Mann's friends, and even designed the covers for several of Mann's books.[57] The model for the numismatic expert Dr. Kranich (198) is certainly the director of the Munich Numismatic Collection, Professor Georg Habich, who, like Kranich, suffered from severe asthma.[58] The change of the name from Habich [Habicht = hawk] to Kranich [= crane] is not only a play on bird names; it is a play on sounds characteristic for Mann.

Another member of the Kridwiss circle is the professor of literary history, Georg Vogler, "who had written a much esteemed history of German literature from the point of view of racial origins, wherein an author is discussed and evaluated . . . as the genuine blood-and-soil product of his real, concrete, specific corner of the Reich" (363). One can easily recognize in this figure the literary historian Joseph Nadler.[59] From 1912 to 1928 there appeared Nadler's four-volume

55. In 1924 Mann wrote an essay "On the Theory of Spengler" (*Past Masters and Other Papers*). See also below, pp. 106, 154.

56. Krey, "Die gesellschaftliche Bedeutung . . . ," p. 312.

57. See *Briefe* 1:478. TM perhaps intended the name Sixtus to suggest the Latin form Preetorius.

58. I am indebted to Prof. Willy Schwabacher for identifying Kranich.

59. Various researchers have helped with these identifications, among them Lesser (*Thomas Mann*, pp. 400–401); H. Mayer (*Von Lessing bis Thomas Mann*, p. 396); P.-P. Sagave (*Réalité sociale idéologie religieuse dans les romans de Thomas Mann*, pp. 115 ff.).

Literaturgeschichte der deutschen Stämme und Landschaften ["Literary History of the German Tribes and Landscapes"]. It appeared in a new edition from 1939 to 1941 with some revisions, and this may have prompted Mann to renew his acquaintance with Nadler's unabashedly and aggressively nationalistic theories. Nadler's chronological divisions alone reveal his orientation; the four volumes have the following subtitles: *Volk* (800–1740); *Geist* ["Spirit," "Soul"] (1740–1813); *Staat* ["State"] (1813–1914); and finally *Reich* (1914–40). The author's attitude emerges most clearly from the "guiding thoughts" set forth at the beginning and end of the preface to the last volume. The following quotation shows how Georg Vogler's — *alias* Joseph Nadler's — study of German literature "from the point of view of racial origins" turns into a dream of world dominion:

The transformation of the Old German Reich to the New Reich via the Prussian state, represents for the race [*Volk*], the spirit of the race, a homecoming — after twice being reduced to its innermost core — what was once a world-race became again a world-race. . . . The evolution of the Germans through history from world-race to state, from state to *Reich*, from *Reich* to world-race draws the entire globe into a great procession of spirits. The peoples of the inhabitable continents are obliged by destiny to participate in this transformation. They accompany the procession, hospitable and inimical, moved and moving, giving and receiving. World poetry — this is the poetry of the German world-race — but no matter in what latitude it appears, it springs from the unmoving center of German racehood. That alone can give rise to world poetry and take the credit for it.[60]

Another figure in the Kridwiss circle taken from reality is the poet Daniel zur Höhe. This portrait is based on Stefan George's disciple Ludwig Derleth. Mann himself reveals this in his reply to an article in the *Hudson Review* by Joseph Frank.

Mr. Frank assumes that the figure of the poet Daniel zur Hoehe is a caricature-portrait of Stefan George. That is not so. It is true that the figure was chiefly drawn after a live model, which, however, was only a pupil and disciple of Stefan George by the name of Derleth. By the

60. J. Nadler, *Literaturgeschichte des Deutschen Volkes*, 4:1, 6. It is easy to see why Mann disapproved of Nadler's narrowminded conception of poets and literature. Nadler's concluding judgment on the Mann brothers is worth mentioning as a cultural curiosity: "Whether or not the older of the two brothers, Heinrich, took more after his mother and the younger, Thomas, more after his father; whether or not each reacted differently to the artistic *bohème* of Munich which had become their home: ultimately they both landed, whether uninhibited or protesting, in that world league of the unprincipled who have neither a fatherland nor a people of their own" (*ibid.*, p. 235).

way, the very same character already figures in an early short story of mine entitled "At the Prophet's." [61]

Mann lifted several passages from his own story; self-quotation is, after all, part of the montage technique.

"At the Prophet's":
Christus imperator maximus was his name; he enrolled troops ready to die for the subjection of the globe; he sent out embassies, gave inexorable ultimata, exacted poverty and chastity and with a sort of morbid enjoyment reiterated his roaring demand for unconditional obedience. . . . "Soldiers," he cried . . . "I deliver to you for plundering — the world!" [62]

Doctor Faustus:
The signatory to these proclamations was an entity named *Christus Imperator Maximus,* a commanding energumen who levied troops prepared to die for the subjection of the globe. He promulgated messages like Orders of the Day, stipulated abandonedly ruthless conditions, proclaimed poverty and chastity, and could not do enough in the hammering, fist-pounding line to exact unquestioned and unlimited obedience. "Soldiers!" the poem ended, "I deliver to you to plunder — *the World!*" [364]

It has been shown that Ludwig Derleth's Catholic manifesto contains parallels to the poet's terroristic proclamations.[63] One of Derleth's proclamations (1904) closes with the words, "Soldiers, I deliver to you for plundering the world." [64] It is understandable that Daniel zur Höhe has been interpreted as a portrait of Stefan George; the disciples not only imitated their master's ideas but also his manner and his clothing. The Kridwiss circle cannot, however, be considered a faithful copy of George's esoteric little band, although ideological connections exist. An allusion to the aestheticism characteristic of the George circle can be seen in Daniel zur Höhe's repeated pronouncement that something is "beautiful" (264) or "has beauty" (498). Although George never took up the cause of National Socialism, he and particularly the members of the Kosmiker-Bund in Munich entertained many ideas which flourished in a much cruder form among the Nazis.[65]

61. Mann gave this information in reply to J. Frank's article, "Reaction as Progress: or, The Devil's Domain," *Hudson Review,* 2 (1949–50): 38–53. Mann's comment was on p. 320 of the same issue.
62. *Stories of Three Decades* (New York, 1948), p. 288.
63. Lesser, *Thomas Mann,* p. 404.
64. L. Derleth, *Proklamationen,* p. 130.
65. The rôle of the George circle in the development of National Socialism is much disputed, as G. P. Landmann's George bibliography indicates.

For a time George had his headquarters in Schwabing, the quarter of Munich where at that period many extremists in art, music, literature and politics lived. When Mann was living in Schwabing and becoming known as a man of letters, he could hardly avoid contact with these circles, even though he determinedly kept his distance and often emphasized that he was independent of all literary coteries.[66] From Georg Fuchs's book on Schwabing, *Sturm und Drang in München um die Jahrhundertwende* ["Storm and Stress in Munich at the Turn of the Century"] (1936), one gets the definite impression that the Kridwiss circle displays features of that period, although the action in *Doctor Faustus* takes place fifteen years later and the mood is less extreme than it seems to have been in reality. Fuchs tries to demonstrate that both Bolshevism and National Socialism originated in Schwabing — Lenin was active there in the 1890's — and that everything that occurred there was wrapped in a mysterious, demonic obscurity:

Schwabing has been compared to the Blocksberg, and what we have to report of our experiences in Schwabing only goes to show that it was indeed a unique meeting place for all the demons of a world thrown off balance by unheard of catastrophes: a witches' Sabbath.[67]

It is not easy to describe the actual demonic elements, or, as Fuchs puts it: "no one knew exactly where, no one knew exactly how, no one knew exactly what, no one knew exactly if it were true at all; but mysterious whispers were afoot." [68]

The prototypes for certain members of the Kridwiss circle are at home in a slightly later period, post-World War I Munich. Here we find the model for Breisacher in the Jewish scholar Oskar Goldberg, who in 1925 published *Die Wirklichkeit der*

Summarizing Oskar Benda's *Die Bildung des Dritten Reiches*, which appeared as early as 1931, Landmann writes: "Assigns the origin of Fascism and National Socialism to George" (*Stefan George und sein Kreis: eine Bibliographie*, p. 162). Claude David also deals with the question in his study, "Stefan George: Aesthetes or Terrorists?" published in the United-Nations-sponsored *The Third Reich*, pp. 287–315. David emphasizes that although George was an aesthete and an artist, not a politician, he had a certain significance for the Nazi movement.

66. "The Years of My Life," (*Meine Zeit*), p. 254. See F. Lion, *Thomas Mann*, p. 59. The following quotation from Mann's *Sketch of My Life* (p. 33) applies to the period around the turn of the century: "Still, I did begin to frequent a few Munich drawing rooms where there was literary and artistic atmosphere: in particular that of the poetess Ernst Rosmer, the wife of the well-known lawyer Max Bernstein."

67. G. Fuchs, *Sturm und Drang in München um die Jahrhundertwende*, p. 99.

68. *Ibid.*, p. 107.

Hebräer ["The Truths of the Hebrews"], in which he advocated a primitive Nietzschean age still immune to slave morality. Dr. Egon Unruhe, the "philosophic paleozoologist" (363) has been identified as the Munich professor of paleontology Edgar Dacqué.[69] The characters around Sixtus Kridwiss modeled on real persons provide, like the other real material, an air of authenticity and exactitude. In addition, these characters have the symbolic function of representing the coming Nazi ideology and prefiguring the catastrophe toward which Germany is moving. But the symbolic role of these characters does not end here; the Kridwiss circle also points backward. The names Mann gives them are almost all taken from the Reformation period. A name like Georg Vogler sounds natural and provides a good pseudonym for Joseph Nadler,[70] but Georg Vogler was also a "Chancellor in Ansbach" with whom Luther corresponded. Among Luther's numerous other correspondents one also finds the names Heinrich Bullinger and a "judge in Torgau," Anton Unruhe. One can establish Mann's source for these names. In his own copy of Luther's letters he underlined a large number of names which he later uses for characters in his novel.[71] And the names in the Kridwiss circle are not the only ones that link the present with the time of the Reformation. Other names taken from Luther's letters are Schlaginhaufen, Scheurl, Zink, Spengler, von Riedesel and the names of the minor characters

69. O. Goldberg, *Die Wirklichkeit der Hebräer*. Lesser (*Thomas Mann*, p. 401) provides this identification. See also Sagave, *Realité sociale*, p. 115. Lesser links Unruhe with Dacqué, while Sagave considers him a mild caricature of Bachofen (p. 116). Milch ("Thomas Mann's 'Doktor Faustus'," p. 235) does not connect Breisacher with Goldberg but speaks instead of a "genuine lyric poet" whom Mann has tastelessly caricatured; perhaps he means Karl Wolfskehl.
70. Prof. Michael Mann particularly emphasized in a personal discussion on August 5, 1961 that similarity of sound was often decisive for Mann's choice of pseudonyms. He cited the names Nackedey and Rosenstiel as examples.
71. *The Story of a Novel* tells us that Mann was reading Luther's letters while working on DF (pp. 24, 77). In the edition used by Mann (*Martin Luthers Briefe*, sel. and ed. R. Buchwald), underlinings occur on the following pages: 2:129, Baworinski; 2:151, Bullinger; 1:42, 230, 255, Dungersheim (actually Dungersheim von Ochsenfart, called Ochsensfart in the letters, but appearing under both names in the editor's commentary); 2:138, Kegel; 2:158, 162, Ölhafen; 2:115, Osiander; 2:43, von Plausig; 2:133, 154, Probst; 2:134, von Riedesel; 1:18, Scheurl; 2:121, Schlaginhaufen; 2:159, Schneidewein (Ursula Schneidewein, *ibid.*); 1:133, Spengler; 1:209, Spiegel; 2:85, von Teutleben; 2:152, Unruhe, 2:60, Vogler; 2:111, Zink; 2:132, Zwilling. Bullinger is also named in Scheible's *Doktor Johannes Faust* (p. 72).

Kegel, Osiander, Zwilling and Spiegel. Then there are Adrian's brother-in-law Schneidewein — the name Ursula Schneidewein occurs in Luther — and Zeitblom,[72] as well as Helene Zeitblom's maiden name, Ölhafen. Some other names from the Kridwiss circle are taken from the same period, though not directly from Luther. Among these is Holzschuher; in the novel he is an art historian and Dürer-scholar, in reality he was a Nuremberg patrician who participated in the *Reichstag* at Augsburg of 1547 and was painted by Dürer.[73] Ines Rodde's husband, Institoris, the art historian and worshipper of the Renaissance, also takes part in the Kridwiss discussions; his name is that of the author of the *Malleus maleficarum*,[74] a contemporary of the original Dr. Faustus.

We thus have every reason to assume that Mann intends to arouse the reader's associations with the Reformation period. The Kridwiss chapter in fact includes three different time levels: the time of the central action around 1920; the coming period of National Socialism; and the time of Luther and the historical Dr. Faustus. We shall show later that this division into different time levels is typical of several sections and motif-complexes of the novel. A conscious principle seems to be at work which should prove of great importance for our analysis of the underlying concept of the book.

THE STUDENT SOCIETY WINFRIED

Another group featured in the novel, which Mann describes in such a way that his sources are identifiable, is the student society Winfried, of which Adrian is a member while a student at Halle. In the chapter dealing with this society, various time levels can be recognized, as was the case with the Kridwiss Circle.

72. Lesser (*Thomas Mann*, p. 433 f.) and Sagave (*Réalité sociale*, p. 94) have found the name Zeitblom in Luther's letters. There are also other interpretations, not necessarily excluding the possibility of a link with Luther. F. Kaufmann, for instance, sees the name Zeitblom as an allusion to the fifteenth-century Swabian painter of the same name who painted "serene" devotional paintings ("Dr. Fausti Weheklag," p. 21). Others think that Mann simply wanted to express the idea of a "serene creature of the times," as Olschewski puts it (" 'Doktor Faustus,' " p. 165).

73. See for instance the *Allgemeine deutsche Biographie* (Leipzig, 1881), 13:32.

74. *Malleus Malleficarum* or the *Hexenhammer* was issued toward the end of the fifteenth century by the two Papal Inquisitors Heinrich Institoris and Jacob Sprenger to help combat witchcraft. See Mayer, *Thomas Mann*, p. 367, and *Von Lessing bis Thomas Mann*, p. 390.

From 1904 to 1905 Adrian is enrolled as a theology student in Halle and occasionally attends the meetings of a society of young Christians. Zeitblom devotes an entire chapter (14) to the description of this theologians' society, in order to give the reader an impression of the intellectual climate in Halle. The seventy students of the group meet in Mütze's tavern to talk and make music. They also undertake walking tours, together or in smaller groups, to "enjoy the beauty of God's green creation" (112). Now and then, Adrian and Zeitblom accompany the smaller groups, and Mann lingers over their walks in the Thuringian Forest and the student bull sessions. The whole section on the Winfried Society is something of a digression, doing nothing to advance the action. It has, however, an important symbolic function and thus merits careful analysis.

Three components of this chapter can be traced back to their sources: the picture of university life in Halle and of the student group; the ideas discussed by the Winfried members; and finally the names of the students involved.

What did Thomas Mann know of the life of the German student and specifically of the theology student at the beginning of the century? He had had experience with students in Munich, but since his formal studies had been limited to two semesters as an auditor at the Polytechnical Institute, he was acquainted with the academic world largely as an outsider. Aware of the gaps in his knowledge, Thomas Mann turned to Paul Tillich, who was then teaching at Union Theological Seminary in New York. Tillich had been a theology instructor in Berlin and had studied in Halle during the very years that concerned Mann. Mann mentions with his customary precision in *The Story of a Novel* that he sent a letter to Tillich "to ask about the procedures of studying for the ministry," and received an answer.[75] But as usual he does not reveal the use to which he put this letter. The letter can now be studied in the Thomas Mann Archives in Zurich. It contains a detailed description of Tillich's own studies, of the theological faculty in Halle, of the professors, and of the Student Society Wingolf; Thomas Mann changed the name only slightly.[76] Thomas

75. Pp. 25, 39.
76. The letter, dated "New York, May 23, 1943," is quoted with the now deceased Professor Tillich's kind permission. Mann's own letter asking for information is lost. R. Engländer mentioned in a conversation that he sees the change from Wingolf to Winfried as an allusion to Richard Wagner's daughter-in-law Winfried, who declared her solidarity with National Socialism.

Mann does not merely use the facts given in the letter; as in other cases we have already discussed, he weaves entire sentences into his narrative.

Part of Tillich's information appears in the chapter describing Halle and Adrian's experiences as a student of theology. A few quotations will indicate Mann's method:

Tillich:
The theology curriculum was structured as follows: during the first few years the historical and exegetical subjects came foremost, in the middle years the systematic subjects and at the end the practical ones (the science of preaching, curacy, religious instruction, etc.). But thanks to academic freedom, one could follow one's preference for certain subjects or professors and dispense with the usual order . . . but philosophy was regularly one of the subjects for the first examination in theology.

Doctor Faustus:
In the curriculum of a theology student the first years the emphasis is on history and exegesis, history of the Church and of dogma, Assyriology and a variety of special subjects. The middle years belong to systematics; that is to say, to the philosophy of religion, ethics, and apologetics. At the end come the practical disciplines, the science of preaching, catechesis, the care of souls, Church law, and the science of Church government. But academic freedom leaves much room for personal preference. . . . [94] Philosophy, the regular course for the first examination in theology. . . . [93]

The survey Zeitblom gives of the different schools of theological opinions at Halle is likewise based on Tillich's letter:

Tillich:
Liberal theology, as it was then called, represented by such names as Ritschl, Harnack and Troeltsch, had taken over the historico-critical methods of the secular field of historical scholarship, whereas the conservative school clung to a strict concept of revelation and tried to defend the traditional form of exegesis.

Doctor Faustus:
In its conservative form, holding to revelation and traditional exegesis, it [theology] sought to save what was to be saved of the elements of Bible religion; on the other hand it liberally accepted the historico-critical methods of the profane science of history and abandoned to scientific criticism its own most important contests: the belief in miracles, considerable portions of Christology, the bodily resurrection of Jesus, and what not besides. [89–90]

It failed to provide us with insight into the "demonic" nature of human existence which

The scientific superiority of liberal theology, it is now said, is indeed incontestable, but its

I have portrayed in the theological system I developed between the World Wars, partly with the help of Reinhold Niebuhr, and which has by now largely proved its superiority over liberal "moralism" and humanism. We found that the conservative tradition had retained more true understanding of human nature and of the tragic character of existence than the liberal bourgeois ideology of progress.

theological position is weak, for its moralism and humanism lack insight into the daemonic character of human existence. Cultured indeed it is, but shallow; of the true understanding of human nature and the tragic nature of life the conservative tradition has at bottom preserved much more; for that very reason it has a profounder, more significant relation to culture than has progressive bourgeois ideology. [90]

One of Adrian's theology professors, Dr. Kumpf, bears certain traits of Halle's real Professor Martin Kähler:

Tillich:
In my day the typical Hallensian theology was a combination of middle-of-the-road conservatism and Ritschlianism. By far the most imposing representative of the conservative wing was Martin Kähler, in his youth an enthusiastic student of German classical poetry and philosophy; he boasted of having known all of Goethe's weightier works by heart; later he had been deeply affected by the revival movement of the mid-nineteenth century, and undertook to defend the Pauline gospel of sin and justification against the aesthetic humanism of the great "heathen" Goethe, as he called him. . . . My friends and I have him to thank for the realization that our thinking is a broken reed in need of "justification," and that for this reason dogmatism is an intellectual form of phariseeism.

Doctor Faustus:
Theologically speaking, Kumpf was a representative of that middle-of-the road conservatism with critical and liberal traits to which I have referred. As a student he was, as he told us in his peripatetic extempores, dead set on classical literature and philosophy and boasted of having known by heart all of Schiller's and Goethe's "weightier" works. But then something had come over him, connected with the revival movement of the middle of the previous century, and the Pauline gospel of sin and justification made him turn away from aesthetic humanism. . . . Kumpf had convinced himself that our thinking too is a broken reed and needs justification, and precisely this was the basis of his liberalism, for it led him to see in dogmatism an intellectual form of phariseeism. [95–96]

A comparison of the above sets of quotations shows how Thomas Mann introduced tiny changes to attain an ironic distance which Paul Tillich's honest and respectful description lacks: Mann simply inserts quotation marks here, a word there, which turn Tillich's information into exaggeration: "Schiller's and Goethe's" instead of simply "Goethe's." Or he adds a phrase like "Kumpf had convinced himself. . . ."

Mann's details on conditions in Halle coincide with those given by Tillich, such as the digressions, the "extra punches" (95), so beloved of the students, that Professor Kähler — or Kumpf — scatters throughout his lectures.[77] The description of the student society Winfried relies heavily on Tillich's letter, which says:

> You might be able to use my experiences as a member of the "Wing-olf" League of Christian Students. The summer of 1907, when I was the "leader" of this club, which numbered about seventy members, still seems the decisive period in my life. My professors are partly to be thanked for what I have become as a theologian, as a philosopher and as a person, but most of it is due to the club, for the post-midnight theological and philosophical debates and the pre-dawn personal conversations remained crucial for my entire life. Music played an important role, as did the Romantic relationship to nature, something I always contrast in my lectures here with the Americans' Calvinistic alienation from nature. It is to this Romantic nature cult that I owe my hikes with the other fraternity members through Thuringia and to the Wartburg.

Mann does not directly quote these words of Tillich's, but he elaborates them in *Doctor Faustus*, primarily in the passages on pages 114–15.

Mann devotes most of his chapter on the Winfried Society to the students' discussions during their hikes. The ideas are not taken from Tillich's letter but from a source that dates from a period thirty years later than the one Tillich describes. The ideas have much in common with those discussed in the Kridwiss circle; they likewise anticipate Nazi modes of thought. These conversations, which Mann records with mocking irony, are nevertheless more abstract and idealistic than the Kridwiss discussions, and for that reason they are much less repellent.

What do Adrian and his companions discuss as they rest in the haymow after a day's hiking? The students speak in a quasi-philosophical academic jargon of the "great" subjects: art, religion, philosophy, politics. They meditate on the form of their

77. Tillich writes: "We went to his lectures for the sake of what we students called his 'ex-cursus,' his digressions from the fixed subject matter." Prof. Johannes Lindblom, who studied theology in Halle around the beginning of the century, has had the goodness to confirm Kumpf's similarity to Martin Kähler. He points out how aptly the Halle milieu is portrayed (see "Möten med TM," *Sydsvenska Dagbladet Snällposten*, Aug. 12, 1960 and "Inledande grundtankar i Martin Kähler teologi."

own existence, youth, seeing German youth as an incarnation of the "spirit of the German people." To them "youthful courage" (118) typifies the German people, and they ponder the German people's propensity to "plunge into the elemental," its religiosity (115 ff). Konrad Deutschlin is the most zealous defender of the German spirit and German youth; he also defends the majesty and dignity of the nation-state against the European economic community advocated by another student, Matthaeus Arzt. Deutschlin objects that, in a European welfare state which has solved all its economic problems, the feeling for spiritual values would wither away. Some of the students raise warning voices against Deutschlin's superpatriotism; Adrian refuses to acknowledge that youthfulness and spirituality are specifically German traits and repeatedly points to the role of France and Italy as leaders in historical development. Hubmeyer warns against idolizing the folk, but he admits that a "capacity for enthusiasm" and a "need for faith" are positive qualities. Dungersheim cautions against enveloping the warlike German in a "myth of doubtful genuineness" (124) and invokes Christ as the true "lord of the heavenly hosts." This warning obviously prepares us for the proclamations of Daniel zur Höhe.

It would be an oversimplification to see the students' discussions as simply foreshadowing National Socialist ideology, but a connection plainly exists. Sagave maintains that the students' nationalistic opinions should be read as an echo of Bismarck and Nietzsche,[78] but in fact many of the ideas stem from a later phase of German nationalism. This becomes abundantly clear when we examine the source Mann used for this section. Mann quotes verbatim long passages from a circular letter which appeared periodically and was called *Die Freideutsche Position* ["The Free-German Position"]. Mann used an issue from the year 1931. The pamphlet was published by the *Freideutsche Kameradschaft* [Free-German Fraternity], one of the so-called "free" student fraternities that had sprung up at most German universities. Among other activities, the group sponsored "work weeks" devoted to the discussion of specific topics; their publication contained reports on these symposia.[79]

78. Sagave, *Réalité sociale*, p. 107.
79. *Die Freideutsche Position*. Rundbriefe der freideutschen Kameradschaft, Nr. 4, Winter, 1931. The back pages of the pamphlet give information on the organization.

It is extremely difficult to summarize the contents of the pamphlet in question because the style of the reporting is so diffuse. The same general problems are discussed as in the Winfried sessions. Mann's use of this source is an exceptionally revealing example of montage; for one passage he welds eight different sections from the source into one, while elsewhere he takes over entire paragraphs unchanged.

Freideutsche Position:
Economic organization of society as a social ideal obviously has its origins in an enlightened and autonomous mode of thinking which, as yet unaffected by knowledge of the power of the human instincts, hopes to develop a just order by means of perspicacity and human reason; the concepts "just" and "socially useful" might be used synonymously. . . . Political organization (as opposed to economic organization) refers to the state, wherein power is exercised without reference to considerations of usefulness, and wherein entirely different qualities figure, such as honor and dignity. . . . At the peak of the economic pyramid stand the entrepreneurs' representatives and the trade union secretaries.

Doctor Faustus:
"But we must be clear on this point, Matthaeus," said he, "that the social ideal of an economic social organization comes from autonomous thinking in its nature enlightening, in short from a rationalism which is still by no means grasped by the mighty forces either above or below the rational. You believe you can develop a just order out of the pure insight and reason of man, equating the just and the socially useful, and you think that out of it new political forms will come. . . . Political organization refers to the State, a kind and degree of control not conditioned by usefulness; wherein other qualities are represented than those known to representatives of enterprises and secretaries of unions; for instance honor and dignity." [120]

"Can a new people arise out of an economic society? In the Ruhr I see only assembly centers of men and no new national cells. Take the local train from Leuna to Halle some day. You will see clusters of workmen who may well be discussing tariff questions, but who have certainly not drawn any sense of national strength from their common activity" [Friedrich Säckel]. — "In economics the nakedly finite rules more and more nowadays."

". . . can a new nationality rise out of an economic society? Look at the Ruhr: there you have your assembly centers of men, yet no new national cells. Travel in the local train from Leuna to Halle. You will see workmen sitting together, who can talk very well about tariffs; but from their conversation it does not appear that they have drawn any national strength from their common activity. In economics the nakedly finite rules more and more." [121]

Here, because of their innate capacity for enthusiasm, out of their need for faith, a phenomenon of visible reality is taken for revealed truth, for instance the idolized national state is mistaken for the utopian state. Thus we must examine as to their genuineness the new groupings which are being offered everywhere, to see whether what forms the bonds is real or only the expression of a certain structural romanticism that creates its own ideological connections in a nominalistic or fictionalistic way . . . . reveal real mystical forces which lie behind the confession of faith contained in the word "Germany." . . . We do not possess common contents, only personal substance.

"Capacity for enthusiasm is very fine and a need for faith very natural to youth; but it is a temptation too, and one must look very hard at the new groupings, which today, when liberalism is dying off, are everywhere being presented, to see whether they have genuine substance, and whether the thing creating the bond is itself something real or perhaps only the product of, let us say, structural romanticism, which creates for itself ideological connections in a nominalistic not to say fictionalistic way. I think, or rather I am afraid, that the deified national State and the State regarded as a utopia are just such nominalistic structures; and the recognition of them, let us say the recognition of Germany, has something not binding about it because it has nothing to do with personal substance and qualitative content." [121]

Mann describes the Winfried Society's nocturnal discussions as becoming increasingly abstract; all the expressions in quotation marks are taken directly from the *Freideutsche Position*:

. . . it went on deep into the night, on and on, with "bipolar position" and "historically conscious analysis," with "extra-temporal qualities," "ontological naturalism," "logical dialectic," and "practical dialectic": painstaking, shoreless, learned, tailing off into nothing — that is, into slumber. [124]

In addition to his sources on academic life and student attitudes, Mann had one major source for the characters' names. All of them stem from the Reformation period, many of them, like the names in the Kridwiss circle, from the edition of Luther's letters used by Mann. The leader of the Winfried Society is called Baworinski, after Benedikt Baworinski, the "head of the Bohemian brethren," with whom Luther corresponded.[80] Other names from the same source are Dungersheim,

80. Luther, *Briefe*, 2:129.

Probst and von Teutleben.[81] Names from the same period which cannot be found among Luther's letters are Hubmeyer and Schappeler — leaders of the Anabaptist movement; Arzt — a captain of the Swabian League in Augsburg; and Deutschlin, after a man called Teuschlein who helped introduce the Reformation into Rothenburg.[82] The change in spelling is probably intended to make the nationalistic tendencies represented by Deutschlin more apparent.

Mann reinforces the reference to the Reformation period by a concrete allusion to Luther in the form of Professor Kumpf (who also, as already mentioned, resembles Martin Kähler as described by Tillich). In his "tabletalk" and his advocacy of wine, women, and song, Kumpf obviously takes after Luther; the roll he throws at the devil is a jest on Luther's inkwell (97–98).[83] Kumpf's identity with Luther becomes even more certain when we find that much of his language comes straight from Luther's works.[84] Mann underlined several passages in his edition of the letters, and they reappear in Kumpf's speeches:

Luther:
. . . and foul work's afoot.[85]

Doctor Faustus:
He said "There's foul work" instead of "there's something wrong." [95]

(Mann adds the explanation "there's something wrong," which he found in an editor's note.) In the following expression Kumpf echoes Luther's spicy language:

Luther:
By God, may the Devil shit on them, Amen.[86]

Doctor Faustus:
"And may the Divil shit on him, Amen!" [96]

81. See above, n. 71.
82. See *Bibliographie zur deutschen Geschichte im Zeitalter der Glaubensspaltung 1517–1585*, ed. K. Schottenloher, 2:326.
83. Lesser, *Thomas Mann*, p. 445; Mayer, *Thomas Mann*, p. 351. Mayer notes that Kumpf is also a caricature of Treitschke.
84. Lesser (*Thomas Mann*, pp. 394, 445–46) shows that Kumpf's language has echoes of Luther's *Table Talk* and letters and of Grimmelshausen's *Simplicissimus*. There are also traces of the latter work in Adrian's speech (see Mayer, *Thomas Mann*, p. 351). G. Orton has pointed out that many of Kumpf's expressions and most of the oaths are taken from *Simplicissimus*, in fact from a limited number of pages. Orton suspects therefore that Mann did not use Luther's letters ("The Archaic Language in Thomas Mann's 'Doktor Faustus,'" pp. 71, 75). Actually Mann combined several sources for Kumpf's style.
85. Luther, *Briefe*, 2:85.
86. *Ibid.*

Kumpf gives vent to his lust for life in terms strongly reminiscent of Luther:

Luther:	Doctor Faustus:
. . . he is a sad, sour spirit who especially cannot abide to see a heart merry or at rest in God.[87]	"There he stands in the corner . . . the sad, bad guest,* and cannot stand it to see us merry in God with feasting and song!" [97]

At times Adrian's manner of speech recalls Luther. An example is the letter from Leipzig in which he parodies Kumpf for Zeitblom's benefit:

Luther:	Doctor Faustus:
Be therefore comforted and suffer the rod from thy father gladly, for it shall benefit thee in its own good time.[88]	Albeit first our friendly hert and good will, trusting and playing that thou maist almost joyfully bear the rod and in tract of time be so holpen thereby. . . . [139]**

In Mann's copy of the Luther letters certain forms of words and certain phrases are underlined; we find them again in Adrian's letters. Among these are the place names "Saala" (p. 216 of the 1947 Stockholm edition, not rendered into English on p. 139), "Haala" (Stockholm, 219), "magstu" (ibid., 216; rendered in English as "maist thou," p. 139), and the expression "What is afoot betwixt me and Satan" (141).[89] We also hear such echoes of Luther in Adrian's great farewell speech as "out of the desolation of this retreat" (496), and "I have ever busied myself as a worker and did never arrest" (501).[90]

By putting Luther's words into Adrian's mouth, Thomas Mann suggests a connection between Luther and the original Faust; in fact this was one of his pet ideas, expressed both in

87. Ibid., p. 83.
* Translator's note: The German text would be more literally rendered by "sad, sour spirit."
88. Ibid., p. 43.
** Translator's note: The English translation distorts Adrian's words and spellings into word-plays: "Herz" becomes "hert," "verhoffe" "playing," instead of "praying," etc., thus rendering the passage as a travesty rather than a parody.
89. Ibid., pp. 200, 166, 88. Sagave (Réalité sociale, p. 91) has noted borrowings from Luther's letters. Lesser (Thomas Mann, p. 444) quotes wordings taken from the writings of Luther's contemporaries, e.g., from Ulrich von Hutten.
90. Luther, Briefe, 2:93, 146.

the novel and in "Germany and the Germans,"[91] written while he was working on *Doctor Faustus*. The two figures are linked by a characteristic Germanness, but their similarity goes deeper. Mann read Heine's essay on the Faust legend in connection with *Doctor Faustus*[92] and underlined the following passages:

> It is highly significant that the home of Faust, Wittenberg, should also be the birthplace and laboratory of Protestantism.[93]

> It [the Renaissance] could come to fruition more easily in Italy than in Germany, where it encountered the iconoclastic fanaticism of what we should like to call the evangelical Renaissance when the Judaic spirit was reborn as a result of the new translation of the Bible.[94]

To be sure, Adrian Leverkühn studies in Halle rather than in Wittenberg, but Zeitblom gives us the following pointer:

> There was thus good intellectual justification when, after studying for two semesters in Jena and Giessen, I decided to draw my further nourishment from the breast of Alma Mater Hallensis. And my imagination saw an advantage in the fact that it was identical with the University of Wittenberg, the two having been united when they were reopened after the Napoleonic Wars. (86)

We can thus see that the section on student life in Halle contains references to two time levels besides the one on which the immediate events of the novel take place. As with the Kridwiss circle, Mann hints at the coming of National Socialism and recalls the Reformation period. The figure of Kumpf suggests one connection between the Reformation and Nazism by being both a reincarnation of Luther and a zealous nationalist.[95] But it is Adrian Leverkühn who provides the real unity. Later we shall discuss what Mann intended by superimposing these different historical ages. The chapters on Halle do not advance the action any more than does the Kridwiss section, but they both help set Adrian's symbolic identity in sharp focus.

Mann's use of language in the chapters on Adrian's student years in Halle expresses his intention to articulate three time levels. As Mayer has pointed out, three separate styles can be distinguished: Zeitblom's pure, "classical" prose, the students'

91. "Germany and the Germans," *Thomas Mann's Address at the Library of Congress*, pp. 52–55.
92. *Story of a Novel*, p. 110.
93. H. Heine, *Sämtliche Werke*, ed. R. Frank, 3:161.
94. *Ibid.*, p. 167.
95. See Sagave, *Réalité sociale*, p. 85.

44

abstraction-ridden jargon (taken from the *Freideutsche Position*, a source Mayer was not aware of), and the archaic phraseology modeled on Luther.[96]

MATERIAL FROM THE FAUST LEGEND

The external frame for *Doctor Faustus* — made up of the places, milieus, and secondary characters — is for the most part authentic: for it Mann has borrowed elements from concrete reality. This is also true of the novel's central figure. A number of different sources have gone into the description of Adrian's character and fate. In fact, almost every detail can be found somewhere in real life or in literature; what is original is the new whole that Mann has constructed.

Mann's sources for his main character vary widely. Some provide the data and the general outlines of Adrian's life and development, others contribute details for the picture of his character and personality. Some source material is assigned to Adrian, in the form of direct quotations from one of Adrian's models. Some of the source material serves to create a certain atmosphere around Adrian, for example to raise echoes of the life and times of the original Doctor Faustus, thus enabling the reader to see Adrian as a modern Faust.

To help conjure up the Faustian atmosphere, Mann also borrows from the fine arts. He draws most extensively on Albrecht Dürer, whom he describes in another context as a typical representative of the medieval German atmosphere of "passion, odor of the tomb, sympathy with suffering, Faustian *melencolia*." [97] In the little essay on Dürer which contains these words, Mann also states that Dürer inevitably suggests Nietzsche to him.[98] It thus becomes clear what Dürer's significance is for the novel. Leverkühn draws inspiration for his apocalyptic oratorio from Dürer's series of woodcuts (354), one plate of which he describes in detail. But Dürer also appears in other contexts: as already indicated, Kaisersaschern bears some of the features of Dürer's Nuremberg, and the engraving above Adrian's piano in Halle is a reproduction of the magic square in Dürer's "Melencolia" (92).[99]

96. Mayer, *Von Lessing bis Thomas Mann*, p. 401.
97. "Dürer," *Past Masters and other Papers*, p. 151.
98. *Ibid.*, p. 150.
99. Sometimes Mann also drew his fictional characters after Dürer portraits. Thus F. Kaufmann ("Dr. Fausti Weheklag, p. 18) and Mayer (*Von*

45

On the one hand, Adrian belongs to the realm Mann calls that of "Faustian melencolia"; on the other, Adrian represents "a kind of ideal figure, a 'hero of our time,' a person who bore the suffering of the epoch." [100] Thomas Mann announces firmly that he used no one real, concrete model for his "hero." [101]

This "hero of our time" is, however, first and foremost a reincarnation of the old Doctor Faustus. A basic source for the portrayal of Adrian's figure and fate is, of course, the old Faust chapbook.[102] Mann describes how he plunged himself into the study of Scheible's edition of the Faust legends; [103] the results of this study are apparent in the novel. Adrian and the original Faust are both peasants' sons who go to the university to study theology but gradually slip into more equivocal fields. Both sell their souls to the devil with a time clause of twenty-four years. The important events within that time span coincide

Lessing bis Thomas Mann, p. 387) find features from Dürer's "Melanchthon" in Jonathan Leverkühn, from the "Germans of Venice" or the "Portrait of a Virgin" in the mother, and from "Hieronymous of Augsburg" in the uncle.

100. *Story of a Novel,* p. 88. The idea that Mann, Adrian and Zeitblom are identical has been discussed by, among others, Lesser (*Thomas Mann,* 465 ff.), Mayer (*Thomas Mann,* pp. 325 ff.) and J. M. Lindsay, (*Thomas Mann,* p. 116). Lindsay cites an interesting remark of Mann's in a letter dated October 30, 1948 to the editor of the *Zürcher Student:* "If I have endowed this Adrian Leverkühn with anything of my own, it is the sense of the comic and the tendency toward parody." To P. Amann, Mann writes on October 21, 1948, [given erroneously as November 21 in the English translation], "Zeitblom is a parody of myself. In Adrian's attitude toward life there is more of my own than one might think — or than the reader is intended to think." (*Letters to Paul Amann, 1915–52,* tr. R. and C. Winston, p. 115). H. B. Boeninger has examined the symbolic identity of Zeitblom and his models ("Zeitblom, Spiritual Descendent of Goethe's Wagner and Wagner's Beckmesser.") See also E. Kirsch, "Serenus Zeitblom."

101. *Story of a Novel,* p. 88.

102. On Mann's relation to the chapbook, see: G. Bianquis, "Thomas Mann et le *Faustbuch* de 1587"; H. Slochower, "The Devil of Many Faces," and the less thorough treatment by B. Blume (*Thomas Mann und Goethe,* p. 129); E. M. Butler ("The Traditional Elements in Thomas Mann's *Doktor Faustus*"; W. A. Berendsohn ("Faustsage und Faustdichtung"); and H. Politzer ("Of Time and DF.")

103. *Story of a Novel,* p. 138–39. The edition mentioned above (Stuttgart, 1847), did not come into Mann's hands until the work on *DF* was already well advanced. He had been using another copy loaned by the Library of Congress (*Story,* p. 22). The charge lists for the period have unfortunately not been preserved, and one cannot determine which edition Mann borrowed. R. Benz's *Historia von D. Johann Fausten* from his series *Die Deutschen Volksbücher* gives the clearest summary of the heterogeneous Faust matter, in strict chronological order. We therefore use it as a basis for the following sketch of the Faust legend.

even to the chronology. An outline of the chronology of both works yields striking similarities:

Chapbook:	*Doctor Faustus*:
Faust signs the pact with his own blood (13f).[104]	As a result of a syphilitic infection, the disease enters Adrian's bloodstream, 1906.
The devil reveals himself in different shapes and emits extreme cold (49f).	The devil appears to Adrian in Palestrina, 1911.
Faust descends into hell and journeys to the stars during the eighth year (53ff, 58ff).	Adrian dives into the sea and reports on the universe, 1913.
Pilgrimage: the sixteenth year of the pact (64ff).	Journey to the estate of Madame de Tolna, 1924.
Second pact with the devil in the seventeenth year (176).	Fitelberg's visit, 1923.
In the seventeenth year Faust becomes a procurer (177).	Adrian brings Marie and Rudi together.
Faust's amorous adventures during the nineteenth and twentieth years (180).	Adrian's relationship with Marie, 1925–26.
In the twenty-third year Faust begets with Helena a beloved son (182).	Echo visits Adrian, 1928 (cf. p. 501).
Faust's farewell speech in the twenty-fourth year (193f).	Adrian's farewell speech, 1930.

In addition to these more striking correspondences, Mann borrows many details from the chapbook, for example, certain proper names. Thus Pfeiffering becomes the pseudonym for Polling, as mentioned earlier, and the Rohmbühel also takes its name from this source. The name Praestigiar, by which Adrian calls the dog Kaschperl in his farewell speech, belonged to the dog of the original Dr. Faustus.[105] In the same speech Adrian uses the name Hyphialta for Hetaera esmeralda; the word is underlined in Mann's copy of the Scheible edition:

It is the general opinion of the old Church fathers and teachers that

104. The page numbers in this column refer to the Benz edition.
105. Bianquis, "Thomas Mann," p. 58; Scheible, *Das Kloster*, pp. 168, 156. It is interesting to note that Agrippa of Nettesheim, who according to the *Story of a Novel* (188) also belongs to the Faustian realm, owned a dog which revealed itself on closer inspection as the devil; see Scheible *Doktor Johannes Faust*, p. 50, n. 36.

man and woman devils take the form of incubi, succubae, ephialtae or hyphialtae and have intercourse with human men and women.[106]

The stylistic echoes and verbatim quotations are numerous. Here are but a few examples:

Chapbook:
"Especially dear gentles and brethren, I can yet put me in remembrance of our schooldays from youth up, since we did study together at Wittenberg . . ."[107]

Doctor Faustus:
"Esteemed, in especial dear and beloved brethren and sisters . . . called by my leal famulus and special friend, which yet knoweth how to put me in remembrance of our schooldays from youth up, since we did study together at Halla . . ." [496]

"Betook himself then to Cracaw in Poland . . . and found there those of his own kind who trafficked in Chaldaean . . . *figuris, characteribus, coniurationibus, incantationibus,* and whatsoever names conjury and nigromancy may bear."[108]

"So . . . have I borne me, and let nigromantia, camina, incantatio, veneficium, and what names so ever be all my aim and striving." [500]

". . . so that, be 24 years elapsed from the date of this pact, he shall have full power to deal and dole with me, to move and manage, be it in life, soul, flesh, blood or goods and that for all eternity," and he renounces "all living creatures, all the Heavenly Host and all men, and that must be."[109]

"When the houre-glasse runs out, then I shall have good power to deal and dole with, to move and manage the fine-created Creature after my way and my pleasure, be it in life, soul, flesh, blood or goods — to all eternity!" [249]
". . . if thou renay all living creature, all the Heavenly Host and all men, for that must be." [248]

The old Faust chapbook is obviously a major source for Thomas Mann's novel. But what did he find in Goethe's *Faust*? Surprisingly little, when one considers that Thomas Mann loved and studied Goethe all his life. Certainly there are some correspondences between Mann's and Goethe's *Faust*, but they can be traced back to their common origin in the

106. Scheible, *Doktor Johannes Faust*, p. 198.
107. *Ibid.*, p. 90.
108. *Ibid.*, p. 114–15.
109. *Ibid.*, p. 137.

chapbook. They are, moreover, indirect or disguised allusions; one cannot properly speak of montage from Goethe's *Faust*.[110] Different interpretations have been offered to explain why Mann's treatment of the Faust legend is so free of Goethe's influence. Some scholars maintain that Thomas Mann deliberately ignored Goethe's *Faust*, having already based an earlier novel on it — *The Magic Mountain*.[111] Others argue that the absence of all references to *Faust* is an inverted allusion; *Doctor Faustus* would thus be the retraction of *Faust*, as Adrian Leverkühn's Faust oratorio is the retraction of Beethoven's Ninth Symphony.[112] But the discussion of these fundamental questions will have to be postponed to a later chapter.

SCIENTIFIC SOURCES

One of the similarities between Goethe's *Faust* and Mann's *Doctor Faustus* can be found in the characters of the heroes' fathers. Both are ponderers, given to speculating on the mysteries of nature.[113] Jonathan Leverkühn and his partially reprehensible passion for experimentation are described in detail. Some of Adrian's Faustian urges appear already in his father and become all the more impressive by repetition. We have

110. Olschewski (" 'Doktor Faustus,' " pp. 18 ff.) discusses the significance of Goethe for *DF* and gives a survey of the work of previous contributors to this problem.

111. See Erika Wirtz, "Zitat und Leitmotiv bei Thomas Mann." Berendsohn ("Faustsage und Faustdichtung," p. 377) and Bianquis ("Thomas Mann," p. 58) consider the chapbook a more important influence than Goethe's *Faust*, while Lesser (*Thomas Mann*, pp. 446 ff.) emphasizes the correspondences between Mann and Goethe. See also J. Müller, "Faust und Faustus," and H. W. Reichert, "Goethe's *Faust* in Two Novels of Thomas Mann." W. D. Williams argues that Mann in no way wanted to advocate a conception of life opposed to Goethe's. Just as evil in Goethe's *Faust* is a necessary element of life and an incentive to creative activity, in *DF* sin is necessary before eternal forgiveness can be attained ("Thomas Manns Doktor Faustus," pp. 273, 279).

112. This interpretation is favored by Blume (*Thomas Mann und Goethe*, p. 129), Mayer (*Thomas Mann*, pp. 341 ff.), Butler ("Traditional Elements," p. 23), E. Hilscher ("Thomas Mann und Goethe," p. 736), F. Kaufmann ("Imitatio Goethe," p. 252). Cf. also Anni Carlsson, "Das Faustmotiv bei Thomas Mann," pp. 352 ff.

113. "My father was a worthy man who worked in the dark, / Who in good faith but on his own wise / Brooded on Nature and her holy circles / with laborious whimsicalities," says Goethe's Faust (*Goethe's Faust*, tr. Louis MacNeice, p. 38). Jonathan Leverkühn is characterized as a "speculator," (*DF*, pp. 17, 455), a name that occurs, as Bianquis ("Thomas Mann," pp. 55) discovered, in the Faust chapbook (Scheible, *Doktor Johannes Faust*, p. 114).

already indicated that Jonathan recalls the times of the original Dr. Faustus: his appearance is reminiscent of Dürer's portrait of Melanchthon. His interest in the secrets of nature and his experiments in a homemade laboratory link him with other Faust figures. His "scientific" researches take him into the fields of chemistry, physics, and biology. Zeitblom gives a thorough account of the older Leverkühn's books on "exotic lepidoptera and sea creatures" (13). Despite the allusion to earlier times, Mann bases his account on modern scientific material: two splendidly illustrated works with scientific commentary. The first is *Falterschönheit*, introduced by the Swiss zoologist Adolf Portmann; Mann wove whole sections of this work into his novel:

Portmann:	Doctor Faustus:
In contrast to red, yellow, or black, blue is usually not a true color; rather it arises from very fine, intricate little furrows and other surface configurations formed by tiny scales. This microstructure breaks and reflects the light in such a way that only the most intense blue light reaches the eye of the observer, while all other rays are excluded by virtue of a complicated process. The scientist calls such a blue "structural blue"; one which, like the blue of the sky, is not created by any demonstrable pigment.[114]	The most splendid color they displayed, a dreamlike lovely azure, was, so Jonathan instructed us, no true color at all, but produced by fine little furrows and other surface configurations resulting from artificial refraction of the light rays and exclusion of most of them so that only the purest blue light reached the eyes. [14]

Portmann's remark on the blue of the sky provided Mann with Jonathan's calm answer when his wife asks worriedly if the butterfly's azure color is a mere illusion: " 'Do you call the blue sky a cheat?' answered her husband looking up backwards at her" (14). The description on the next few pages adheres closely to Portmann, although Mann makes small but significant changes. The following quotations show how Mann manages to suggest that the insects are somehow human. He even hints at a moral sense, thus preparing for the development the butterfly motif will undergo as the butterfly becomes the symbol for a woman:

114. *Falterschönheit: Exotische Schmetterlinge in farbigen Naturaufnahmen*, pp. 15–16.

Portmann:
"These insects," Wallace reports in his *World of the Tropics*, "are usually large, easily recognizable, and visible from a distance, often gorgeously colored and decked out with all possible spots and colors. They fly slower and never try to hide, but no bird, spider or lizard, no ape will touch them, although all these animals like as a rule to eat butterflies." [115]

Doctor Faustus:
Not only were they exceptionally large, but also colored and patterned with unusual gorgeousness; and Father Leverkühn told us that in this apparently challenging garb they flew about in perfect security. You could not call them cheeky; for they never hid, yet never an animal — not ape or bird or lizard — turned its head to look at them. [15]

Mann's small additions — "challenging," and "cheeky," here make all the difference between neutral scientific description and artistic evocation.*

Mann also borrowed Portmann's explanation for the striking behavior of these butterflies. *The Story of a Novel* [116] does not even mention this source, which, after all, furnished one of the central motifs of *Doctor Faustus*. The section on Hetaera esmeralda goes as follows:

Portmann:
"One of these clear-wings," reports Bates, "is especially beautiful — namely the Hetaera Esmeralda; it has one spot only of opaque coloring on its wings, which is of a violet and rose hue; this is the only part visible when the insect is flying low over dead leaves, in the gloomy shades where alone it is found, and it then looks like a wandering petal of a flower." [117]

Doctor Faustus:
One such butterfly, in transparent nudity, loving the duskiness of heavy leafage, was called Hetaera esmeralda. Hetaera had on her wings only a dark spot of violet and rose; one could see nothing else of her, and when she flew she was like a petal blown by the wind. (14)

115. *Ibid.*, p. 18. C. S. Brown found the description of the butterfly Hetaera esmeralda in the work of the English naturalist H. W. Bates, *The Naturalist on the River Amazons*, 1:104. Mann's direct source is, however, Portmann, who himself quotes Bates when describing the butterfly (Brown, "The Entomological Source of Mann's Poisonous Butterfly").

* Translator's note: The German original also refers to the butterflies' flight as "somehow depressing."

116. In a section of *The Story of a Novel* which he later deleted (MS, p. 29), Mann mentions that he worked through an *Allgemeine Biologia*, in which he was especially interested by the "fraud of osmotic growths." He gives no closer information on this work, but most textbooks discuss such phenomena. Thus Jonathan Leverkühn's experiment with the shellacked glass rod and the chloroform drop is described in Max Hartmann's *Allgemeine Biologie: eine Einführung in die Lehre vom Leben*, pp. 212–13.

117. *Falterschönheit*, p. 16, quoting Bates (*The Naturalist*), p. 52.

By the addition of "transparent nudity" to Portmann's description, Mann anticipates the motif of sensuality which will appear with the figure of the little prostitute. When Hetaera esmeralda first appears in *Doctor Faustus*, it is as a South American butterfly of the genus *Morphos*. But the name becomes connected with the girl who infects Adrian, and a symbolic identity is established between the girl and the butterfly; the identity is underlined by their fluttering nature and the deceptiveness of their beauty. The name also gives rise to a tone row: h [b-flat] -e-a-e-ess [e-flat], which occurs as a leitmotif in Adrian's compositions and comes to symbolize sensual temptation and the pact with the devil. And this symbolic net, which stretches throughout the novel, can be traced back to a book of zoological plates!

Mann's source for the descriptions of the creatures of the sea is another book of plates, *Kunstgebilde des Meeres, Muscheln und Schneckengehäuse* ["Artifacts of the Sea, Mollusks and Snail Shells"] with an introduction by Arnold Masarey. In Mann's descriptions of the colors and mysterious patterns of the shells one can recognize several of the plates from this book — small, pleasing water colors by Paul A. Roberts. Mann's account of the uses of shells follows Masarey closely:

Masarey:
According to a superstitious interpretation, shells belonged to the indispensable inventory of witches' kitchens and apothecary shops during the early Middle Ages. . . . Thus they were to be found in use as splendid tobacco boxes . . . as containers for repulsive poisons and their antidotes. They enjoyed pious veneration as liturgical use-objects: jewel-studded shell cabinets intended as monstrances or reliquaries, Communion chalices, and such things.[118]

Doctor Faustus:
In the Middle Ages they had belonged to the standing inventory of the witches' kitchen and alchemist's vault: they were considered the proper vessels for poisons and love potions. On the other hand, and at the same time, they had served as shrines and reliquaries and even for the Eucharist. What a confrontation was there! — poison and beauty, poison and magic, even magic and ritual. [16]

Symbolically and thematically, the section on Jonathan Leverkühn's biological studies establishes the major motifs for Adrian's life. The father's interest in sea creatures broadens as a motif when Adrian descends into the depths. Adrian's fan-

118. *Kunstgebilde des Meeres*, pp. 11, 12.

tastic excursions in the company of Professor Capercailzie come directly from the old chapbook. There we read how Faust journeys during the eighth year to hell and to the stars, and Adrian claims to have investigated the sea and the universe in 1913, the eighth year after his pact with the devil.[119] Both undertake their voyages with an incarnation of the devil.[120]

Although the passage on Adrian's deep-sea adventures directly parallels the chapbook, Mann takes the details from a modern source, a newspaper article about the ocean explorations of Dr. William Beebe. Mann used an unsigned article from the *Prager Presse* with the heading "The Wonders of the Depths. A New Depth Record: 830 Meters Below the Surface." Mann's clipping lacks the full date, but the article is datelined "Bermuda, August 13" and probably refers to a descent undertaken by Beebe on August 11, 1934 near the island of St. George.[121] Adrian's description coincides to a large extent with the report in the *Prager Presse*. Mann underlined several of the phrases in red and uses them in the novel:

Prager Presse:	*Doctor Faustus*:
. . . eight sea miles east of St. George . . .	. . . some nautical miles east of St. George . . . [266]
. . . films made through quartz windows by the use of high-voltage searchlights.	. . . provided with a supply of oxygen, a telephone, high-voltage searchlights, and quartz windows all round. [267]

Mann borrowed all his statistics from the article. The diving bell has for instance "only one point two inside diameter" (267) and is subject to "a pressure of five hundred thousand tons" (267). There are several word-for-word correspondences; the phrase "wonders of the depths," the title of the article, appears in Mann's text (266). The descriptions of deep-sea creatures contain slight modifications of the wording of the article. At the top of the clipping Mann has noted: "suited for predatory way of life by huge mouths, powerful jaws, tele-

---

119. See above, p. 47. Hans Joachim Mette points out this similarity to the chapbook but demonstrates that the motif of descent and ascent comes from the Greek romance of Alexander ("Doktor Faustus und Alexander. Zur Geschichte des Descensus- und Ascensus-Motivs," p. 29).

120. Cf. Lesser (*Thomas Mann*, p. 445), Blume (*Thomas Mann und Goethe*, p. 129). On the etymology of the name Capercailzie, see V. A. Oswald, "Full Fathom Five: Notes on Some Devices in Thomas Mann's 'Doktor Faustus.' "

121. W. Beebe, *Half Mile Down*, pp. 213 ff., 195.

scope eyes, light-shedding organs." Beebe gives similar descriptions of such sea monsters; [122] Mann may have found these details either in the newspaper or in Beebe's book, but at any rate he speaks in *Doctor Faustus* of "predatory mouths; obscene jaws, telescope eyes" (268). [123]

As a counterpart to his tales of the depths, and parallel to the journey to the stars in the chapbook, Adrian gives Zeitblom a brief course in astronomy. Here, too, Mann leaned heavily on newspaper and magazine articles. The beginning of this section is based on an article by R. D. Potter in *The American Weekly*, "We Live Inside a Globe, Too." Mann weaves in the title itself: "In a hollow ball . . . we all and sundry pass our days" (270), as well as the following passages:

Potter:	*Doctor Faustus*:
. . . our galaxy may be watch-shaped.	It was shaped more or less like a flat watch; . . . But this disk was only comparable to the
. . . our galaxy . . . is shaped like a huge orange. Most of it is empty space. [124]	flat round surface which results when one cuts an orange in half . . . in whose spaces, mostly empty spaces . . . [270]

Many factual passages echo the article, among them the phrases "thirty thousand light-years" (270), and "the whole diameter of the galactic hollow ball came to two hundred thousand light-years" (271).

Adrian's further remarks are based on "Is the universe expanding?" by Emo Descovich, printed in 1934 in the *Neue Freie Presse*. Mann made extensive use of Descovich's information, again changing some of it and leaving certain parts unchanged. In the following passage the words in italics are quoted directly from the article; Mann underlined them in his clipping:

. . . the cosmos . . . *for nineteen hundred million years, has been in a state of furious expansion — that is,* of explosion. Of this we

122. *Ibid.*, p. 220.
123. Anni Carlsson in "Der Meeresgrund in der neueren Dichtung," picks out similarities between Adrian Leverkühn's deep-sea expedition and H. C. Andersen's satiric fairy tale in verse, "The Diving Bell." She states, however, that Mann did not know the fairy tale, so that any similarities are accidental. The character of the deep-sea journey as a descent to the kingdom of the dead — in the sense of an initiation rite — familiar to us from the *Joseph* novels is discussed by M. Yourcenar, "Humanism in Thomas Mann," p. 163.
124. R. D. Potter, "We Live Inside a Globe, Too," p. 4.

were left in no doubt, due to the *red-shift* of the light . . . the stronger alteration of color of this light *toward the red end of the spectrum* is in proportion to the greater distance from us of these nebulae. [272] [125]

For the latter part of the section on Adrian's astronomical studies Mann leans on an article under the "Science" heading in *Time*. The article contains underlinings which reappear more or less verbatim in *Doctor Faustus*. This is an example:

Time:	*Doctor Faustus*:
. . . containing methane and ammonia gases which surround planets such as Jupiter, Venus and Mars.[126]	. . . containing much methane and ammonia, like Jupiter, Mars, and Venus. [274]

These expeditions into the realm of modern science accord with Adrian's Faustian nature. We have here a clear example of how heterogeneous fragments can be arranged to form a meaningful whole, just as the sand on the glass plate "grouped and arranged itself in astonishingly precise and varied figures and arabesques" [18] when one stroked the edge with a cello bow. Mann transforms rather banal newspaper articles or paragraphs from reference books into organic parts of a great work of art. Indeed, part of the magic of the novel is that he fuses such disparate and unlikely elements into a single pattern.

NIETZSCHE AND INSPIRATION THROUGH DISEASE

Until now we have been looking at only those details of Adrian's character and biography that go back to the original Dr. Faustus and his times. But in creating a modern Faustus, Mann could not be satisfied with a figure rooted in the days of superstition, magic, and demonology. This atmosphere provides a necessary historical background, but Mann modernizes it in several significant ways.

A connection immediately suggests itself between Adrian and Arnold Schönberg. It is well known that Mann "borrows" Schönberg's twelve-tone technique and attributes its creation to his Adrian; Mann was more or less forced to add an explanatory postscript to the second and subsequent editions of the novel. But Adrian is definitely not a portrait of Schönberg, as

125. E. Descovich, "Dehnt sich das Weltall aus?"
126. Anonymous article in *Time*, Feb. 21, 1944.

Mann emphatically states in his answer to Schönberg's outraged protest:

The idea that Adrian Leverkühn is Schoenberg, that the figure is a portrait of him, is so utterly absurd that I scarcely know what to say about it. There is no point of contact, not a shade of similarity, between the origin, the traditions, the character, and the fate of my musician, on the one hand, and the existence of Schoenberg on the other.[127]

Michael Mann offers the explanation that Schönberg was primarily offended because his twelve-tone technique seemed to be "involved with a sick-minded fictional character or even with German National Socialism." [128]

Disease, in fact, is what links Adrian Leverkühn to the powers of darkness and gives him the strength with which Mephistopheles traditionally invested Faust. Mann very early conceived the idea of a gifted artist who deliberately contracts syphilis. He recounts in *The Story of a Novel* that he looked through old papers for material on Faust and found a "three-line outline of the Dr. Faust of 1901." [129] Another plan, dated 1905 and only slightly expanded, is among Thomas Mann's papers:

Novella, or for "Maja." Figure of the syphilitic artist: as Dr. Faust, pledged to the devil. The poison works as intoxication, stimulant, inspiration; he is filled with ecstatic enthusiasm and creates works of genius; the devil guides his hand. But finally the devil fetches him: luetic paralysis.[130]

It is not hard to understand how Thomas Mann's general attitude toward art and the artist should lead him to conceive of resurrecting the old magician and charlatan Faust as a modern artist in the grips of illness. Ever since *Tono Kröger*, Mann had been portraying the artist as a dubious being located on the borderline between two worlds, one narrow but wholesome, the other permeated with disease and demonic elements. A more lighthearted view of the artist as charlatan appears in the Felix Krull story. Krull is, after all, one of Mann's artist figures — and it might be mentioned here that Mann himself was nicknamed the "magician" by his family. But in *Doctor*

127. "Thomas Mann's Answer," in *Saturday Review of Literature*.
128. M. Mann, "The Musical Symbolism in Thomas Mann's Doktor Faustus," p. 318.
129. P. 17.
130. See P. Sherrer, who dates the sketch 1905, "Thomas Mann und die Wirklichkeit," p. 85.

Faustus the old theme has been reborn, and the ironic, coquettish pose has given way to deepest seriousness.

Because Adrian's syphilitic infection is of such extraordinary importance, Mann was determined to plot the course of the disease according to correct medical information. He borrowed details from the biographies of many persons who had suffered from the disease, but in addition he sought expert medical advice. A doctor friend, Martin Gumpert, provided him with technical literature,[131] and he or another doctor drew up a brief summary of the symptoms and usual course of the disease; this report has been found among Mann's papers, and a few comparisons with the novel will show how faithfully Mann followed his authorities. The doctor's report reads as follows:

Luetic paralysis results from physical destruction of the brain mass by the spirochetes . . . paralyzation of the pupils . . . headaches. Psychic irritability — to the point of sudden frenzied states. Vague speech — frequent unconscious slips of tongue, inability to pronounce difficult words.[132]

Zeitblom mentions several of these symptoms: Adrian constantly suffers from headaches; he displays sudden, violent agitation at Echo's approaching death (476 ff.); Zeitblom also notices the abnormal fixity of expression that results from paralysis of the pupils (484). Adrian's farewell speech offers examples of "frequent slips of the tongue," when he repeatedly corrects himself and blunders in his corrections (496, 501). The doctor's account continues:

General state of health more or less affected. Headaches, dizziness, lack of appetite, weakness. Periods of improvement even without treatment.

These, too, are among Adrian's symptoms. Zeitblom describes a period when Adrian's condition shows remarked improvement, except that he succumbs to occasional dizzy spells accompanied by headaches (158). But in one detail Mann strays from his medical source: with Adrian all secondary symptoms fail to manifest themselves, as Zeitblom "can confirm and maintain against any professional doubts" (158).

Mann's idea of linking artistic genius with syphilis was suggested by the case of Nietzsche, and insofar as it is permissible to speak of a model for Adrian Leverkühn, that model is Nietz-

131. *Story of a Novel*, p. 62.
132. The report comprises five handwritten pages, unnumbered and undated. The handwriting is not Mann's.

sche. Mann comments on the parallel in a letter published a year after *Doctor Faustus*:

> *Doctor Faustus* has been called a Nietzsche-novel, and indeed, the book, which for good reasons avoids mention of Nietzsche's name, contains many references to his intellectual tragedy, even direct quotations from the history of his illness. It has also been said that I had bisected myself in the novel, and that the narrator and the hero each embraced a part of me. That, also, contains an element of truth — although I, too, do not suffer from paralysis.[133]

The connection between Adrian and Nietzsche is at once apparent to anyone acquainted with Nietzsche's biography, and the issue has already been dealt with at length in the literature on *Doctor Faustus*.[134] Here it is sufficient to summarize briefly the major points of similarity.

Like Nietzsche, Adrian Leverkühn grows up in an old German city whose culture has been largely formed by Protestantism.[135] Both reveal unusual talents and are destined for the university. Both transfer to the University of Leipzig in order to accompany a favorite professor. They contract syphilis under exactly similar conditions and succumb after a period of intense creative activity to *paralysie générale* and total insanity. Both use a friend to conduct a courtship, which, however, fails. Finally, both are nursed during their last years by their mothers. Adrian and Nietzsche both die on August 25th at the age of fifty-five.

In addition to these specific biographical echoes, *Doctor Faustus* contains many of Nietzsche's favorite thoughts and concepts. Nietzsche's philosophy had formed an integral part of Mann's intellectual world for a good half century and left its traces in almost every one of his works. But in *Doctor Faustus* Mann is looking at the phenomenon Nietzsche from a new perspective; he goes so far as to make the devil enunciate certain cardinal principles of Nietzsche's. Mann had revised

133. "Thomas Mann's Answer," p. 23.
134. See for example Lesser, *Thomas Mann*, pp. 433–42; Mayer, *Thomas Mann*, pp. 322–23; J. C. Blankenagel, "A Nietzsche Episode in Thomas Mann's Doktor Faustus."
135. Cf. E. Bertram on Nietzsche's Naumburg, "The Germany of Luther, of Dürer and of the oldest German music, provincially pious and at the same time inflexibly protesting Germany" (*Nietzsche: Versuch einer Mythologie*, p. 182). B. A. Sørensen has demonstrated the great extent to which Mann's Nietzsche image was dependent on Bertram; both Mann and Bertram emphasize the importance of the natal city and give a similar characterization of these old cities ("Thomas Mann's Doktor Faustus: Mythos und Lebensbeichte," p. 84).

his view as a result of renewed and intensive study of Nietzsche's writings and the literature on him. This study also led to the essay "Nietzsche's Philosophy in the Light of Recent History," written immediately after the novel.[136] In *The Story of a Novel* Mann mentions some of the works on Nietzsche that he consulted while writing *Doctor Faustus*, but by no means all.[137] His working library included several editions of Nietzsche's works and about twenty-five books on Nietzsche; a good number of quotations from these books found their way into the novel.[138] Compared with the deeper correlation between Adrian and Nietzsche, these quotations may seem merely peripheral additions, but since they clearly demonstrate how Mann goes about his montage process, a few examples may prove helpful.

An interesting feature of these borrowings is that while Adrian occasionally quotes or paraphrases Nietzsche, passages taken from the Nietzsche literature are always assigned to Zeitblom. For Zeitblom stands in the same relation to Adrian as Nietzsche's biographers to Nietzsche. Yet one must also realize that Zeitblom, because of his mysterious identity with Adrian, participates in some of Nietzsche's attributes. Like Nietzsche, he is a classical philologist, although his conception of classical literature differs in essential points from Nietzsche's.[139] Zeitblom is closer in his attitude to Nietzsche's friend and colleague Erwin Rohde. Two passages from Rohde's letters to Nietzsche's friend Overbeck reappear in Zeitblom's narrative and lend weight to the hypothesis that Zeitblom is partly modeled on Rohde:

Rohde:	Doctor Faustus:
An indescribable atmosphere of *aloofness*, something that struck me then as completely	. . . the indescribable atmosphere of aloofness which he carried about wherever

136. *Last Essays*, pp. 141–77. Thomas Mann calls the Nietzsche essay "the essayistic postlude to *Faustus*" (*Story of a Novel*, p. 232 [translation amended]).

137. Pp. 11, 19, 96, 223.

138. The authors of the most important works on Nietzsche that Mann owned are as follows (for full details see Bibliography): L. Andreas-Salome, E. Bertram, R. Blunk, H. W. Brann, P. Deussen, P. G. Dippel (1934), O. Flake, E. Förster-Nietzsche, K. Joël, W. A. Kaufmann (1950), L. Klages, F. Krökel, K. Liebmann, R. M. Lonsbach, A. Mittasch, P. J. Möbius, F. Muckle, E. F. Podach (1930, 1932), H. Prinzhorn, K. Reinhardt, H. A. Reyburn, W. Shubart, J. Sommer, W. Weigand (1893).

139. M. Colleville points out that Zeitblom, like Nietzsche, does his military service in Naumburg ("Nietzsche et le 'Doktor Faustus,'" p. 344).

uncanny surrounded him. Something was present in him which had not been there before, and much was missing which had been present earlier. As if he came from a country where no one else lives.[140]

. . . had also become physically shriveled, weak and small, although with healthy coloring. . . . Anyway, they are far too much taken in by appearances, and almost completely by the half-imbecilic Ecce homo expression.[141]

he went. In increasing degree, more and more perceptible and baffling as the years went by, it wrapped him round and gave one the feeling that he came from a country where no one else lived. [411]

He seemed grown smaller, which might be due to the bent and drooping posture, from which he lifted to me a narrow face, and Ecce-homo countenance, despite the healthy country color, with woeful open mouth and vacant eyes. [509]

Zeitblom also echoes other Nietzsche friends. In the following passage Zeitblom follows Paul Deussen's evocation of a visit to his sick friend on his fiftieth birthday:

Deussen:
His mother led him in. I congratulated him, informed him that he was turning fifty today, and handed him a bouquet. He did not grasp any of what I was saying. Only the flowers seemed to arouse his interest for a moment, then they, too, lay forgotten.[142]

Doctor Faustus:
Of what I said to him about his birthday, the meaning of my visit, he obviously understood nothing. Only the flowers seemed to arouse his interest for a moment, then they lay forgotten. (509)

Even the solemnity and pathos in the novel's last sentence — where one would certainly expect an author to speak in his own voice, not in hidden allusions — contain a reminiscence from the Nietzsche literature. Zeitblom's parting words on his departed friend are a variation on a letter written by Nietzsche's friend Julius Langbehn after receiving the news of Nietzsche's death.

Langbehn:
With Nietzsche I have lost a brother. God be merciful to his poor soul.[143]

Doctor Faustus:
"God be merciful to thy poor soul, my friend, my Fatherland." [510]

140. The letter was published by Erich F. Podach in *Gestalten um Nietzsche: mit unveröffentlichten Dokumenten zur Geschichte seines Lebens und seines Werks*, p. 59. See W. Boehlich, "Thomas Manns 'Doktor Faustus,'" p. 592.

141. Podach, *Gestalten*, p. 63.

142. Deussen, *Erinnerungen an Friedrich Nietzsche*, p. 97.

143. Podach, *Nietzsches Zusammenbruch*, p. 134.

Adrian uses the words of Nietzsche in the letter which describes to Zeitblom the experience in the Leipzig brothel. Mann here paraphrases a letter in which Nietzsche describes to Deussen a very similar adventure:

Nietzsche:	Doctor Faustus:
I suddenly found myself surrounded by a half-dozen creatures in tulle and gauze, who were looking at me expectantly. I stood there speechless for a while. Then I instinctively went over to the piano, the only thing in that company with a soul, and struck a few chords.[144]	. . . on them sitting your nymphs and daughters of the wilderness, ribaudes, laced muttons all, six or seven, morphos, clear-wings, esmeraldas, et cetera, clad or unclad, in tulle, gauze, spangs. . . . I stood, not showing what I was feeling, and there opposite me I see an open piano, a friend, I rush up to it across the carpet and strike a chord or twain, standing up. [142]

H. W. Brann, in his book *Nietzsche und die Frauen* ["Nietzsche and Women"], which Mann read and extensively underlined, writes of Nietzsche's brothel visits and the infection he contracted: "Nietzsche seems in both cases to have deliberately sought out the infection — for the sake of self-mortification." [145] This very thought causes Zeitblom to pause, deeply stirred by the possibility that Adrian's behavior might have a higher spiritual purpose (154 f). Mann put a mark in the margin beside Brann's contention that "Nietzsche's dealings with prostitutes must have been limited to rare, fleeting encounters." He also noted Brann's insistence on the "strong and lasting influence made on Nietzsche's imagination by the experience in the Cologne brothel." [146] These statements are as applicable to Adrian as to Nietzsche.

Certain turns of phrase in the discussion between the devil and Leverkühn reveal their Nietzschean origin. Zeitblom insists that he is transcribing Adrian's exact words (221), but in fact the devil's tirade on inspiration echoes Nietzsche's *Ecce Homo*: [147]

Ecce Homo:	Doctor Faustus:
Has anyone at the end of the 19th century any distinct notion	"Who knows today, who even knew in classical times, what

144. Deussen, *Erinnerungen an Friedrich Nietzsche*, p. 24.
145. Brann, *Nietzsche und die Frauen*, p. 208.
146. *Ibid.*, p. 207.
147. Colleville, "Nietzsche et le 'Doktor Faustus,'" pp. 348–49.

61

of what poets of a stronger age understood by the word inspiration? . . . an ecstasy so great that the immense strain of it is sometimes relaxed by a flood of tears. . . . the feeling that one is utterly out of hand, with the very distinct conscious-ness of an endless number of thrills and titillations descending to one's very toes . . .[148]

inspiration is. . . . What he wants and gives is triumph over it, is shining, sparkling, vainglorious unreflectiveness! . . . A genuine inspiration . . . received by the possessed one with faltering and stumbling step, with shudders of awe from head to foot, with tears of joy blinding his eyes . . ." [237]

It may at first seem remarkable that Mann chose as a model for Adrian Leverkühn a nonmusician, even if he embodied the other typical German and Faustian features which Mann wanted to portray in his hero. In "Germany and the Germans" Mann says:

It is a grave error on the part of legend and story not to connect Faust with music. He should have been musical, he should have been a musician.[149]

Mann intends his Faust-novel to rectify this mistake, and Nietz-sche turns out to fit this context after all. He often expresses the conviction that music is an inseparable component of what-ever is specifically German.[150] Nietzsche himself loved music and both played the piano and composed — as a youth — in the style of the Romantics.[151] He also deserves recognition as a philosopher of music and friend and adviser to Richard Wagner. Ernst Bertram summarizes Nietzsche's relation to music thus:

When Nietzsche awakened to consciousness, it was as a musician; as a musician the youth was gripped by the most intense enthusiasm of his life; ripe for decay, he still thought of himself and described himself as a musician.[152]

In an essay Thomas Mann likewise contends that Nietzsche might well be counted a musician.[153]

The motif of courtship in *Doctor Faustus* has, as already suggested, its forerunner in the life of Nietzsche. Adrian's abor-

148. Nietzsche, *Complete Works* (New York, 1924), 17:101–2. Cf. Mann, *Last Essays*, p. 147.
149. "Germany and the Germans," p. 51.
150. E. Bertram, (*Nietzsche*, p. 108) speaks of the "identity of music and Germanness that the young Nietzsche constantly experiences."
151. *Ibid.*, p. 104.
152. *Ibid.*, p. 103.
153. "Dostoevsky — in Moderation," p. xii.

tive proposal to Marie Godeau through Schwertfeger alludes either to Nietzsche's rejected proposal to Lou Andreas-Salomé or to the episode with Mathilde Trampedach and Hugo von Senger.[154] Mann thinks it natural that this detail should recall Nietzsche when so many aspects of the novel refer to him.[155] But, Mann continues, the biographical reference does not exhaust the significance of the courtship motif, for it also has literary forerunners; the motif is familiar to us from Shakespeare; in fact Marie Godeau bears some resemblance to the Dark Lady of the sonnets and to the dark-eyed Rosaline. In *The Story of a Novel* Mann points out several direct quotations from Shakespeare, which he smuggled into the passages that describe Adrian's marriage plans and the courtship. Other quotations have also been traced.[156] Mann further mentions reading Frank Harris's *The Man Shakespeare and His Tragic Life Story*.[157] Several of Harris's theories and even entire passages turn up in the fictional world of *Doctor Faustus*. A few examples will indicate how Mann goes about using his unacknowledged borrowings.

Frank Harris's comments on Rosaline appear in slightly modified and expanded form when Zeitblom offers his interpretation of a scene in *Love's Labour Lost*:

Harris:	Doctor Faustus:
. . . there Biron tells us that among the three of the Princess's women he loves "the worst of all." Up to this moment we have only been told kindly things of Rosaline and the other ladies. . . . The suspicion grows upon us . . . that Shakespeare is speaking of himself and of a particular woman; else we should have to admit that his portraiture of Rosaline's character was artistically bad, and bad without excuse, for why should he lavish all the wealth of unpleasant detail on a mere subsidiary character?[158]	There can be no doubt that the strangely insistent and even unnecessary, dramatically little justified characterization of Rosaline as a faithless, wanton piece of female flesh — a description given to her only in Biron's speeches, whereas in the actual setting of the comedy she is no more than pert and witty — there can be no doubt that this characterization springs from a compulsion, heedless of artistic indiscrepancies, on the poet's part, to take poetic revenge for them. [216]

154. See for example Brann, *Nietzsche und die Frauen*, pp. 150, 44.
155. *Story of a Novel*, p. 33.
156. *Ibid.*, p. 34–35. See also F. Kaufmann, *Thomas Mann*, p. 201.
157. *Story of a Novel*, p. 35.
158. F. Harris, *The Man Shakespeare and His Tragic Life Story*, 2d rev. ed., p. 224.

When Rosaline replies "The blood of youth burns not with such excess/As gravity's revolt to wantonness," Zeitblom repeats Frank Harris's judgment to the letter:

Harris:	*Doctor Faustus*:
This remark has no pertinence or meaning in Rosaline's mouth. Biron is supposed to be young in the play, and he has never been distinguished for his gravity, but for his wit and humor. . . . The two lines are clearly Shakespeare's criticism of himself.[159]	For he is young and not at all grave, and by no means the person who could give occasion to such a comment as that it is lamentable when wise men turn fools and apply all their wit to give folly the appearance of worth. In the mouth of Rosaline and her friends Biron falls quite out of his role; he is no longer Biron, but Shakespeare in his unhappy affair with the dark lady. [216]

Although these allusions to Shakespeare do not belong to the central group of motifs, they are so striking that they seemed worth mentioning.

FURTHER DISEASED GENIUSES

Mann's criteria for the modern Faust might be summarized as follows: he should be an artist of genius, deeply rooted in the German cultural tradition; his inspiration should gain intensity through the effects of syphilis; his medium of expression should be music. Nietzsche fulfills all but the last requirement. Nietzsche was, however, not the only model for Adrian. Adrian is a composite of several composers, both pure geniuses and syphilitics, the foremost among them being Beethoven.

Mann was familiar enough with the literature on Beethoven to know that Beethoven's illness was often hinted to be of venereal origin. The first wholesale attempt to interpret Beethoven's life and work in terms of syphilis was undertaken by Ernest Newman in *The Unconscious Beethoven*,[160] which Mann read with rapt attention, marking every passage dealing with Beethoven's illness. In one such passage Newman quotes Grove to the effect that Beethoven's deafness was "most probably the result of syphilitic affections at an early period of his

159. *Ibid.*, p. 230.
160. Newman, *The Unconscious Beethoven*. Mann mentions the book in *Story of a Novel*, p. 90.

life." [161] In his determination to establish his theory, Newman suggests that the peculiarities of Beethoven's last compositions are directly connected with his deafness and isolation, and thus indirectly connected with syphilis.

However, Beethoven has more than personal significance for *Doctor Faustus*. As human beings Adrian and Beethoven have little in common; the biographical parallels are small and inessential. We begin to see the deeper bond between Adrian and Beethoven during a discussion of the relation of music to the word, when Adrian tells an anecdote borrowed from Newman about Beethoven's technique of composition:

Newman:	*Doctor Faustus*:
"He is composing," was the answer. "But he is writing words, not notes." "That is his method; he usually indicates in words the course of the ideas in a composition, at the most adding a few notes in between." [162]	"What is he writing there in his notebook?" it had been asked. "He is composing." "But he is writing words, not notes." Yes, that was a way he had. He usually sketched in words the course of ideas in a composition, at most putting in a few notes here and there. [163]

Newman's was not the only Beethoven source that Mann consulted. He mentions in *The Story of a Novel* that he read the major biographies by Schindler and Bekker and, what is equally important, studied Beethoven's compositions under the guidance of Adorno. [163] Most of the material Mann gained from these sources pertains to music and will be treated in a later section, but certain general aspects of Beethoven's life belong in our present discussion.

Anton Schindler's Beethoven biography seems to have had influence on the overall character of *Doctor Faustus*. It is the work of a reverent disciple, who tries to gloss over unedifying aspects of the maestro's life and work. The very situation reminds us of *Doctor Faustus*: the faithful, admiring, and rather

161. Newman, *The Unconscious Beethoven*, 1st ed., p. 47. (Since the copy of the second edition used by Mann cannot be found, all references are to the original edition.) Newman rests his theory about Beethoven's disease on the testimony of earlier Beethoven biographers who had contact with persons who had known Beethoven. His leading source is the five-volume work by A. W. Thayer, *Beethoven's Leben* (1866–78).

162. *The Unconscious Beethoven*, p. 149. This anecdote also appears in another work with which Mann was familiar: J. Bahle, *Eingebung und Tat im musikalischen Schaffen*, p. 182. Mann's wording is, however, closer to Newman's.

163. *Story of a Novel*, pp. 49, 69, 47.

limited apostle places his master before himself and with trembling hand sets out to record the life history of his "departed Friend." We are dealing here not with quotations but with a general agreement in style, tone, and manner of expression. Schindler's officious and garrulous introduction, in which he explains how he came into possession of certain papers and why he is the only qualified biographer, bears a striking similarity to Zeitblom's. Schindler begins by stating that he will be dealing with "facts, most of which one must have experienced on the spot and at the side of this great man," and he stresses his own position as that of an ever-present "helping hand": [164] "It was my duty from that time to his death to do his bidding wherever and whenever he needed me; what he asked of me went before everything else." [165] Zeitblom, too, sees it as his task to provide information which will help the reader understand Adrian's plight; he expresses his relation to Adrian in similar terms: "Have I not said more than once that the life I am treating of was nearer to me, dearer, more moving than my own?" (176), and speaks of the "always cherished desire to serve, to help, to protect him" (253). When Zeitblom's hand trembles at the necessity of continuing his narrative, the equivalent passage in Schindler's book reads: "if only I could here lay down my pen and entrust the continuation to another person." [166]

Details like the following suggest further similarities between Adrian and Beethoven: Beethoven's mysterious illness — Schindler declines to be specific — causes him to seek out several doctors, but for various bizarre reasons none of them so much as begins treatment; this has its parallel in Adrian's ill-starred visits to the three doctors (156 ff.).[167] Adrian's relation to Frau von Tolna might be seen as reminiscent of Beethoven's to the Hungarian countess, Marie Erdödy. Schindler writes: "I know only that this friend of the arts built for her friend and teacher a lovely temple in the park of one of her castles in Hungary, and its entrance is adorned with an appropriate inscription." [168]

164. Schindler, *Biographie von Ludwig van Beethoven* (Münster, 1840), pp. 7, 8.
165. *Ibid.*, pp. 96–97.
166. *Ibid.*, p. 101.
167. *Ibid.*, pp. 179–80. Schindler also mentions (p. 156) a Countess Schafgotsch; Mann uses the name for the quartet that plays Beethoven's Opus 132 in Leipzig (*DF*, p. 159).
168. *Biographie von Beethoven*, pp. 68–69.

The Frau von Tolna episode in *Doctor Faustus* is likewise shrouded in mystery, although it has an additional source, more detailed than Schindler's account. The story of Frau von Tolna and Adrian repeats in many respects that of Frau von Meck and Tschaikovsky, as Mann himself remarks in *The Story of a Novel*.[169] Mann's papers for *Doctor Faustus* include a brief newspaper clipping that deals with Frau von Meck; Mann underlined the following passage:

She offered him money. In her absence Tjajkovskij visited her home in the country and her magnificent residence in Moscow. . . . She travelled to foreign countries in order to be in the same town with him. But they never met! [170]

But we must return to Beethoven. Although Mann was principally reading for musical details, certain passages that he marked indicate an interest in Beethoven's private circumstances. Schindler says of Beethoven's love life, "Beethoven never married, and strangely enough never had a love affair either." [171] Mann wrote in the margin, "Doesn't mean 'was never in love,' " a distinction that reminds us of Zeitblom's interpretation of Adrian's union with Hetaera esmeralda. Mann also saved clippings that refer to Beethoven's personal life and his illness.[172]

Others besides Nietzsche and Beethoven, however, fit the specifications set by Mann for the hero of *Doctor Faustus*: it is indeed remarkable how many talented artists share their fate. Certainly the combination of creativity and syphilis was at one time fairly common, although not so common as suggested by Brunold Springer in *Die genialen Syphilitiker* ["The Inspired

169. P. 33.
170. L. Altmann, "Our Great Symphonies Written by Lonely Men." Mann could also find material for his portrait of Frau von Tolna in his son Klaus's *Pathetic Symphony: A Novel about Tschaikowsky*. V. A. Oswald has provided an ingenious analysis of the role of Frau von Tolna: "Thomas Mann's *Dr. Faustus*: the Enigma of Frau von Tolna." D. Devoto points out several similarities in the careers of Tschaikowsky and Adrian; see "Deux musiciens russes dans le *Doktor Faustus* de Thomas Mann."
171. This is not to be found in the 1840 edition (above) but in *Anton Schindlers Beethoven-Biographie*, ed. A. C. Kalischer, p. 136, n. 83, which Mann used.
172. The question of Beethoven's syphilis is discussed in an anonymous article on his *Gesprächbücher* in the *Prager Presse*, Oct. 7, 1935; Mann underlined various details. E. Engelberg, who briefly touches on the relationship between Adrian and Beethoven, sees literal reminiscences of Beethoven's "Heiligenstadt Testament" in *DF*. See "Thomas Mann's Faust and Beethoven."

Syphilitics"].[173] Ernest Newman mentions this imaginative theoretician and concludes that

> No one is safe from Springer. Setting out from the comprehensive assumption that, as he puts it, "civilization is syphilization," he explains in terms of this disease the lives and thoughts and actions of a large number of representative men, from Pope Alexander VI in the fifteenth century and Leo X in the sixteenth through Ulrich von Hütten [sic] and Benvenuto Cellini and Mirabeau and Napoleon and E.T.A. Hoffmann and Beethoven and Heine and Schopenhauer and Schumann and Manet and Maupassant and Daudet and Nietzsche and Hugo Wolf and many others, down to Woodrow Wilson and Mussolini.[174]

Although Mann displays nothing like Springer's zeal for completeness, he does show a tendency to interpret the illness of various geniuses in this direction and to set up Adrian Leverkühn as a clearly "representative" figure. In many cases Mann has no need to force such an interpretation; the facts speak for themselves. It would, however, be ridiculous to see every inspired "syphilitic" as a prototype for Adrian. We will discuss here only those cases which could furnish other biographical details or contribute somehow to the world of motifs and ideas that go to make up the novel.

The biography of Hugo Wolf offers certain parallels to Adrian's. He contracted the same disease as Adrian and died insane. His life as an artist is marked by the same violent alternation between intense creativity and deep depression.[175] During his last illness, Wolf, like Adrian (507), tried to drown himself. In *The Story of a Novel* Mann mentions studying Wolf, his letters as well as Newman's biography.[176] Traces of these sources can be found in the form of quotations. The borrowings from Wolf's letters deal primarily with the artist's anguish that he is constantly at the mercy of the ebb and flow of inspiration. The devil's speech on art and the artist contains an obvious quotation:

Wolf:	*Doctor Faustus*:
It's a dog's life when one can't work. If I could only croak in good style, it would suit me fine.	" 'Oh, flat and stale! Oh, a dog's life, when a man can do nothing! . . . If I could croak

173. Springer, *Die genialen Syphilitiker*.
174. *The Unconscious Beethoven*, p. 46, n. 1.
175. A French medical dissertation cites Wolf as a typical example of manic inspiration: H.-H.-O. Hécaen, *Manie et inspiration musicale*.
176. Pp. 22, 26. E. Newman, *Hugo Wolf*.

May hell take pity on me. . . .	in good style! May hell pity me,
And I feel that I am one of	for I am a son of hell!' " [236]
those sons of hell.[177]	

The violent alternation of productivity and apathy also characterizes Robert Schumann's later years, when insanity was increasingly gaining the upper hand. Like Adrian and Hugo Wolf, Schumann made an abortive attempt at suicide: he flung himself into the Rhine. Mann's underlinings in Richard Batka's Schumann biography indicate his interest in such correspondences; the following passage, for instance, is obviously pertinent to Adrian:

. . . conceived the grandious plan of composing the score to Goethe's Faust, and summoning all his energy composed a score for the major part of that powerful last scene; then, in the fall, came the inevitable relapse. A nervous affection set in; he was prey to obscure demons.[178]

Schumann's contact with the demonic realm had particular significance for Mann. He clipped a newspaper article which quotes Clara Schumann's description of her husband's disorder.[179] She mentions his hallucinations, which strikingly resemble Adrian's: "Raved all night. Angels were floating around him, sang him a theme, which he wrote down. In the morning the angels turned into demons making blood-curdling music. Forms of tigers and hyenas." "During the night violent self-accusation — called himself a criminal. Hallucinations with a strong religious tinge." [180] She also mentions his "halting speech," "hunched posture," and "the abnormal dilation of his pupils," typical symptoms that also occur in Adrian.

Among the diseased geniuses relevant to *Doctor Faustus*, though not serving as immediate models, are Dostoevsky and Kierkegaard. Mann tends to interpret these two figures' illnesses in such a way that they fit the pattern of luetic paralysis. Mann sets forth his opinion on Dostoevsky in the introduction he wrote in July, 1945 to an American edition of that writer's short novels.[181] He gives his own explanation of Dostoevsky's epilepsy: [182]

177. Wolf's letter to Grohe dated December 30, 1890, *Hugo Wolfs Briefe an Oskar Grohe*, ed. H. Werner, p. 51.

178. R. Batka, *Biographie Schumanns*, p. 61. Mann underlined most of this passage.

179. Undated newspaper clipping headed "Zur Veröffentlichung von Robert Schumanns Violinkonzert."

180. Cf. *DF*, pp. 501–2, 477–78.

181. *Story of a Novel*, p. 131.

182. Lilli Venohr argues convincingly that Mann accepts the version of

I don't know what neurologists think of the "sacred" disease, but in my opinion it is definitely rooted in the realm of the sexual, it is a wild and explosive manifestation of sex dynamics, a transferred and transfigured sexual act, a mystical dissipation. I repeat that I regard the subsequent state of contrition and misery, the mysterious feeling of guilt, as even more revealing than the preceding seconds of bliss for which "one is ready to exchange his life." No matter to what extent the malady menaced Dostoevsky's mental powers, it is certain that his genius is most intimately connected with it, that his psychological insight, his understanding of crime and of what the Apocalypse calls "satanic depths" . . . are inseparably related to the disease.[183]

Mann's thoughts lead directly from Dostoevsky's disease to Nietzsche, whom "one can very well imagine as an epileptic," although his disease was different:

He shared the fate of many artists and particularly of a notable number of musicians (among whom he belongs after a fashion): he perished from progressive paralysis, a malady of unmistakably sexual origin.[184]

The introduction reveals Mann's deep involvement with the thematic complex of *Doctor Faustus* — and shows how much his preliminary researches for the novel add to the essay. Thus Mann appropriately takes up the case of Hugo Wolf and analyzes the particular type of syphilitic's inspiration which is so characteristic for this composer and which Mann also sees in Schumann. Mann then quotes the passage from Nietzsche's *Ecce Homo* given above in connection with the devil's remarks on inspiration. Mann's digression on the syphilitic creativity of Nietzsche and Hugo Wolf must be read as a footnote to his explanation of Dostoevsky's epilepsy; his linking of the three men reveals what interests him about Dostoevsky: his participation in the "Faustian" realm.

It is thus no accident that Adrian's interview with the devil echoes the devil's visit to Ivan Karamasov, a fact that has not gone unnoticed.[185] Dostoevsky is "pertinent," as Mann expresses it. But the fever vision of Ivan Karamazov colors more

Dostoevsky's illness offered by Mereschkowsky, whom Mann much admired. See *Thomas Manns Verhältnis zur russischen Literatur*, pp. 46 ff.

183. "Dostoevsky — in Moderation," p. x–xi.

184. *Ibid.,* p. xii. For literal correspondences to this essay see *DF*, pp. 242, 243.

185. See Blume, *Thomas Mann und Goethe*, p. 127; Lesser, *Thomas Mann*, p. 387; Faesi, *Thomas Mann*, p. 151. More thorough studies are Eva-Maria Pietsch, "Thomas Mann und F. M. Dostojewski," pp. 118 ff. and Venohr, *Thomas Manns Verhältnis . . .* , pp. 75 ff.

the general tone and mood of the scene in Palestrina than the details. Both Dostoevsky and Mann have a devil who appears as a rather peculiarly dressed gentleman, settles himself in a corner of the sofa, uses the familiar form of address, and articulates in an ironic jargon ideas which the hero recognizes as his own.[186] When the devil appears, Adrian has just been reading Kierkegaard's essay on Mozart's *Don Giovanni*. Kierkegaard is, of course, highly relevant to *Doctor Faustus* and has already been mentioned by the Winfried members as a thinker who calls attention to the demonic side of life (118). The devil now praises Kierkegaard for recognizing the kinship of music to the demonic and for loving music so intensely (242). The reference is to one of Kirkegaard's guiding concepts: in the connection of music with the erotic realm, music becomes a medium for the expression of sensuality. Adrian and the reader have already been prepared for these ideas by the lectures of the theology instructor Schleppfuss.

As an inspired artist with insight into the demonic nature of music, Kierkegaard deserves a place in the novel's complex of motifs. Mann says of Kierkegaard's relevance, "The novel's congruence to Kierkegaard's philosophy, of which I had had no knowledge, is most remarkable."[187] Added to this general congruence is the fact that Kierkegaard's knowledge resulted from the struggle with an illness of rather ambiguous nature. Interpretations of the "thorn in the flesh" that he mentions vary widely,[188] but the argument of Georg Brandes commands our closest attention, for in the summer of 1944 Mann took up Brandes' essay on Kierkegaard before reading anything by Kierkegaard himself.[189] He marked in Brandes' book several

186. Mann could find the same concept of the devil in Heine's writings: "We [the devils] have no shape that is exclusively ours; according to your fancy [Faust's] we borrow any shape you wish to see us in; we will always have the appearance of your thoughts" (Heine, *Sämtliche Werke*, 3:163). Christian Buddenbrook also has hallucinations of an uninvited guest who appears at dusk in the corner of the sofa: "Perhaps it happens to you that you come into your room when it is getting dark and see a man sitting on the sofa, nodding at you, when there is no man there?" (*Buddenbrooks*, tr. H. T. Lowe-Porter, 2:182).

187. *Story of a Novel*, p. 104.

188. Some scholars believe that this phrase refers to Kierkegaard's being humpbacked, e.g., R. Magnussen, *Det Saerlige Kors*, p. 11; others suspect homosexual leanings, venereal disease, etc. See L. Zeuthen, *Søren Kierkegaards hemmelige Note*, p. 18.

189. *Story of a Novel*, p. 85. Mann seems to have received the impetus for his Kierkegaard studies from Adorno, who lent him his book *Kierkegaard: Konstruktion des Ästhetischen*.

passages which attribute Kierkegaard's illness to sexual origins,[190] and others that hint at Kierkegaard's occasional struggles with approaching insanity. Brandes never goes so far as to portray Kierkegaard as a syphilitic, but Mann probably saw Brandes' vague indications in this light. Adrian Leverkühn is, in Mann's expression, "exemplary," that is, a representative rather than an individual figure. It is therefore natural that his life should unite elements from the lives of many famous artists, but when one speaks of models for Adrian, one must assume that Mann *intended* a connection or an allusion. Interpretations which cite Hölderlin, Rimbaud, or Rilke or even painters like Cézanne and Picasso as models seem rather farfetched.[191] It is more logical to seek references to musicians like Alban Berg and Igor Stravinsky,[192] so long as one recognizes that Mann borrowed only small details and did not establish any deeper kinship between these figures and Adrian.

MUSIC HISTORY AND THEORY AS SOURCES

Mann felt that his novel about a musician should contain a great deal of real musical material, and he went about acquiring his knowledge of music by careful and extensive study of sources.

190. "This contradiction [i.e. that the disease took on both a physical and a psychic character], when seen together with all his previous statements, indicates something sexual, for that is precisely what affects both body and soul and would be an essential matter to consider before contracting a marriage" (Georg Brandes, "Skandinavische Persönlichkeiten," *Gesammelte Schriften*, 3:2, 303). Mann marked the quotation in the margin.

191. Müller mentions Hölderlin ("Thomas Manns *Doktor Faustus*," p. 166). The other figures are suggested by P. B. Rice in "The Merging Parallels: Mann's *Doktor Faustus*," p. 208. It must be stressed that what they have in common has nothing to do with illness. Karl Heim discovers that, as youths, Adrian and Stravinsky share such things as the first musical impressions, the quick habit of learning, the fact that neither studies at a conservatory; see K. Heim, "Thomas Mann und die Musik," pp. 328, 331. Cf. I. Stravinsky, *Chronicle of My Life*, pp. 11, 28. Mann mentions that he had read this book (*Story of a Novel*, p. 11), and the numerous underlinings in his copy indicate a thorough study. Several passages in *DF* echo Stravinsky, e.g., Kretschmar's explanation that music had reached its greatest expressiveness in orchestral composition (*DF*, p. 150, Stravinsky, *Chronicle*, p. 39).

192. Lesser (Thomas Mann, p. 467) regards Adrian's journey to hear the Austrian premiere of Strauss' *Salomé* in Graz (*DF*, p. 154) a detail borrowed from the biography of Alban Berg. He also considers the name of the bassoon player Griepenkerl an echo of Berlioz' memoirs; cf. E. Newman, ed., *Memoirs of Hector Berlioz from 1803 to 1865*, tr. R. and E. Holmes, pp. 302, 340. Mann seems to have studied the 1935 edition carefully; see *Story of a Novel*, pp. 39, 54, 63.

These were later integrated in the usual manner into Mann's fictional context.

Again we will have to distinguish several distinct types of sources. During the course of a long life, Mann had acquired a knowledge of music which did credit to a man of letters. It was more than the fruit of listening and reading; at various times he pursued musical studies, and he played the violin.[193] With this solid foundation, Mann set out to deepen his insight into the history and theory of music by reading broadly and intensively and by talking and corresponding with the professional musicians among his friends and relatives. *The Story of a Novel* gives a full account of these efforts.

Critical opinions differ in their assessment of the manner in which Mann appropriated his musical source material. Some observers cannot praise Mann's musical judgment and knowledge highly enough, while others accuse him of misunderstandings and distortions. Even if this problem is not of central importance for us, it is interesting to hear a few of the experts.

In an unpublished study, "Die Musik im Roman Thomas Manns"[194] ["Music in Thomas Mann's Fiction"], the music historian Hans Grandi offers a thorough inventory of the musical material in the novel. He finds that Mann was well acquainted with the pertinent literature and possessed an extraordinarily solid knowledge of music, occasional errors such as his estimate of Beethoven's relation to the fugue notwithstanding. Grandi considers such mistakes insignificant. He points instead to descriptions of real compositions so accurate that they permit the piece in question to be immediately identified; examples are the evocation of the *Meistersingers* prologue (133) or the allusion to Saint-Saëns' "Danse macabre" (42).[195] He holds that Mann's descriptions of Adrian's compositions leave nothing to be desired in the way of clarity and "authenticity," and he concludes that

The compositions are an exemplary achievement, from both the musical and the literary point of view, giving the professional musician and the music lover alike a clear intellectual conception of each work and calling forth emotional response of a particularly high order.[196]

193. E. & K. Mann, *Escape to Life*, p. 79. Cf. J. C. de Buisonjé, "Bemerkungen über Thomas Manns *Doktor Faustus*," p. 185.
194. H. Grandi, "Die Musik im Roman Thomas Manns."
195. *Ibid.*, p. 136 ff. See *Story of a Novel*, p. 103.
196. Grandi, "Die Musik," p. 168.

Several musicians testify that Mann has captured the essence of modern music's predicament. The music critic and composer H. H. Stuckenschmidt summarizes his impressions of *Doctor Faustus* as follows:

In a heartrending way this story has come to be a part of me, for it is set to a great extent in my most intimate surroundings, it portrays and pleads for my causes, and enunciates the ideas of my generation, the musical avant-garde.[197]

On the negative side, J. L. Stewart, for example, declares that Mann has a totally false conception of the twelve-tone method, and that the concepts of "determinism" and "breakthrough" spring solely from this misunderstanding.[198] But critics like Stewart fail to realize that Thomas Mann may have deviated from his sources deliberately. We shall see later that Mann's "false" picture of the Schönberg technique — or of Adorno's interpretation of it — stems from Mann's use of musical terminology to illuminate a literary problem; he sometimes has to twist the terminology to make it fulfill its symbolic function.

But we are concerned here with the nature and sources of Mann's musical material. The most comprehensive treatments of this subject can be found in two unpublished dissertations. The first is Grandi's abovementioned "Die Musik im Roman Thomas Manns," and Karl Heim's "Thomas Mann und die Musik" ["Thomas Mann's Use of Music"], surveys the musical aspects of Mann's major works and offers a close analysis of *Doctor Faustus*. Both examine the significant passages on music, discuss Adrian's compositions, and attempt to define Mann's view of the central concerns of modern music. Despite the similarity in method, Heim and Grandi occasionally reach different results. Heim does not always find Mann's musical exposition convincing. He considers the description of Beethoven's sonata, Opus 111, highly unsatisfactory but does not criticize the chapter as a whole, having made a simple but important discovery that answers much of the criticism leveled against the novel; Heim detects the literary theme behind the musical one and concludes that music in *Doctor Faustus* has "a poetic function in the service of the higher reality of the

197. Letter of Stuckenschmidt to Mann's brother-in-law, the conductor Klaus Pringsheim, published by the latter in "Der Tonsetzer Adrian Lever-Kühn: ein Musiker über Thomas Manns Roman."
198. J. L. Stewart, "On the Making of *Doctor Faustus*," pp. 340–41.

novel."[199] Unfortunately Heim's incisive remarks are often coupled with random thoughts and hasty associations. He interprets the letter L in the title of Adrian's *Love's Labour's Lost* as the "Luciferian initial"; the three L's corrrespond to other triads he claims to discover in the novel's structure.[200] But he provides little supporting evidence for his interpretations.

Grandi and Heim have laid a useful foundation for the study of the musical thematics of *Doctor Faustus*. But some of their observations and conclusions need to be revised and supplemented. The material now available in the Zurich Archives reveals Mann's determination to "document" everything. Mann was apparently interested not only in exactitude and "authenticity," but also in historical veracity; he intended to portray specific lines of development in the history of music. In fact, if one arranges all the composers in the novel chronologically, the list of about seventy composers includes the foremost names in Western music from the late Middle Ages to Adrian's debut in our own times.[201] Moderns mentioned include Auric, Poulenc, and Stravinsky. Although all these musicians fit naturally into the narrative, the chronological distribution of the names makes it seem clear that Mann chose them according to a conscious principle.

Mann is not content to go back to the year 1200, when composers began to be known by name; he evokes even earlier stages in the development of Western music by describing the boys' singing with Hanne (27 ff.). Here Mann lets Zeitblom observe that vocal music originated in the anonymous folksong; and when the names of Pythagoras and Ptolemy occur, the reader is reminded of the founding of music theory in ancient times.

If the many real composers mentioned are intended to provide an air of authenticity, Mann achieves this end perhaps even more successfully by his references to contemporary musicians, among them the great conductors known for launching modern music, whom Mann entrusts with introducing Adrian Leverkühn's work to the public.[202] Mann also mentions several

199. Heim, "Thomas Mann," p. 274.
200. *Ibid.*, p. 310; see also p. 288.
201. G. Bergsten, "Musical Symbolism in Thomas Mann's 'Doctor Faustus,' " This essay is based on the second German edition of *DF*, from which Mann deleted the names of several composers.
202. Engländer shows that Mann chose wisely, for example when he picked Otto Klemperer — an enthusiastic interpreter of modern music in

famous orchestras and such ensembles as the Pro Arte String Quartet and the Flonzaley Quartet (403). Mann probably needed no further source than his frequent attendance at concerts, but to reinforce his own memories he also gathered reviews of performances by musicians whom he wished to use in *Doctor Faustus*.[203]

In other ways, too, Mann situates Adrian's work within the authentic world of modern music. Adrian has dealings with real music journals and music publishers — the Viennese publishing house Universal Editions is an example — and some of his compositions are performed at such real music festivals as the one in Donaueschingen (389). The source of Mann's detailed knowledge of these festivals can be traced: he heavily underlined the chapter on the festivals in *Music Here and Now*, a work written for the layman by Mann's friend, the Austro-American composer and writer Ernst Křenek.[204]

Mann's intention of sketching the development of music from the earliest times to the present further reveals itself in his treatment of musical instruments. A survey of all the instruments in *Doctor Faustus* and the properties attributed to them yields a fairly complete picture of the evolution from such ancient instruments as the Nordic bronze trumpet and primitive drums to later forms such as the saxophone and the celesta.[205] This large assortment of instruments might result simply from the description of Adrian's compositions. Primitive instruments would merely indicate that Adrian, like Stravinsky, appropriates elements of primitive music. But such an explana-

the 1920's — to conduct the premiere of the *Apocalypsis cum figuris* in 1926 (MS of the lecture series "Thomas Manns Faustusroman som musikalisk spegelbild," p. 16).

203. In a clipping from the Zurich newspaper *Die Weltwoche* dated Nov. 12, 1943 Mann underlined the following phrases, the first of which refers to Hindemith's Symphony in E♭ Major: "performed last year in Geneva . . . under Ansermet" (cf. *DF*, p. 178); "to the Zurich Tonhalle Orchestra and its masterful conductor, Dr. Volkmar Andreae" (cf. *DF*, p. 184).

204. TM mentions in *The Story of a Novel* that he studied Křenek's book while working on *DF* (pp. 39, 90). See E. Křenek, *Music Here and Now*, pp. 262 ff.

205. In my abovementioned article in *Orbis Litterarum* the musical instruments occurring in *DF* are listed by category. See also J. Müller-Blattau, who suggests but does not pursue a similar approach in "Die Musik in Thomas Manns *DF* und Herman Hesse's *Glasperlenspiel*," pp. 146–46. Engländer thinks the description of the musical instrument collection is an allusion to the private collection of Paul de Wit in Leipzig ("Thomas Manns Faustroman," p. 135).

tion cannot fully account for Mann's devoting considerable space to the instrument-maker Niklaus Leverkühn's instrument collection (40 ff). We know in addition that Mann studied Volbach's handbook on musical instruments.[206] In his copy of Volbach, Mann particularly marked the dates for the construction or development of various forms of instrument.[207]

The evolution of music that Mann indicates by the inclusion of composers, musicians, and musical instruments remains largely superficial. More significant aspects emerge from the discussions of music theory and music history. For these, too, Mann drew on numerous sources. We are concerned primarily with the written sources, but it should be emphasized that the musical sections of the book owe much to information imparted in conversation and to discussions of musical problems. Among the musical mentors mentioned in *The Story of a Novel* are Bruno Walter and the philosopher and music historian Theodor Wiesengrund-Adorno.

A major written source to be considered is Paul Bekker's *Musikgeschichte* ["History of Music"], which Mann received from the author as early as 1927 but studied purposefully while working on the novel.[208] Mann borrowed many ideas and formulations from Bekker, as the following quotations will indicate.[209]

Adrian's observations on the mathematical basis of early polyphonic song agree fully with Bekker's:

Bekker:	Doctor Faustus:
But if this mathematical element is especially apparent here, one must not forget that the material is itself the most impressively sensuous that can be: the warm breath of the human voice.[210]	But then they had these penitential practices sung, delivered over to the sounding breath of the human voice, which is certainly the most stable-warm imaginable thing in the world of sound. [68]

By changing Bekker's "warm" to "stable-warm," Mann calls up the memory of the stable girl Hanne, thus blending Bekker's observations into the texture of the novel. Later Breisacher

206. *Story of a Novel*, p. 29.
207. F. Volbach, *Das moderne Orchester: I. Die Instrumente des Orchesters: ihr Wesen und ihre Entwicklung.*
208. *Story of a Novel*, p. 23. The full title of Bekker's book is *Musikgeschichte als Geschichte der musikalischen Formwandlungen.*
209. Several scholars, among them Heim and Grandi, note that Mann uses Bekker, but they do not indicate to what extent.
210. Bekker, *Musikgeschichte*, p. 58.

echoes Bekker when he speaks of the great sixteenth-century masters of polyphonic vocal music; small changes suffice to produce a scornful tone:

Bekker:
And certainly the musicians of this period make the concept of vocal polyphony most "humanly" apprehendible to us; that is why they strike us as the greatest masters of this style.[211]

Doctor Faustus:
"These gentlemen brought us the conception of the vocal polyphonic art, 'humanly' at first, oh yes, and seemed to us therefore the greatest masters of this style." [281]

And on the subject of the glissando:

Bekker:
Sound . . . then, becomes denaturalized. If the natural form of song is a howl gliding over several notes, deliberate stylization fixes it firmly on one note. . . . Thus the first step is to divide up the whole tonal range, originally present as a sort of chaos, into areas defined according to established laws. This division of sounds according to exactly predetermined conditions is called a *tonal system*. The creation of such a tonal system as the normative metric system of musical pitches is the prerequisite for and first sign of a true creative process in music.[212]

Doctor Faustus:
. . . to fix to one single note the singing which in primeval times must have been a howling glissando over several notes, and to win from chaos a musical system. Certainly and of course: ordering and normalizing the notes was the condition and first self-manifestation of what we understand by music. [374]

In addition to the numerous literal or almost literal quotations,[213] Mann makes use of such arguments advanced by Bekker as that song or the human voice requires formal organization. In Bekker's words, we need the restrictions of form as "a necessary correlation" to the human voice, which is "the *human being itself*, the human being in complete nakedness." [214] This thought appears with slight changes in Kretschmar's lectures (68, 146).

Mann admits that he learned a great deal about modern

211. *Ibid.*, p. 65.
212. *Ibid.*, pp. 20–21.
213. *Ibid.*, pp. 23, 40–41, 112, 231 and *DF*, pp. 9, 280, 76, 372.
214. Bekker, *Musikgeschichte*, p. 59.

music and especially about the contributions of Arnold Schönberg from Adorno.[215] He studied the manuscript lent him of
Adorno's *Philosophie der neuen Musik* ["Philosophy of Modern
Music"]; he felt it exactly coincided with the atmosphere and
intellectual world of his Faust novel. Mann straightforwardly
admits his debt of gratitude:

The analysis of the row system and the criticism of it that is translated into dialogue in Chapter XXII of *Faustus* is entirely based upon
Adorno's essay. So are certain remarks on the tonal language of the
later Beethoven, such as occur early in the book in Kretschmar's
sputterings: the comments on the uncanny relationship that death
establishes between genius and convention.[216]

Mann's indebtedness to Adorno has been pointed out several
times, but no one specifies how many passages Mann quotes
verbatim.[217] Mann employs here the same process of piecing
together that has been observed in the Winfried section. Thus
page 192 is a composite of passages from pages 55, 62, 63 and 68
of Adorno's book.[218] Here is one of the larger of these "puzzle"
sections:

Adorno:
These four modes can in turn
be transposed to all twelve
notes of the chromatic scale, so
that forty-eight different versions
of the basic series may be used
in a composition. . . . And
finally, a composition can also
be based on two or more
series, on the analogy of the
double and triple fugue.[219]

Doctor Faustus:
So then you have four modes,
each of which can be
transposed to all the twelve
notes of the chromatic scale, so
that forty-eight different
versions of the basic series may be
used in a composition. . . . A
composition can also use two
or more series as basic material,
as in the double and triple
fugue. [192]

Mann allows himself the joke of investing the devil with features of Adorno during part of the debate with Adrian: he
becomes an intellectual music theoretician and critic with
glasses, "who himself composes" (238). We are thus hardly sur-

215. *Story of a Novel*, p. 42.
216. *Ibid.*, p. 46.
217. In an unpublished essay Lesser has traced parallels between *DF*
and Adorno's *Philosophie der neuen Musik* and Adorno's article "Spätstil
Beethovens," *Auftakt*, June 5, 1937. Grandi, Heim, and Stewart also point
out phrases borrowed from Adorno. See also F. Kaufmann, *Thomas Mann*,
p. 292 n.
218. T. W. Adorno, *Philosophie der neuen Musik*, 2d ed.
219. *Ibid.*, p. 63.

prised to find this devil quoting the *Philosophie der neuen Musik* with conviction. Here are a few examples:

Adorno:
There is no longer the demand, and in the pre-liberal era production becomes possible largely through the chance of a Maecenas.[220]

Doctor Faustus:
Lack of demand? And as in the pre-liberal period the possibility of production depends largely on the chance of a Maecenas? [239]

The diminished seventh, which is out of place in salon music, is right and full of expression at the beginning of Beethoven's sonata, Op. 111. . . . But Beethoven's whole technical niveau, the tension between consonance and the harshest dissonance known to him . . . the dynamic conception of tonality as a whole lends the chord its specific weight.[221]

The diminished seventh is right and full of expression at the beginning of Op. 111. It corresponds to Beethoven's whole technical niveau, doesn't it? — the tension between consonance and the harshest dissonance known to him. The principle of tonality and its dynamics lend to the chord its specific weight. [239]

Thomas Mann continues in this manner for pages, sometimes quoting, sometimes paraphrasing. Here and there one of Adorno's many Latinate terms is replaced by an earthy German one, which seems more appropriate to the devil.

Wendell Kretschmar likewise bears a resemblance to Adorno, not in character, appearance, or opinions, but in his manner of playing the piano. Part of Kretschmar's lecture on Beethoven's Opus 111 consists of his grotesque performance of playing the sonata while simultaneously providing commentary (53–56). Kretschmar's mighty exaggerations certainly have another source besides Adorno, but his actual method of musical analysis probably goes back to an experience described in *The Story of a Novel* as follows: "Then Adorno sat down at the piano and, while I stood by and watched, played for me the entire Sonata Opus 111 in a highly instructive fashion. I had never been more attentive." [222] Mann playfully pays his debt to Adorno by working Adorno's patronymic, Wiesengrund (meadowland), into Kretschmar's explication of Opus 111 (55).[223]

220. *Ibid.*, p. 103. The part of the sentence beginning "and as . . ." has been omitted from the 2d edition but was underlined by Mann in the manuscript.
221. *Ibid.*, p. 39.
222. P. 48.
223. *Ibid.*

One of Adorno's duties was to provide Mann with suitable reading on music. He recommended Julius Bahle's *Eingebung und Tat im musikalischen Schaffen* ["Inspiration and Deed in Musical Creation"], which Mann in his journal calls "important." [224] Bahle's book did not furnish so much material as the works of Bekker and Adorno, but a few phrases reappear in *Doctor Faustus*. The devil's comment on inspiration paraphrases Bahle's quotation of Richard Strauss:

Bahle:	Doctor Faustus:
The melodic idea usually comprises two to four bars. The subsequent bars are the result of consciously working toward a goal.[225]	"The idea, then, a matter of three, four bars, no more, isn't it? All the residue is elaboration, sticking at it." [237]

Bahle, or the devil, uses Beethoven as an illustration of this process:

Bahle:	Doctor Faustus:
And in his notebooks marginal comments occur constantly such as "meilleur," "better," "good," which clearly reveal his value judgments.[226]	"Take Beethoven's notebooks. There is no thematic conception there as God gave it. He remoulds it and adds 'Meilleur.' " [237]

Another work on music theory used by Mann is John Redfield's *Music, a Science and an Art*.[227] The underlinings in Mann's copy are scanty, and limited to the chapter "Harmonic Possibilities," particularly the section on the genesis of the various scales. Dates are often underlined, likewise the names Pythagoras and Ptolemy; this book is probably the source for Adrian's interpretation of the Ptolemaic scales:

Redfield:	Doctor Faustus:
The most perfect scale at present known is the natural scale sometimes called the "just," devised about 150 A.D. by Claudius Ptolemy, the astronomer and mathematician.[228]	He expressed great pleasure over the fact that it was an astronomer and mathematician named Ptolemy, a man from Upper Egypt, living in Alexandria, who had established the best of all known scales, the natural or right one. [160]

224. *Ibid.*, p. 42.
225. Bahle, *Eingebung und Tat*, p. 201.
226. *Ibid.*, p. 248.
227. *Story of a Novel*, p. 90.
228. J. Redfield, *Music, a Science and an Art* (1949 ed.), pp. 185–86. Mann used the 1941 edition.

Mann found a convenient source of information in his musician son Michael. Michael could share his firsthand knowledge of the education of a musician and explain to his father certain specific problems with which the novel was to deal. The Zurich Archives possess letters that Michael evidently wrote in reply to the "letters of inquiry" that Mann addressed to his son as well as to his learned friends. A long letter dated July, 1943 contains detailed descriptions of different musical forms from the canon to the fugue, with handbook definitions of terms and brief musical examples.[229] One cannot expect to find such a schematic text quoted verbatim in *Doctor Faustus*, but there is substantial evidence that Mann studied the letter with care. As an example of the canon, Michael analyzes the old song, "O, wie wohl ist mir am Abend," the very canon that Hanne teaches Adrian and his brother; it is described at considerable length in the novel (28). Adrian's youthfully enthusiastic explanations of the chord and its possibilities (73 f.) are also partly based on Michael's letters.[230]

Mann asked Michael for information on the viola d'amore, Zeitblom's instrument. In his answer, Michael mentions that it is difficult to find works originally composed for this instrument. Among those he mentions are "six sonatas by Attilio Ariosti, a contemporary and friend of Handel's."[231] In the Schlaginhaufen salon Zeitblom then plays "a sonata by Ariosti, the friend of Handel" (227). Michael refers to versions of compositions written for other instruments, and Zeitblom accordingly plays a piece that Haydn wrote for the viola di Bordone (227). In a later letter Michael mentions that his researches have turned up a number of compositions for the viola d'amore, a list of which he is sending to his father.[232]

When dealing with various composers and their work, Mann copies entire pages from various musicologists. One example is the remarkable passage describing Wendell Kretschmar's lec-

229. The letter of July 6, 1943 is quoted here with the kind permission of Professor Michael Mann.
230. Michael Mann recommended various reference works to his father and indicated which essays would be most useful. In the above letter he suggests *The Macmillan Encyclopedia of Music and Musicians* and *Grove's Dictionary of Music and Musicians*. The Archives possess a typed list, probably from Michael Mann, of "Musical articles from the Encyclopedia Britannica by Donald Francis Tovey." These articles deal among other things with musical forms from "Aria" to "Variations"; some are marked with a red cross, Mann's usual way of indicating important items.
231. Michael's letter to Mann, May 22, 1945.
232. Michael's letter to Mann, May 29, 1945.

tures on the religious leader and musical systematician Johann Conrad Beissel. This section is borrowed in its entirety from an American article by H. T. David that came Mann's way just before he began the chapter containing this lecture. Mann says of the discovery:

> At the same time I stumbled across some curious information, in some magazine, concerning spiritual music among the Seventh-Day Baptists of Pennsylvania, with emphasis on the strange figure of Johann Conrad Beissel, whom I then and there decided to include in the lectures with which Kretschmar the Stammerer opens up the world of music to young Adrian (and to the reader) — the buffoon "systematician" and schoolmaster whose memory haunts the whole novel.[233]

Mann's statement by no means indicates the extent of his debt to the article. The following examples are very revealing:

David:
Beissel's style was one of exalted mysticism, full of metaphors, dark allusions to passages in the Scriptures, and a rather exaggerated erotic symbolism. His first products included a tract on the Sabbath with the characteristically cryptic title *Mystyrion Anomalias* [The Mystery of Lawlessness] . . . a set of 99 *Mystische und sehr geheyme Sprüche.*[234]

Doctor Faustus:
His style was high-flown and cryptic, laden with metaphor, obscure Scriptural allusions, and a sort of erotic symbolism. A tract on the Sabbath, *Mystyrion Anomalias*, and a collection of ninety-nine *Mystical and Very Secret Sayings* were the beginning. [64]

He decreed that there should be masters and servants in each tune. Taking the tonic triad as the melodic center of any given tonality, he designated the tones of that chord as masters and the remaining tones of the scale as servants. The accented syllables of a text would ordinarily be presented by a master, the unaccented by a servant.[235]

He decreed that there should be "masters" and "servants" in every scale. Having decided to regard the common chord as the melodic center of any given key, he called "masters" the notes belonging to this chord, and the rest of the scale "servants." And those syllables of a text upon which the accent lay had always to be presented by a "master," the unaccented by a "servant." [65]

233. *Story of a Novel*, pp. 39–40.
234. H. T. David, "Hymns and Music of the Pennsylvania Seventh-Day Baptists," p. 4.
235. *Ibid.*, p. 6.

Once he had entered the field of music, he cultivated it with the assiduity characteristic of all his pursuits. He collected his comments on music and had them printed as a preface to the *Turteltaube*.[236]	This man cultivated the field of music, once he had entered it, with the same persistence with which he pursued all of his other aims. He put together his thoughts on theory and published them as a preface to the book of the *Turtle Dove*. [66]

The page in *Doctor Faustus* that follows consists to a large extent of an equally faithful translation, this time of a section of the David article, which in turn quotes a certain William Fahnestock's memories of the otherworldly singing of Beissel's congregation. Mann adheres to his source by having his speaker, Kretschmar, draw upon a firsthand account, but makes Kretschmar's informant his father, thus integrating the episode into the world of the novel.

It would be tedious to quote all the passages that Mann lifts from the article on Beissel, but the above quotations show how far Mann's technique could be carried.

Another form of montage occurs in Kretschmar's lecture on Beethoven's piano sonata, Opus 111. We remarked above that Kretschmar's manner of commentary is copied from Adorno's, but Adorno's influence does not stop there. He wrote comments into Mann's score of the sonata, and one can trace how Mann takes up his notes on technical details and develops them further. In spite of his thorough study of the sonata, Mann commits certain blunders when describing it,[237] but we shall demonstrate that the mistakes can be attributed to the symbolic position the sonata occupies within the novel.

Mann often elaborates metaphorically on Adorno's factual remarks. Where the motive d-g-g occurs in the eighth bar of the second movement of the sonata, Adorno's note reads: "The

236. *Ibid.* A. Briner, in an article "Conrad Beissel and Thomas Mann," tries to trace the sources for Mann's description of Beissel, but he overlooks the direct source which Mann mentions in *The Story of a Novel.* Briner works on the premise that Mann "recalls only that on a visit to the Library of Congress some time previously he had been given a publication on Beissel, but he cannot remember any author or title" (24). In reality this visit to the Library occurred in the summer of 1945 in connection with the lecture on Germany (*Story*, pp. 120–21.). The section on Beissel had already been written. Mann had stumbled on the Beissel article two years earlier and at once resolved to work it into the novel (*Story*, p. 39).

237. Heim, "Thomas Mann," p. 307. Other scholars do not share this opinion. Gerd Hoffmann, for example, calls the Kretschmar lecture "a wonderful introduction to Beethoven's Op. 111"; see "Die Musik im Werk Thomas Manns," p. 567.

motive in its original, (objective) form: at the end of the first half of the theme." In *Doctor Faustus* we find "The arietta theme [is] . . . reducible to a motif which appears at the end of the first half, like a brief soul-cry — only three notes, a quaver, a semiquaver, and a dotted crotchet . . ." (54). This "soul-cry" is of great symbolic import. According to Kretschmar it can be scanned as "fare thee well," that is, as a cry of parting which expresses the central message of a sonata that bids farewell to the traditional sonata form (55 f.). Mann found this idea in Bekker's biography of Beethoven, in which he underlined the sentence "With Opus 111 Beethoven takes leave for good of the form of the piano sonata."[238]

A single note in the Arietta gives Mann a pretext for subtly refining the idea of farewell. In the first variation, the figure c-c♯-d-g-g appears, described by Adorno as "the humanized leave-taking variation in the finale." Of the note c♯ he says, "The decisive, added note is c♯." Mann's novel treats the musical phenomenon pointed out by Adorno in the following characteristic manner:

With the motif passed through many vicissitudes, which takes leave and so doing becomes itself entirely leave-taking, a parting wave and call, with this D G G occurs a slight change, it experiences a small melodic expansion. After an introductory C, it puts C sharp before the D, so that it no longer scans "heav-en's blue," "mead-owland," but "O-thou heaven's blue," "Green-est meadowland," "Fare-thee well for aye," and this added C sharp is the most moving, consolatory, pathetically reconciling thing in the world. It is like having one's hair or cheek stroked, lovingly, understandingly, like a deep and silent farewell look. [55]

When one realizes that the musical categories in *Doctor Faustus* must be interpreted symbolically, the literary significance of this tender concern for the motif of parting becomes clear; but we shall be returning to this point.

Much could be said about the material Mann drew from works on Beethoven. It is noteworthy, for instance, that Mann consistently marked those passages that referred to any of the following compositions: the sonata Opus 111; the *Missa Solemnis*, especially the Credo; the Ninth Symphony; and the last string quartets, particularly the one in A major, Opus 132.[239]

238. Bekker, *Beethoven*, p. 192.

239. One should include among these works the annotated programs such as *New Friends of Music: Program Book*, 1943–44, vol. 3. Mann read this with great care. See also Bekker, *Beethoven*, p. 401.

Of great symbolic importance for *Doctor Faustus* is Weber's opera *Der Freischütz*. It first crops up in the brothel scene when Adrian rushes to the piano and strikes a chord progression.[240] The action recalls Nietzsche's experience, but Mann expands it by describing the chords: they accompany the hermit's prayer in the Weber opera, and the description is taken verbatim from Hermann von Waltershausen's little book on the opera:

Waltershausen:
In the prayer of the hermit that follows, a surprising modulation leads back to a shining C major (note the entry of timpani, trumpets and oboes on the six-four chord on C) . . . the semitone-rise always means an extraordinary brightening and is perhaps the greatest intensification of which music is capable.[241]

Doctor Faustus:
. . . modulation from B major to C major, the brightening semitone step, as in the hermit's prayer in the finale of the *Freischütz*, at the entry of the timpani, trumpets, and oboes on the six-four chord on C. [142]

The interview with the devil contains a further reference to the opera. Adrian decides that he is dealing with "black Kaspar, which is one of the names, and so Kaspar and Samiel are one and the same" (227). Adrian proceeds on the basis of association to describe Samiel's motif in the opera. His wording might, of course, be based on direct study of the score, but since Mann has already quoted von Waltershausen, it seems probable that the same book served as model for this passage;

Waltershausen:
With a frightful C-minor triad in sudden fortissimo (low strings, trombones, low bassoons, clarinets and oboes, — Weber discovered the importance of the latter) — Samiel steps out of his abyss.[242]

Doctor Faustus:
"Where then is your C-minor fortissimo of stringed tremoli, wood and trombones, ingenious bug to frighten children, the romantic public, coming out of the F-sharp minor of the Glen as you out of your abyss — I wonder I hear it not!" [227]

ADRIAN LEVERKÜHN'S COMPOSITIONS

Zeitblom devotes considerable time and energy to evoking his friend's compositions. A few he mentions only in passing while

240. *DF* contains several allusions to *Der Freischütz*: pp. 78, 227, 498.
241. H. v. Waltershausen, *Der Freischütz*, pp. 113, 114.
242. *Ibid.*, p. 99.

lingering over others, describing the stages of their composition, their structure and instrumentation as well as their fate at the hands of publishers and concert audiences. Many music experts speak with admiration of Mann's ability to portray a nonexistent piece of music so convincingly; others consider Mann's descriptions a bluff, if a skillful one. Of course, not even the most practiced musician could construct a musical sequence simply on the basis of Mann's data, but neither was that his intention. On the other hand, the compositions are sometimes analyzed with such precision of detail that Mann seems to have had before him a clear musical image.

Can we trace the sources of Adrian's compositions? It would be foolish to expect a novelist to execute a composition in actual notes before one of his characters composes it, whereas we may safely assume that he can formulate verbal documents such as letters or poems. Thus, borrowed details on composition do not necessarily express the same intentions as those operative in Mann's purely literary montage. But since we are still dealing with material transported from reality into the fictional world of the novel, we must consider a few representative cases in our analysis. The musicologist is better equipped to cope adequately with this subject than the literary historian. Heim and Grandi have tracked down numerous models.

The prototypes for Adrian's compositions fall into several categories. The easiest method for Mann was to proceed from a real composition and give a more or less disguised description. In some cases Mann determined the intellectual content and symbolic function of a composition and then created a musical event out of these elements. Not infrequently we find both methods combined. For assistance with the more freely constructed compositions Mann consulted professional musicians. In *The Story of a Novel* he describes Adorno's contribution to Adrian's violin concerto: his friend helped him achieve a clear conception of "the technical aspects of the opus, the 'parody of being carried away,' of which I had had only a very impressionistic idea." [243]

Instead of discussing Adrian's first major composition, *Ocean Lights* (151), as an individual work, Mann treats it within the

243. *Story of a Novel*, p. 205. See *ibid.*, p. 117. P. G. Dippel maintains that the original impetus for the music was Mann's, later confirmed by Adorno; see Dippel, "Thomas Mann und die Musik," p. 692.

history of style. Zeitblom characterizes the piece as an exquisite example of musical impressionism, and in fact the title immediately suggests a connection with one of the outstanding documents of orchestral impressionism, Debussy's *La mer*.[244] Certain similarities to Stravinsky's *Firebird Suite* of 1908 have also been discovered.[245]

For Adrian's large body of songs, different parallels and models can be found. Adrian follows Stravinsky in composing settings to poems by Verlaine,[246] and the Keats hymns have been seen as a reference to Schönberg's cycle *Pierrot lunaire*.[247] The Brentano songs might be considered a parallel to Wolf's settings of German romantic poets like Mörike and Eichendorff, although musically, as R. Engländer points out, they bear more resemblance to the art songs of Gustav Mahler.[248] But here again Schönberg is the primary model, for Adrian himself asserts that the Brentano songs represent the nearest he has come to "strict style," which is, after all, based on Schönberg's twelve-tone technique. One should recall Schönberg's "Fifteen Poems by Stefan George for voice and piano" (1909), in which Schönberg breaks definitively with traditional tonality. One of Adrian's songs, "O lieb Mädel, wie schlecht bist du" (155 f.) is based on the symbolic letter progression h-e-a-e-e-flat (Hetaera Esmeralda), which becomes a leitmotif in Adrian's work. Mann had read of such a musical *ideé fixe* in Ernest Newman's edition of Berlioz' memoirs, where the composer discusses the Estelle motif in the *Symphonie fantastique*.[249] Here Mann found a musical figure used to symbolize a beloved woman.

Ernest Newman describes another sort of symbolic formula, this one occurring in Beethoven's works. In many of the slow movements a small figure of three rising notes appears, apparently carrying a fixed emotional content. Newman speaks of "this unconscious tyranny of the formula over the musician's imagination,"[250] but in Adrian's case the formula is not an

244. Krey, ("Die gesellschaftliche Bedeutung . . . , p. 321) sees certain similarities to Max Reger's Böcklin suite.
245. Heim, "Thomas Mann," p. 336.
246. *Ibid.*, p. 368.
247. Lesser, *Thomas Mann*, p. 358.
248. Engländer, "Thomas Manns Faustroman," p. 136. Zeitblom himself points out Mahler's influence on Adrian's songs (*DF*, p. 162).
249. Berlioz, *Memoirs*, pp. 98–99. It is interesting that Berlioz was inspired to write the *Symphonie fantastique* by reading Goethe's *Faust* (*ibid.*, p. 98).
250. Newman, *Beethoven*, orig. ed., p. 80.

unconscious pattern but a calculated device. This accords with Mann's intention of portraying Adrian as Beethoven's opposite; where Beethoven lets himself be inspired, Adrian's works are consciously constructed.[251]

Zeitblom dwells on Adrian's oratorio *Apocalipsis cum figuris* (373 ff.), describing Adrian's method of work, mentioning the literary sources, giving deep consideration to such musical elements as the fugue sections, the glissando, and the relationship between dissonance and harmony. He discusses the respective roles of the chorus and the orchestra, and he even selects individual passages of the text and surveys the musical means by which Adrian obtains certain effects. Stravinsky's operatic oratorio *Oedipus Rex* has been mentioned as a model for this work; like Adrian's work it was first performed under the direction of Otto Klemperer (377).[252] Richard Strauss's *Death and Transfiguration* is not out of the question, and Berlioz' *Symphonie fantastique* seems to have suggested Adrian's handling of the motifs; Berlioz himself had the idea of composing an "apocalyptic" work.[253]

Adrian's next major composition is the opera suite *Gesta Romanorum* (315 f.). Mann concentrates largely on its literary background, but the music is reminiscent of Stravinsky's *Histoire du soldat* or his ballet *Petruschka*;[254] the idea of a marionette play apparently stems from Kleist (305). In *The Story of a Novel* Mann mentions that he was reading Kleist's essay on marionettes while working on the *Gesta* chapter, and Mann's edition contains many underlined passages, among them the concluding lines, which appear only slightly paraphrased in Adrian's comments on "breakthrough" (321 f.).[255]

The work of Schönberg hovers in the background of everything Adrian composes, once he outgrows experimentation and finds his own style. But one can also find references to specific works of Schönberg; thus the "scarcely playable" trio for violin,

251. In his 1930 edition Mann underlined a footnote on pp. 71–72 in which Newman suggests that almost every composer has a secret musical configuration that turns up like a fingerprint in every work.

252. Heim, *"Thomas Mann,"* p. 379.

253. J. Boyer, "A propos du rôle de la musique dans le 'Doktor Faustus' de Thomas Mann," p. 138.

254. *Ibid.*, p. 137.

255. *Story of a Novel*, p. 145; H.v. Kleist, *Sämtliche Werke und Briefe*, ed. W. Herzog, 5:2.

viola, and cello (457) is based on Schönberg's trio for strings, Opus 9.[256] It might seem superfluous to seek sources for Adrian's violin concerto, since we know that Adorno provided the musical description. Zeitblom also points out musical echoes of Beethoven's A-minor quartet, Opus 132 and Tartini's *Devil's Trill Sonata* (410). However the piece also has a modern prototype; Richard Engländer has detected a link between Adrian's concerto and one by Schönberg's disciple Alban Berg, who was the same age as Adrian and wrote a violin concerto "in which something personal, all-too personal is intended to find expression."[257] The similarity is not accidental, for among the papers on *Doctor Faustus* is a newspaper review of Berg's "violin concerto dedicated 'to the memory of an angel.'"[258] The angelic element fits in with Adrian's concerto, and some of the phrases in the review would be applicable to the fictional composition: "highly affective music," "a carefully structured work," "unearthly beauty and transfiguration." Mann describes the theme of the first movement of Adrian's concerto likewise, as one of those "manifestations capturing head and shoulders, bordering on the 'heavenly'" (410).

Adrian's last work, the cantata *The Lamentation of Doctor Faustus* (485 ff.), has a more clearly symbolic function in the novel than any of the other compositions. This work, too, is related to existing works, although more on the basis of ideas than of technical details. Not surprisingly, individual features of Adrian's cantata are suggested by the "farewell" works of several different composers. Thus similarities have been found to Tschaikovsky's *Symphonie pathétique*, finished only a few months before his death. Its name, expressing the idea of suffering, brings to mind the *Lamentation*, and in fact the last movement is marked "Adagio lamentoso"; there all the groups of instruments seem to take their leave until only the basses and celli remain.[259] In the *Lamentation*, too, the orchestra

256. Heim, "Thomas Mann," p. 386. In *The Story of a Novel* (p. 217) Mann mentions that he borrowed Schönberg's opinion that the new trio was "impossible but rewarding" and attributed it to Adrian. Other elements of Adrian's trio likewise fit Schönberg's; see *DF*, p. 457.
257. Engländer, "Thomas Manns Faustroman," p. 136.
258. The review, signed "P.Mg.", appears under the heading "Neue Musik in Basel" in *Die Weltwoche* (Zurich), n.d.
259. Heim, "Thomas Mann," p. 391. Engländer sees a connection between the end of the *Lamentation* and Mahler's *Lied von der Erde*; see "Thomas Manns Faustroman som musikalisk spegelbild," p. 24.

gradually falls silent, and the piece ends with a solitary cello note (491). Adrian's cantata raises further associations in the history of music; Zeitblom mentions a return to Monteverdi's *Lamento* (486 ff.), and critics have also invoked Monteverdi's opera *Arianna*, although this is an early work.[260]

The most important model for the *Lamentation* is, however, Beethoven's Ninth Symphony. The connection is primarily on the symbolic level, but certain technical correspondences deserve mention. The *Lamentation* takes an hour and a quarter to perform, the time required by Beethoven's Choral Symphony. Since the *Lamentation* symbolically negates the Ninth Symphony, many elements of the Beethoven work appear in inverted form. Thus Adrian's work is referred to as an "Ode to Sorrow" (490), the obvious counterpart of Schiller's "Ode to Joy," which forms the textual basis for Beethoven's choral passages. Beethoven's vocal sections rise up out of the purely instrumental introduction, and the theme of the chorus is sounded by the celli; in Adrian's work the orchestra silences the human voice, and the cantata ends on a cello note, making the reversal complete.

In the decisive moment when Adrian describes the *Lamentation* as a retraction of Beethoven's Ninth Symphony, he uses the phrase "it is not to be" (478). One could regard these words [italicized in the German text] as a negative allusion to the motto Beethoven chose for the first theme of the fourth movement of his string quartet, Opus 135.[261] This motto, "It must be," has been much discussed in the literature on Beethoven. Some interpret the motto as the result of a quarrel with his housekeeper, others as an expression of the same faith that pervades the Ninth Symphony.[262] When he analyzes the *Lamentation*, Zeitblom recalls the conversation in which Adrian said "it is not to be," and adds:

How the words stand, almost like a musical direction, above the choral and orchestral movements of "*Dr. Fausti Wehe-klag*." [490]

The allusion to Beethoven here becomes obvious.

Adrian Leverkühn's extensive literary interests put him in close touch with the realm of his own author. Naturally enough,

---

260. Grandi, "Die Musik . . . ," p. 145.

261. Earlier, when the devil says "for that must be" (*DF*, p. 248), he is quoting from the chapbook.

262. The anecdote can be found in Schindler, *Biographie von Beethoven*, 1840 ed., p. 263, but H. Mersmann, *Die Kammermusik II: Beethoven*, p. 185 offers a more profound interpretation of the incident.

Mann takes a sympathetic interest in the literary foundations of Adrian's compositions; in fact, most of Adrian's work reveals a "tendency to marriage with the word, to vocal articulation" (161). But Mann gives a more general explanation for this tendency: it is the guiding principle throughout the history of German music:

> It was very natural that music should take fire at the word, that the word should burst forth out of music, as it did towards the end of the Ninth Symphony. Finally it was a fact that the whole development of music in Germany strove towards the word-tone drama of Wagner and therein found its goal. [164]

Adrian's early work consists to a large extent of that typically German form, the art song. He sets old Provençal and Catalan lyrics (162), Dante, Shakespeare, Blake, Shelley, Keats, Klopstock, Brentano, Verlaine, and others. The descriptions of these compositions give Mann a pretext to quote extensively from the poems in question. In some cases the quotations are not designated as such; Thomas Mann himself then generously points them out in *The Story of a Novel*.[263] The clearly marked quotations cannot properly be thought of as montage, but their function is obviously to authenticate Adrian's compositions. One of the typewritten versions of the novel contains still further quotations and interpretations; these were later cut, probably on the advice of Erika Mann.[264] Mann observes that she persuaded him to curtail his "overindulgence in Brentano songs." [265]

263. P. 35.

264. Thus Mann originally used poems by Novalis which were later omitted entirely, and quoted more extensively from Keats than in the final version (*DF*, p. 264). The MS (p. 355 *verso*) contains a very interesting analysis of the Brentano poem "Der Jäger an den Hirten," only mentioned in the published version (*DF*, p. 182: "The Huntsman to the Shepherds"); Zeitblom sees his own relation to Adrian mirrored in the poem. The MS also contains Zeitblom's analysis of a Brentano poem ("Frühlingsschrei eines Knechtes aus der Tiefe") (p. 350), which he considers revealing of Adrian's innermost feelings. After quoting the poem Zeitblom says, "The poem is noble and of great intensity, but the music into which it is plunged, which is wrung from it makes one want to kiss these burning, work-scarred hands. And tears are unleashed — unleashed in me, although I am not a pious man — when the last lines breathe out their sweet, spiritual sigh:

'Dass des Lichtes Quelle wieder
rein und heilig in mir flute
träufle einen Tropfen nieder,
Jesus, mir von deinem Blute!' — "

("That the font of light again/ May flow within me, sacred, pure,/ Grant me, Jesus, in my pain/ One drop of blood, I ask no more.")

265. *Story of a Novel*, p. 205.

We need not discuss the cases in which the novel names its own literary sources, and we have already mentioned the Shakespeare quotations hidden in the description of Adrian's opera *Love's Labour's Lost*. But there remain a few compositions for which Mann used unmarked quotations, unnoticeable to the unsuspecting reader.

The series of dramatic "marionette fantasies," the *Gesta Romanorum*, is a borderline case (315 ff). The novel mentions the collection of legends from which Adrian takes his text after making its acquaintance through his friend Schildknapp; Mann read this collection avidly while working on the novel.[266] This collection of legendary tales served, Zeitblom remarks, as "the source of most of the romantic myths of the middle ages" (315). The editor of Mann's edition, Grässe, makes this very statement in his foreword.[267] The collection consists of 181 chapters followed by an appendix containing further stories; it apparently appealed to Adrian's and Mann's "penchant for parody" (316). Mann offers extensive summaries of several of the legends and often adopts Grässe's exact wording.[268] The manuscript of *Doctor Faustus* contains legends which were omitted from the final version.[269] The most carefully told legend was, however, allowed to stand; this is the story of Pope Gregory, later to become the core of Mann's novel *The Holy Sinner*. An example of Mann's faithfulness to his source is the following section from the tale "Of the godless guile of old women":

Gesta:	*Doctor Faustus*:
Now the old woman had a little bitch, which she forced to fast for two days; but on the third day she fed the starved little bitch bread spread with mustard; when it had eaten the bread, its eyes watered all day because of the bitterness. . . . But when they now sat facing one another, the lady saw the	The witch makes her little bitch fast for two days, and then gives it bread spread with mustard to eat, which causes the little animal to shed copious tears. . . . But when the lady looks at the weeping little bitch and asks in surprise what causes its tears. [316]

266. *Ibid.*, pp. 19, 147.
267. *Gesta Romanorum, das älteste Mährchen- und Legendenbuch des christlichen Mittelalters* . . . , ed. J. T. Grässe. H. J. Weigand in his essay "Thomas Manns *Gregorius*," p. 10, points out how closely Mann follows to Grässe's exact wording in the Gregorius section of *DF*.
268. *Gesta*, pp. 143, 147 ff., 152–53, 155–56, 158; see *DF*, pp. 316 ff.
269. The MS of *DF* contains full retellings of the following stories: "Of the poisonous sin upon which we daily feed" (*Gesta*, chap. 11), "Of the incorruptibility of judges" (*Gesta*, chap. 4), and "Of the forgiveness of sins" (*Gesta*, chap. 18).

weeping dog, was greatly
surprised and asked what was the
cause of this prodigy.[270]

Adrian's apocalyptic oratorio likewise has nonmusical
sources. The novel mentions that Adrian drew inspiration from
Dürer's woodcuts of the Apocalypse. On one occasion Adrian
gives a detailed description, and Zeitblom tells the reader which
woodcut Adrian is thinking of (354). Among the literary studies
that precede the composition, Zeitblom mentions, besides the
Bible — he cites Ezekiel as the source of "And end is come, the
end is come" for those who would not recognize it (357) —
Dante; a version of the vision of Paul in Old French; the revela-
tions of two medieval mystics, Mechthild of Magdeburg and
Hildegard of Bingen; and the Venerable Bede. This combination of literary sources is not original with Mann; he found it
in an article by Marta Vogler, which appeared in 1945 in the
Neue Zürcher Zeitung, "Die Jenseitsvorstellungen vor Dante"
["Pre-Dante Conceptions of the Hereafter"].[271] The many
underlinings in the article preserved in the Archives show how
carefully Mann studied it. Mann not only borrowed facts but
quotes several passages:

Vogler:
This sort of inquiry into the
sources would give us the vision
of St. Paul, the Greek text of
which dates back to the fourth
century, and for which a French
verse translation from the
thirteenth century exists. . . .

Doctor Faustus:
. . . a thirteenth-century French
metrical translation of the
Vision of St. Paul, the Greek
text of which dates back to the
fourth century. [355]

One may certainly refer back to
the vision of St. Paul, for in
the second canto of the *Inferno*
Paul is expressly mentioned in
connection with Æneas as one
who has descended to the depths.

"By below I mean in hell. That
makes a bond between people as
far apart as Paul and Virgil's
Æneas. Remember how Dante
refers to them as brothers, as
two who have been down
below?" [355]

. . . the dialogs of Gregory the
Great and the *Historia
ecclesiastica* of the Venerable

. . . then a German version of
*Historia ecclesiastica gentis
anglorum* by the learned monk

270. *Gesta*, pp. 50–51.
271. The article, dated December 1, 1945, is a review of August Rüegg's
*Die Jenseitvorstellungen vor Dante und die übrigen literarischen Voraus-
setzungen der "Divina Commedia": ein quellenkritischer Kommentar* (Ein-
siedeln, 1945).

Bede, which incorporates some of the early Irish visions. One should, of course, mention the source immediately available to Dante, the *Vision Alberici*, the vision of the monk of Montecassino, the only vision native to Italian soil. . . . For these so-called visions, for the most part of the same general type and imbued, despite their wild imaginativeness with a definite purpose, that is, to edify and to arouse fear of punishment.

known as the Venerable Bede: a work in which is transmitted a good part of the Celtic fantasies about the beyond, the visionary experiences of early Irish and Anglo-Saxon times. This whole ecstatic literature from the pre-Christian and early Christian eschatologies forms a rich fabric of tradition, full of recurrent motifs. [356] *

A final literary source for Adrian's compositions is a poetry anthology discovered by Erich Berger: Karl Vossler's translation *Romanische Dichter* ["Romance-language Poets"]. Mann took from it the Provençal and Iberian poems used by Adrian, as well as the "loftiest visions of the *Divina Commedia*" (162). It can be proved that Mann used this anthology: he copies from Vossler a small mistake in a Dante quotation.[272]

SUMMARY

Since this chapter was devoted exclusively to a description of Mann's source material, it inevitably took on the character of a mosaic. And when one studies a mosaic closely, the overall pattern tends to be obscured by the individual chips of stone; yet we quickly discovered that Mann's material fell naturally into several major groups. Seemingly disparate details are bound together in Mann's novel by a chain of associations. As was said at the outset, several manners of organization are feasible; my own method was chosen on the grounds of practical considerations. Simple though it was, this arrangement revealed important unifying elements within the novel, and the fact that

---

* Translator's note: The first edition of *DF* contains references to John of Patmos, Gregory, the papal singing master, Alberich of Montecassino and Dante which are omitted from later versions and from the English translation.

272. *Romanische Dichter*, tr. Karl Vossler. E. Berger points out that the source for the "address, only nine lines long, of the poet to his allegorical song" (*DF*, p. 163) is not, as Mann apparently supposed, the *Divine Comedy*, but the *Convivio*; Vossler prints the strophe out of context with the heading "Allegory." See Berger, "Eine Dantestelle in Thomas Manns 'Doktor Faustus,' " *Randbemerkungen zu Nietzsche, George und Dante*, p. 57.

only a few insignificant details failed to fit into the categories used here, indicates that we were on the track of the principle according to which Mann collected and selected his material.

I certainly make no claim to having traced all of Mann's source materials. In fact, what has been quoted represents only a selection of the known sources. Sources which for various reasons were omitted or passed over hastily do not differ in any significant way from the ones treated more thoroughly.

In concluding, I wish to stress a few important factors. The various physical milieus — the topographical descriptions and occasionally even the interior décors — can usually be traced to actual places. Where Mann changed the place names, the sources of the fictional names and therefore also their symbolic import can be established with a high degree of certainty.

As has been shown, many sorts of relationship exist between the characters in the novel and their real prototypes. In addition to full identity — real persons appearing under their own names — there are many cases of more or less concealed identity. Mann's descriptions make it possible to discover the originals, but the names in the novel are usually symbolic and serve to connect the characters with another sector of reality. Many of these names are taken from Mann's readings. Mann creates simultaneous connections between his characters and several different historical periods; in personality and destiny they belong to the present, even to Mann's personal experience, while their names link them with the past, especially with the Reformation period. By this device Mann deprives his characters of an unambiguous one-to-one identity, and the historically symbolic names take the novel out of the realm of the *roman à clef*. Most intensely symbolic are the two main characters, Leverkühn and Zeitblom, who unite within themselves a whole gallery of outstanding figures from the history of German art and thought.

For a work dealing with the history and critique of culture, Mann naturally wished to have reliable sources; in this respect *Doctor Faustus* does not differ from Mann's other works or from works of this sort by other writers. On the other hand, it seems remarkable and sometimes even astonishing that Mann used, without any changes, entire sections from his sources. Scattered examples of such a procedure can be found in many books, but the sheer mass of quotations in *Doctor Faustus* places this novel in a special category. This accumulation comes to express a definite compositional principle, a principle fundamental to this novel and to Thomas Mann's concept of the novel in his last years.

Mann evidently proceeded with the collection of material for *Doctor Faustus* according to an established plan. He consulted his own library, he wrote to experts for information and bibliographical tips. But in addition to the fruits of this orderly method, Mann gladly accepted anything chance sent his way. Often the date of a source-article or news release indicates that it was published long after Mann began planning the novel; sometimes only a few days or weeks elapsed between Mann's finding the material and his putting it to use in the novel.[273] Despite the lack of time, these scraps seem completely assimilated. Here we encounter one of the secrets of the novel's composition: carefully worked out reflections are combined with lightning intuitions. It seems as if only one criterion had to be met before material could be accepted: it had to be "pertinent" as Mann says in *The Story of a Novel*.[274]

The dates of the various articles and releases used for the novel raise another interesting question. Most of them appeared between 1943 and 1945, and one may safely assume that Mann clipped them with the immediate intention of using them in the novel. But some of the clippings go back to the early 1930's. The pamphlet *Die Freideutsche Position* is dated 1931, and the scientific articles "Dehnt sich das Weltall aus?" and "Die Wunder der Meerestiefe" appeared in 1934.[275] Does this mean that Mann was already thinking of writing a Faust novel? Perhaps not consciously, but the fact that Mann saved the articles and took them with him to America indicates that he expected to use them some day. As was mentioned above,[276]

273. An example would be H. T. David's article on Beissel, published in June, 1943 in the *American-German Review*. Mann read the article around the end of the month (*Story of a Novel*, p. 39) and immediately decided to use it. Chapter 8, containing the lecture on Beissel, was written in the late summer and early fall of the same year. It is even more astonishing how quickly Mann found a use for Marta Vogler's article "Die Jenseitsvorstellungen vor Dante." The article appeared on December 1, 1945 in the *Neue Zürcher Zeitung* and must have taken a good number of days to reach Mann on the West Coast. But the article is quoted verbatim in chapter 34, written after the New Year. Mann had only a few weeks' time to think about the material and see where it would fit into the novel (*Story of a Novel*, p. 156).

274. Similar expressions occur in *The Story of a Novel* on pp. 43, 62, 72, 135.

275. See above, pp. 39, 55, 53.

276. See above, p. 56.

Mann's idea of a novel about a syphilitic writer can be traced back to 1905, and it has been shown that the association of musicality with alienation from politics was present in the *Betrachtungen eines Unpolitischen* (1918).[277] Single motifs and aspects of *Doctor Faustus* were thus conceived long before the actual writing; the conception of the novel as a whole dates from the spring of 1943.

It is hard to say whether Mann expected future readers to detect his method. There are many indications that he not only foresaw the probability but also wanted to provide certain hints. Why else would he give such an extensive bibliography in *The Story of a Novel* and save so many clippings and excerpts? There are other indications as well. For example, Eberhard Hilscher mentions that Mann had intended to let him go through a "stack of preliminary notes to *Doctor Faustus*."[278] Mann's death intervened, and the papers in question are probably those which are now preserved in the Zurich Archives.[279]

Whatever Mann's intentions, we have enough source material available to embark upon a serious discussion of this new principle of composition that makes use of so many quotations; this principle is evidently central to *Doctor Faustus*. One should not be content merely to compare the novel with its sources; one must see it in a larger context and investigate its relation to Mann's earlier works, keeping in mind that Mann thought the novel as a literary form was undergoing a crisis.

277. Engländer, "Thomas Manns Faustusroman som musikalisk spegelbild," p. 16.

278. E. Hilscher, "Begegnung mit Thomas Mann," p. 799.

279. Translating *DF* presents a curious problem. As a result of the quotation technique the novel is veritably untranslatable. Mann supervised the English translation (*Story of a Novel*, p. 204), but the translator did not have access to the English sources that had been used for the novel. The translator thus had to retranslate passages that Mann had himself translated into German, and this naturally led to considerable deviations from the original (cf. the original Beissel article and Mrs. Lowe-Porter's version of it, *DF*, p. 63 ff.). This state of affairs does not, however, prove that Mann wished to conceal his sources.

2

Bases of the Montage Technique

In the fall of 1943, half a year after beginning *Doctor Faustus*, Mann consulted Adorno's study of Schönberg. In *The Story of a Novel* Mann makes a significant comment on the meaning of this work for his novel:

> For what I could draw from it, and what I appropriated from it in order to portray the whole cultural crisis in addition to the crisis of music, was the fundamental motif of my book: the closeness of sterility, the innate despair that prepares the ground for a pact with the devil. Moreover, this reading nourished the musical . . . [constructivism] which had long been my ideal of form and for which this time there was a special esthetic necessity. I felt clearly that my book itself would have to become the thing it dealt with: namely, . . . [constructivistic music].[1]

This explanation contains several terms essential to an understanding of Mann's particular technique of composition. "Whole cultural crisis," "closeness of sterility," and "musical constructivism" — these concepts contain in a nutshell the artistic evolution that led to *Doctor Faustus*. The origin of the work lies in the experience of a general cultural crisis; in art this crisis expresses itself as sterility — lack of inspiration and spontaneous creative energy. This spiritual and intellectual aridity leads to a collapse of the traditional forms of artistic expression. The artists are gripped by a "despair that prepares the ground for a pact with the devil." The artist can find his way out of the crisis by giving up the criteria of spontaneity and inspiration, and, instead, taking refuge in calculated constructivism. The paradigm for this new and revitalizing formalism is Schönberg's twelve-tone technique, and Mann describes its equivalent in literature as "musical constructivism."

As part of this evolution, the art of fiction experiences a crisis in the twentieth century. Unfettered imagination, spontaneous invention of characters and plots is impeded by reflection and

1. *The Story of a Novel,* tr. R. and C. Winston, p. 64 [translation amended].

by the paralyzing feeling that everything the conventional novel can express has already been said. The novel has entered the stage of self-consciousness and intellectualism that Mann designated in 1939 as the stage of "critique." [2] One of the practical results of this development is that the modern novel often substitutes philosophical and aesthetic deliberations for plot and action. The most striking example among Mann's novels is *The Magic Mountain,* but *Doctor Faustus* also contains a large measure of critical discussion. Cultural critique by itself, however, does not take the place of art. Like many of the major novelists of this century, Mann seeks to overcome the crisis by accepting the sense of sterility and finding his way to a consciously "constructed" (in contrast to "invented") novel. The main task of the novelist now becomes that of arranging his material. But if inspiration is completely eliminated, the writer would almost seem to become a sort of engineer. However, the advocates of modern constructivism do not reject the notion of creative inspiration in itself — some kind of inspiration is essential for all art — but only the conventional idea of inspiration, the belief that the noblest form of artistic creation is a spontaneous or "naïve" process. Since Thomas Mann himself had never belonged to the class of artists who create spontaneously, the development of artistic constructivism was of strong interest to him.

If one had nothing but Mann's statement in *The Story of a Novel* upon which to base the hypothesis that the montage technique results from the crisis of the novel, one could be accused of hasty fabrication. However, a glance at Mann's development as a writer and at the artistic climate in which it took place will serve to support such an assumption.

Mann's literary development from *Buddenbrooks* to *Doctor Faustus* certainly shows considerable continuity, but at certain periods the crucial issues manifest themselves with particular urgency; it is these periods we shall examine. At the very beginning of Mann's novelistic career we find him coping with artistic problems which were later to spread to artistic circles in general and cause stormy debates from the First World War

---

2. "Die Kunst des Romans," *Altes und Neues* (hereafter cited as *AN*), p. 399. See H. Koopmann's discussion of the intellectualism of Mann's earlier novels: *Die Entwicklung des "Intellektualen Romans" bei Thomas Mann.* As a result of his topic, Koopmann follows much the same lines as I do in this chapter. See also H. Wolffheim, "Das 'Interesse' als Geist der Erzählung," pp. 362 ff.

until late in the 1920's. Mann himself achieved artistic equilibrium toward the end of this period. There followed in the early 1940's the acute crisis that finds its voice in *Doctor Faustus.*

IN THE WAKE OF NATURALISM

When Mann published his first novel, *Buddenbrooks,* in 1900, nothing suggested that he was to become one of the bold innovators of the twentieth century. The novel remains anchored in the stable world of the *Bürger.* Its adherence to the naturalist pattern tempts one to assign it to the literary milieu of the late nineteenth century. The naturalists were seeking verisimilitude and accuracy of detail, on the assumption that literature had a "scientific" purpose. Far from seeing this literary method as a symptom of degeneracy or sterility, its practitioners were convinced that it represented an important advance over earlier artistic approaches. But the naturalists' world view was not shared by the "decadent" Thomas Mann with his weakness for romanticism, and in fact one can already feel in *Buddenbrooks* the same tension between naturalistic method and metaphysical point of view that characterizes *Doctor Faustus.* A prisoner of social and psychological determinants, Mann's Thomas Buddenbrook acquires inner freedom when he discovers the philosophy of Schopenhauer. As a matter of fact, the literary transition around the turn of the century from naturalism to "decadence" took place largely under the influence of Schopenhauer.

In *Buddenbrooks* Mann describes the Lübeck of his childhood, and his details were so true to life that the book was declared unworthy even of a naturalist. Contemporaries recognized the unmistakable portraits of well-known citizens of Lübeck, and they protested vigorously against the indiscretion of the young artist. He was compared to a certain Herr Bilse, the author of a notorious *roman à clef.* The comparison impugned Mann's honor as an artist, and he retaliated with the brief essay "Bilse und ich" ["Bilse and I"] (1906), in which he presents a capsule definition of his concept of the novel. Mann maintains with considerable acrimony that a writer never creates ex nihilo. Inventiveness and resourcefulness are not to be confused with true poetic imagination and offer no guarantee of artistic value. The poet's task, he says, is not primarily "invention," but "animating"; it does not matter where material comes from, for only in the "artistic utilization of available reality" does the true artist reveal himself. And the writer always presents himself and his own world in his works. "But how can I relinquish myself entirely," he asks finally in terms borrowed from Schopenhauer, "without at the same time relinquishing the world that is my representation? My representation, my experience, my dream, my pain? We are not talking about you, dear readers, never, of that you may be sure, but only about me, about me . . ."[3]

Mann's reasons for his unrelenting adherence to reality are clearly different from those announced in the program of the naturalists. To Mann it makes no difference whether an artist takes his material from reality or invents it out of the whole cloth; what matters is how he assimilates his material and achieves artistic unity. Already at this early stage Mann emphasizes that personal confession forms an important component of artistic creation; in *Doctor Faustus* we find the confessional element carried to extremes.

Mann's juxtaposition of "invention" with "animating" is characteristic of an artist who functions without an overflowing imagination. Writing was always hard work for him, a battle with his material. Mann discusses this particular aspect of art in his essay "The Old Fontane," written in 1910. Here he speaks of the relationship between inspiration and construction in the novel, and he quotes with satisfaction Fontane's statement that divine inspiration comes very infrequently, "Once a year, perhaps, and a year has three hundred and sixty-five days. On the other three hundred and sixty-four the important thing is the critical faculty, the measure of enlightenment."[4] Literary creation requires, according to Mann's quotation of Fontane, "a certain modicum of factual information";[5] artistic production does not take place in a vacuum but, on the contrary, depends to a high degree on specific knowledge.

In this connection we must devote a few words to the novel *Royal Highness* (1909), the least esteemed, by critics and scholars, of all Mann's works, probably with good reason. The tale concerns a young prince, destined to rule an impoverished grand duchy, who marries the daughter of an American millionaire; it reads like light comedy, and, indeed, Mann describes it

3. "Bilse und ich," *AN*, p. 31. See Koopmann, *Die Entwicklung . . .*, pp. 8 ff.
4. "The old Fontane," *Essays of Three Decades*, p. 296.
5. *Ibid.*

later as a "fairy-tale novel." [6] We can hardly expect such a work to embody Mann's unique character and intentions as a novelist. But we are struck by the radical break with the naturalistic style; the motivation for the break emerges clearly from a few letters written about this time. In the summer of 1909 Mann thanks Hugo von Hofmannsthal for his praise of the novel, and says,

You also used the word allegory, and, in contemporary aesthetics, as we both know, the word is in extreme disrepute. Poetic allegory on the grand scale seems to me a noble form, and I believe there is no better way to ennoble the novel than by making it idealized and constructivist. [7]

And half a year later Mann writes to Ernst Bertram:

Thus far . . . you are the only one besides Hofmannsthal who has perceived the constructive element, which is precisely what comprises the new aspiration of the novel. Hofmannsthal had only seen a few installments in the *Rundschau* when he told me, "It is an allegory, an allegorical construction!" [8]

When Mann thus emphasizes the term "construction," he is in complete accord with an important tendency in aesthetics. Around 1910, construction was the password in music and painting although literature had not yet adopted the concept. Construction, to some extent an allegorical construction, was to characterize Mann's next novel, which he only completed fifteen years later.

NEW ARTISTIC GOALS IN THE SHADOW OF WORLD WAR I

During the years following 1912, Mann's production of fiction slackened off. Between the masterpieces *Death in Venice* (1912) and *The Magic Mountain* (1924) he wrote a few novellas and "idylls," [9] but these short pieces reveal that his energies were occupied with other matters. The impact of the war was primarily responsible. Up to the last moment Mann had considered a war out of the question. [10] Faced with the bloody

6. Foreword to the radio play, *Königliche Hoheit* (1954), *Nachlese* (Berlin/Frankfurt a.M., 1956) p. 173.
7. *Briefe*, 1:76 [translated by Richard and Clara Winston].
8. *Ibid.*, 81. See Koopmann, *Die Entwicklung* . . . , pp. 57 ff., 64 ff., 73 ff., 132–36.
9. Among them the *Infant Prodigy* collection, 1914, and in one volume the idylls *A Man and His Dog* and *Gesang vom Kindchen* ["The Song of the Child"], 1919.
10. *Briefe* 1:111 ff. See Klaus Mann, *The Turning Point*, p. 38.

reality, Mann suddenly saw his whole world collapse. He felt obliged to undertake an exhausting "general revision" of all his earlier opinions and principles.[11] The visible result of this revision is the lengthy and heterogeneous work *Betrachtungen eines Unpolitischen* ["Reflections of an Unpolitical Man"] (1918).

The undeniable chauvinism manifested in the *Betrachtungen* narrows Mann's artistic horizon as well as his political one. Mann seems unaware of the advances of modernism on various fronts in Europe, and he restricts his aesthetic discussion largely to music — which he considers the specifically German art form. But what Mann has to say in the *Betrachtungen* about music is of utmost importance for our context: the contrasting of "free" creation with constructivism is an obvious prefiguration of a central theme in *Doctor Faustus*. In the novel, Mann dates the crisis that gives rise to Adrian's "strict style" about 1910 (185, 189 ff).

The *Betrachtungen* do not mention Schönberg because at the time he was known only to a small circle. To exemplify the crisis, Mann instead takes Pfitzner's opera *Palestrina*, which received its premiere on June 12, 1917 in Munich under the baton of Bruno Walter.[12] In a letter dated November 6 of the same year, Mann expresses his enthusiasm for this work:

This summer's premiere of Pfitzner's *Palestrina* in the Prinzregenten-theater was a great event, attracting people in droves. It really is a work of great intellectual and artistic merit, extraordinarily German, by the way, taken from the realm of Faust and Dürer and with its confessional character just the thing for me. I have accordingly heard it a good five times and submitted a well-written study of it to the *Rundschau*.[13]

This "well-written study" is identical with the section on Pfitzner in the *Betrachtungen* and shows how deeply Mann was affected by the opera's central theme of inspiration. Mann observes that Pfitzner considers the present a period of decay in comparison with the 150-year period during which music flourished; Rubinstein's phrase "finis musicae" has become intensely real.[14] The Palestrina of the opera faces this very prob-

11. *Briefe* 1:134 (March 28, 1917).
12. See *Briefe* 1:474. Mayer in *Thomas Mann*, pp. 356–57, mentions the pertinence of Pfitzner's opera for *Doktor Faustus* (hereafter cited as *DF*) but does not examine the question.
13. *Briefe* 1:141.
14. *Betrachtungen eines Unpolitischen*, p. 417.

lem; the sixteenth-century composer relinquishes all hope of inspiration, because "the light of consciousness, deadly, harsh" is paralyzing his creative powers.[15] But then salvation arrives: inspiration in the form of an angelic chorus, whose song he has only to transcribe; thus his masterpiece, the *Missa Papae Marcelli*, is born. At this point in the opera something paradoxical occurs. To portray the moment of inspiration, Pfitzner incorporates a quotation from the historical Palestrina's Kyrie into his modern opera; here Mann could find an example of the quotation technique used in music.

This brief summary of the opera sufficiently indicates the similarity between Pfitzner and Adrian Leverkühn as composers. The similarity becomes even more apparent when Mann describes in the *Betrachtungen* Pfitzner's "great artistry in combining the most nervous variability and piercing harmonic audacity with old-fashioned devoutness."[16] By joining the old with the modern and revolutionary, the hero of the opera becomes a "savior of music."[17] Like Pfitzner's Palestrina, Adrian suffers from a sense of sterility, and like him Adrian seeks to rejuvenate art by knitting the old with the new. But Adrian reaches beyond "old-fashioned devoutness" to the archaic. In a conversation that takes place in the fall of 1910, Adrian says:

". . . we need a system-master, a teacher of the objective and organization, with enough genius to unite the old-established, the archaic, with the revolutionary. . . . However, it could mean something necessary to the time, something promising a remedy in an age of destroyed conventions and the relaxing of all objective obligations — in short, of a freedom that begins to lie like a mildew upon talent and to betray traces of sterility." [189]

Mann here reveals anew his sure sense for the mood of a given period. Around 1910, Europe was beginning to take an interest in the art and culture of primitive peoples. We need only men-

15. See *ibid.*, p. 421.
16. *Ibid.*, p. 409.
17. *Ibid.*, p. 423. Despite these great similarities it would be a mistake to consider Pfitzner a "model" for Adrian. Adrian's music is, after all, based on Schönberg's twelve-tone method, whereas Pfitzner decries the "complete destruction of harmony" (*Die neue Aesthetik der musikalischen Impotenz*, p. 115). This violent polemic also attacks Paul Bekker. In another article Pfitzner takes on yet another music theoretician who provided material for *DF*, Julius Bahle. Considering the relevance of Pfitzner for so many aspects of *DF* it may seem surprising that Mann does not mention him in the novel or in *The Story of a Novel*. The reason can be found in Mann's break with Pfitzner when the latter came out in support of National Socialism. See W. Abendroth, *Hans Pfitzner*, pp. 260 ff., 297–98, 409.

tion such different events as the sensational exhibitions of Negro art and the performances of Stravinsky's *Sacre du printemps*. After completing his "general revision" in the *Betrachtungen*, Mann could turn once again to fiction. The impulse toward *The Magic Mountain* had come as early as 1912,[18] but Mann did not begin serious work until 1919, and then he was plagued with doubts whether he was capable of real art under the existing conditions. In a letter written that year, he says,

Now I am writing away at the "Magic Mountain" novel, whose theme . . . has again cast its spell over me. But the activity of the artist is highly problematical nowadays, when the decline of the entire Western culture seems to be in the offing.[19]

Mann sees his own problems as an artist and those of his generation in the grand perspective outlined by Spengler the previous year in his *Decline of the West*. Spengler's theory that Western culture had outlived itself and was entering a period of sterility was bound to affect an artist with a critical and reflective orientation like Mann's. The musical version of Spengler's theory appeared in Pfitzner's polemic, *Die neue Aesthetik der musikalischen Impotenz* ["The New Aesthetics of Musical Impotence"] (1920). The fear of sterility and the search for new forms can also be seen in such works as T. S. Eliot's *The Waste Land* (1922), with its opposition of aridity and rain, and Rilke's *Duino Elegies* (1922) which evoke the ten years during which he struggled with the powers of inspiration.

Several utterances of Mann's show his preoccupation with the idea of a twilight of art and literature. An essay written in 1924 declares: "The arts lie locked in a crisis which seems at times to be a mortal one, at times to portend the birth of new forms."[20] In 1926 he speaks of "the crisis we all feel the novel to be undergoing," and he observes, "The question whether the conventional novel is still possible will continue to disconcert the producers of novels."[21] In a letter written in 1926, Mann relates his recently finished *Magic Mountain* to the general crisis: "It seems to me that the crisis in art as form or even as idea . . . also finds expression in my books."[22]

What Mann means by a general crisis of the novel in the twentieth century is quite obvious. This century saw the revolu-

18. Mann, "The Making of The Magic Mountain."
19. *Briefe* 1:163.
20. "On the Theory of Spengler," *Past Masters and Other Papers*, p. 218.
21. *Pariser Rechenschaft*, p. 121.
22. *Briefe* 1:256.

tion in the novel that we connect with the names of Kafka and Hesse in Germany, Proust and Gide in France, and Joyce and Virginia Woolf in England, to name only a few of the most notable. Characteristic of these writers' works are self-conscious reflection and constructivism. Gide attains an unprecedented degree of critical reflection in *The Counterfeiters* (1926) and the diary recounting its genesis, *Journal of The Counterfeiters* (1927); and Joyce's novel *Ulysses* (1922) displays a constructivism previously unknown in the novel. Joyce's use of myth is not unique. D. H. Lawrence also felt attracted to primitive religions, and Hermann Hesse's novel *Siddhartha* (1922) is based on Buddhist myths and legends. This interest in mythology was nourished by Freud's theories on patricide, the Oedipus complex and totemism. Mann was familiar with the work of Hesse and Kafka and he corresponded with Gide in the early 1920's, later speaking with admiration of Gide's writings.[23] He did not make the acquaintance of Proust until somewhat later,[24] and he discovered what he had in common with Joyce only when working on *Doctor Faustus*.

Of course Mann's formal innovations in *The Magic Mountain* should not be attributed to the example of these writers. According to Mann it is a question of a "crisis of the entire culture" — a crisis which, within the contemporary novel, appears as dissatisfaction with traditional forms, in the curbing of "invention" by means of critical reflection, and, finally, in a tendency toward experimentation with structure.[25] Mann's *Magic Mountain* is simply one among other products of such a crisis.

The constructivistic aspect of *The Magic Mountain* is apparent in the novel's layout. The hero, Hans Castorp, is suspended between opposite poles or sets of contrasts; "normal" life, the flatland, stands opposed to the isolation of the Berghof

23. On Hesse, see *Briefe* 1:175, 250, 344, 522, also *AN*, pp. 225 ff. Whereas Mann was personally drawn to Hesse, he viewed Kafka's works from a respectful distance; see *Briefe* 1:316 and *AN*, pp. 401, 554 ff. Mann's first letter to Gide, *Briefe* 1:195–96, was written in January, 1922. Two essays on Gide written in 1929 and 1951 show his high esteem for the French writer: *AN*, pp. 521 ff. and 586 ff.

24. In a letter to R. Thieberger (1938) Mann says he "did not make the acquaintance of Proust until long after finishing *The Magic Mountain*" (Thieberger, *Der Begriff der Zeit bei Thomas Mann*, p. 7). In a letter to R. Schickele (1935) Mann expresses a very positive opinion of Proust: *Briefe* 1:402.

25. *Story of a Novel*, p. 64.

Sanatorium; the medieval fanaticism of the Catholic Naphta confronts the enlightened humanism of Settembrini, both so markedly portrayed as types that they almost become allegorical figures. The endless philosophical discussions on culture make the novel critical and reflective, as does the great body of scientific material described in connection with Hans Castorp's researches. Constructivism appears in the technical device of the leitmotif and in the magical numerical structure: the seven chapters of the novel correspond to the seven years of the action, Hans Castorp lives in Room 34, the number of the magic square, and so forth.[26]

Of particular interest for us is the quotation technique employed in *The Magic Mountain*. In earlier works Mann had woven in occasional quotations — an example is *Death in Venice*[27] — but it has been demonstrated that in *The Magic Mountain* the quotations acquire a constructivistic function, linking the novel with Goethe's *Faust*.[28] The reader must recognize the quotations in order to feel their impact. This requirement, as well as the amount of quoted material, distinguishes the novel from *Doctor Faustus*.

INTENSIFICATION OF TENDENCIES

With *The Magic Mountain* Thomas Mann enters a new period. The traditional naturalism of his style gives way to ever bolder and more extensive experiments with the novel form. *The Magic Mountain* still has an "invented" story, but for the *Joseph* novels and the Goethe novel Mann makes use of already existing material. He undertakes specialized studies in the pertinent fields, arranges the material according to a pre-established scheme and often incorporates more or less concealed quotations into his narrative. As Herman Meyer has pointed

26. See for example Wirtz, "Zitat und Leitmotiv bei Thomas Mann." Herman Meyer among others discusses the significance of the number seven in *The Magic Mountain: Das Zitat in der Erzählkunst*, p. 233.

27. See L. Gustafson, "Xenofon and *Der Tod in Venedig*," F. H. Mautner, "Die griechischen Anklänge in Thomas Manns 'Der Tod in Venedig'."

28. H. Meyer, pp. 216–17. Meyer also discusses the technique of quotation in *The Beloved Returns*. This approaches the technique Mann developed in *DF* and later used in *The Holy Sinner*; in the latter the reader is not expected to recognize the quotations. Meyer does not, however, deal with *DF*; he studies instead the technique of quotation in the works of older writers whom Mann prized — Cervantes, Sterne, E. T. A. Hoffmann, and Fontane.

out, Mann makes especially liberal use of the quotation technique in *The Beloved Returns.*[29]

Although the general crisis induced Mann to experiment with the form of his novels of the 1930's, we have no evidence that he was going through a personal creative crisis at this time. He worked purposefully on his great mythic novel, which accorded with the tendency evident at the time to seek out the artistically fruitful myths of primitive cultures. This need of an overcivilized age for spiritual renewal was also asserting itself on the political level, and it is highly significant that the *Joseph* novels are contemporaneous with the National Socialist attempts to revive the old Germanic mythology. Culturally Mann was thus part of a powerful current in Germany, whereas politically he was swimming against the stream. It was in protest against the politically motivated cultivation of Aryan gods and heroes that he buried himself in Oriental religion and biblical history.

Mann's comments in his lecture "Die Kunst des Romans" ["The Art of the Novel"] (1939) illuminate some aesthetic aspects of the *Joseph* novels. Mann notes that the modern narrator substitutes critical consciousness and reflection for the freer, less self-conscious art of old-fashioned story-telling. Quoting Mereshkovsky, Mann speaks of the "transition from unconscious creation to creative consciousness," and remarks that the modern novel has reached "the stage of 'critique,' which follows the stage of 'poetry.' " [30] In this lecture Mann does not, however, mention paralysis of the creative powers, nor does the word "crisis" appear.

But the completion of the *Joseph* novels in the spring of 1943 changes the situation. With this bridge to the past gone,[31] Mann seems to reach a crisis in his personal and creative life which is intensified still further by despondency over political events. In *The Story of a Novel* he quotes a notation from his diary that clearly expresses his personal dilemma:

Only now do I realize what it means to be without the *Joseph* work, the task which always stood beside me, before me, all through this decade. Only now that *The Law* postlude is finished do I become

29. Meyer (p. 264, n. 31) refers in this connection to the unpublished dissertation by G. Lange, "Der Goethe-Roman Thomas Manns im Vergleich zu den Quellen" (Bonn, 1954). Also see E. Cassirer, "Thomas Manns Goethe-Bild," pp. 180 ff.
30. *AN*, p. 399.
31. See p. 4, n. 20.

conscious of the novelty and peril of the situation. It was comfortable, working away on what I had already dredged up. Do I still have strength for new conceptions? Have I not used up my subject matter? And if not — will I still be able to summon up the desire for work? [32]

In this predicament Mann turns again to his old conception of a general crisis of the novel. In a letter to the novelist Alfred Döblin, dated August, 1943, Mann speaks of the "crisis which the novel as an art form is at present experiencing." [33] Mann hardly needed outside suggestion, but his statement bears a definite relation to an article that he had probably read a short while before. Among the papers for *Doctor Faustus* are a few pages torn out of the March, 1943 issue of *Direction*; they contain Charles I. Glicksberg's article "Twilight of the Novel." [34] Mann's numerous underlinings reveal his interest in Glicksberg's hypotheses. Glicksberg's premise is "that the novel has reached a blind alley and may not be able to find its way out." But he describes a possible solution:

Every age calls forth its own appropriate aesthetic and ideological response. Ours takes the form of absorption in the problems of war and peace, fascism and democracy, sociology and economics and politics, and our demand is not for imaginative fantasy but for creative insight based on authentic observation. Not Surrealism but the documentary is the distinctive art form of our time.

We cannot determine how significantly this article affected Mann's plans for *Doctor Faustus*, but the concepts "authentic observation" and "the documentary" are certainly basic to Mann's montage technique. Mann probably took them as corroboration of his method.

Glicksberg sees in James Joyce the typical exponent of the crisis of the novel. During the summer of 1944, a short time after reading Glicksberg's article, Mann discovered Harry Levin's *James Joyce: a Critical Introduction*.[35] Mann mentions that Levin's book touched on many of his own problems. The author of the *Joseph* tetralogy was bound to sympathize with T. S. Eliot's question, quoted by Levin, "whether the novel had not outlived its function since Flaubert and James, and whether *Ulysses* should not be considered an epic." And Levin's thesis might have been formulated specifically for *Doctor Faustus*: "The best writing of our contemporaries is not an

32. P. 18.
33. *AN*, p. 779.
34. I am indebted to Prof. Glicksberg for identifying this article for me.
35. *Story of a Novel*, p. 90–91.

act of creation, but an act of evocation, peculiarly saturated with reminiscences." This is not to say, however, that Joyce actually influenced Mann in the writing of *Doctor Faustus*.[36] Mann did not read Levin's book until a year after beginning his novel, and by that time he had surely established the form the book was to take and the technique whereby it was to be realized. The kinship Mann felt with the author of *Ulysses* simply indicates that *Doctor Faustus* continues the revolution in the art of the novel that was taking place around the First World War. In *Doctor Faustus* Mann treats the crisis in terms of musical theory. As a source Mann could look up his own study of Pfitzner in the *Betrachtungen*. We should also not overlook the fact that Mann's musical adviser in the 1940's, Adorno, expressed in his *Philosophie der neuen Musik* ideas very close to Mann's. If one omits Adorno's sociological observations, the following words could very well have been spoken by Leverkühn. Adorno says of the tendency toward musical "quotation" in the early twentieth century:

It would be superficial to call this tendency Alexandrian and "civil-ized" in the Spenglerian sense of the word, thereby suggesting that the composers have nothing more of their own to say and are clinging like parasites to a lost tradition. Such a concept of originality derives from the bourgeois idea of property; we see unmusical judges handing down sentence on musical "thieves." The reason for this new tendency is a technical one. The number of possibilities for tonal "invention," which seemed endless to the aestheticians of the age of free enterprise, can in fact almost be calculated; tonality is limited on the one hand by the broken triad, on the other hand by the diatonic progression. At the time of Viennese Classicism, when the formal whole was con-sidered more important than melodic "ideas," no one strained against the boundaries imposed by the system. But with the emancipation of subjective melody, the limitations became more and more oppres-sive; composers were expected to have "ideas" like those of Schubert and Schumann, but the sparse material had been so thoroughly worked over that no idea could be conceived that had not been thought of already. Composers therefore accepted the objective fact that their material had been exhausted and made that fact part of their sub-jective relationship to the material; they constructed their themes as more or less obvious "quotations," achieving their effects through reiteration of the familiar.[37]

36. *Ibid.* Mann was apparently more interested in Levin's theories about Joyce than in Joyce's works, which presented too many language difficulties.
37. T. W. Adorno, *Philosophie der neuen Musik* (1958), pp. 168–69, note. The quotation comes from the second part of the book, which was not available to Mann while he was working on *DF*. Since, however, Adorno's verbal influence was great and he was composing this second part while advising Mann, the quotation seems applicable to *DF*.

Adorno uses terms like "idea," "invention" and "quotation" in the same sense as Mann in his *The Story of a Novel* when he discusses literary theory.

In summary, we can say that the manner of construction used for *Doctor Faustus*, including the montage technique, is anticipated to a certain extent in Mann's earlier works. *Buddenbrooks* borrows from reality what Mann calls factual, personal data.[38] In a few shorter works Mann uses acquaintances or members of his family as models.[39] The material for the *Joseph* novels comes from the world of legend and myth, while *The Beloved Returns* is based on historical reality; all these works are thus built around a "factual" core. *The Magic Mountain* reveals Mann's tendency to integrate an almost encyclopedic mass of knowledge into the fictional action, as well as to use direct quotations.

As we have seen, this technique of composition arose, partly out of naturalism, with its demand for veracity and detailed description, partly out of Mann's artistic make-up, in which the critical faculty dominated, and finally out of the crisis of the modern novel.

Yet *Doctor Faustus* in some ways occupies a unique position among Mann's works. In it the montage technique becomes a totally new device.[40] Mann assimilates in the form of either "open" or "hidden" quotations unprecedented quantities of material from the most disparate sources. The use of quotations which the ordinary reader would not recognize is not new in *Doctor Faustus*; *The Beloved Returns* contains quotations from Goethe and his contemporaries which are recognized only by the Goethe specialist. But there is an essential difference between the two works: in *The Beloved Returns* the quotations, both "open" and "hidden," serve to create a period atmosphere, whereas in *Doctor Faustus* the quotations represent widely varied sources, many of them totally unconnected with the historical setting of Faust. "Personal data" are exploited in *Doctor Faustus* more ruthlessly than ever before.[41] The constructivist

38. *Story of a Novel*, p. 32.
39. An example would be the heroine of *Royal Highness* (1909), who was modeled on Mann's wife Katia, or the heroine of *Disorder and Early Sorrow* (1926), based on Mann's youngest daughter, Elisabeth (see *Sketch of My Life*, p. 36). One can sense a more tenuous connection between Gustav Aschenbach of *Death in Venice* (1912) and Gustav Mahler (see *Briefe* 1:185).
40. *Story of a Novel*, p. 31.
41. *Ibid.*, p. 32.

tendency reaches greater complexity than in previous works. Taking the material of the Faust chapbook was only the first step; Mann's goal was to superimpose the Faustian pattern on the life of various historical or contemporary figures, while simultaneously portraying the historical evolution of Germany and the adventures of the novel in his own times.[42] As we shall see, the structure of the novel is more "musical," the development of the motifs more sophisticated than in any of Mann's previous novels.

The explanation for this extraordinary intensification of earlier tendencies can be found primarily in Mann's theme. He had resolved to write the novel of his own times, a novel about his country, and about himself: a confession in the form of a novel. To balance the subjectivity of ruthless self-revelation, and perhaps also to help him withstand the impact of his own insights, Mann needed a solidly objective form. This he found in the montage technique. The technique was thus identical with the basic conception of the book, or, as Mann expresses it,

This montage technique was continually startling, even to me, and gave me cause to worry. Yet it rightly belongs to the conception, to the "idea" of the book; it has to do with the strange and licentious spiritual relaxation from which it emerged, with its figurative and then again literal directness, its character as arcanum and confession, so that, as long as I was working on the book, the concept of its public existence did not enter my mind.[43]

In yet another respect the montage technique is essential to the basic conception of *Doctor Faustus*. Mann's task went beyond that of the ordinary novelist; in order to investigate the history of his country and reconstruct its development, he required exactitude and documentary evidence. Thus Mann can legitimatize the connection he suggests between his own times and the Reformation period with names and phrases from Luther's letters. He authenticates his students' jargon by incorporating samples of abstract discussion found in the *Freideutsche Position*. The particular choice of sources was largely determined by his attitude toward Germany and the German question. This attitude, and the evolution it had undergone in the decade preceding *Doctor Faustus*, will be the subject of our next chapter.

42. *Ibid.*, p. 38.
43. *Ibid.*, p. 32.

3

Thomas Mann
and the German Question

THE AWAKENING OF POLITICAL CONCERN

To understand the ideas behind *Doctor Faustus*, we must take into account more than the merely personal experiences and feelings of Thomas Mann discussed in the introduction. *Doctor Faustus* and *The Story of a Novel* give ample evidence of Mann's passionate sense of participation in the German tragedy, and both works reveal his conflicting sentiments: on the one hand disgust and horror, on the other agonized love, pity, and despair. The development of Mann's political attitudes from the early 1930's up to the writing of *Doctor Faustus* is fairly well documented. Our reconstruction of the chronological progression in Mann's earlier thinking must remain tentative, since we do not yet have access to all the pertinent material. But although the future will probably bring corrections and additions, Mann's various statements on Germany yield a relatively complete picture, provided we take note of the context in which each statement appears.

In 1918 Mann published his *Betrachtungen eines Unpolitischen,* a passionate defense of the German Romantic tradition and German culture against shallow "Western civilization." The *Betrachtungen* still show the predominant influence of the "three-star constellation" — Schopenhauer, Nietzsche and Wagner — that had presided over Mann's youth. During the 1920's a reorientation takes place: Goethe becomes Mann's ideal; active involvement in politics is avoided.[1]

In the face of developments in the late 1920's and early 1930's Mann could no longer refrain from taking a political stand. In October, 1930, after the election victory of the National Socialist Party, Mann delivered a speech in Berlin entitled "An Appeal to Reason," in which he labels the National Socialists

1. W. A. Berendsohn, "Thomas Mann und das Dritte Reich," p. 245.

a serious threat and calls on the German middle classes to throw in their lot with the Social Democrats as the last defenders of a civilized way of life.[2] He goes on to point out the horrifying alliance that National Socialism has concluded with "a wave of anomalous barbarism, of primitive popular vulgarity — that sweeps over the world today,"[3] and he warns Germany to beware of arrogance. If Germany, with its particular "state of mind," wants to reach out for political hegemony, it will become a "world menace."[4] Mann already visualizes Germany as a psychological case; he cautions the German people against giving the world "the spectacle of an ecstatic nervous collapse."[5] Mann's idea of the German catastrophe as a sort of collective nervous breakdown or outbreak of insanity reappears in *Doctor Faustus*, portrayed symbolically in Adrian Leverkühn's disease.

On February 10, 1933 Mann delivered his Munich lecture, "Sufferings and Greatness of Richard Wagner." Following the uproar occasioned by this speech, Mann refrained for several years from such public utterances. But in 1945 he published an interesting work, *Leiden an Deutschland: Tagebuchblätter aus den Jahren 1933 und 1934* ["Suffering for Germany: Leaves from a Journal, 1933 and 1934"]. It would be hard to determine whether these notes represent truly private reflections or were written with publication in mind. They comment with great intensity on the events of the day. Mann denounces Hitler and his followers as "scum" and passionately urges the German people to exorcise the curse of National Socialism. In tone and attitude these notes anticipate the radio talks written almost a decade later. Although these notes are not beamed at a specific audience, they contain the summons to "rid yourself of those fools, dripping with the blood of others, who strut about as your leaders."[6] In an outburst like the following we already hear the Thomas Mann of the radio addresses:

Make an end of it! Écrasez l'infâme! Away with Hitler, the miserable creature, the hysterical cheat, the hollow monster, the un-German trampish swindler of power. . . . Away with "General" Goering, that cutthroat popinjay with his three hundred uniforms. . . . Away with that blubber-mouthed Propaganda Chief of Hell named Goebbels.

2. "An Appeal to Reason," *Order of the Day*, pp. 60 ff.
3. *Ibid.*, p. 55.
4. *Ibid.*, p. 50.
5. *Ibid.*, p. 58.
6. *Leiden an Deutschland*, p. 8.

. . . Away with this shameless philosophaster Alfred Rosenberg. . . . Away with this whole apocalyptic pack, this band of ruffians . . . who . . . have driven Germany into dishonorable isolation, have torn a gulf between Germany and the civilized world and with fatal certainty will plunge the country into physical and moral ruin if they are not stopped.[7]

The journal contains other thoughts that Mann develops in later speeches and essays. As early as 1933 he is saying how difficult he finds the life of exile, how "every nobler aspect of Germany has been abandoned to the torture of homelessness." [8] He calls exile a martyrdom "for which I feel I was never born, but to which my spiritual dignity irresistibly calls me." [9] He distinguishes accordingly between a good, noble Germany and the Germany of the ruling regime. He begins to use quotation marks around the word "German" when the word occurs in connection with the National Socialists.[10]

Here Mann for the first time attempts to explain the developments in Germany psychologically as well as historically. He considers one of the causes to be the unfortunate isolation of the nation; he speaks of the "unhappy, isolated, erring people," [11] brooding in "cramped, unhealthy, phantastical, mischief-breeding self-centeredness." [12] He thinks that the arrogance and prestige-hunger of the nation are rooted in "an inferiority complex that is pure hypochondria." [13] When the German peoples' fateful solitude and its longing for recognition combine with its constitutional "lack of gift for politics" [14] and what Mann calls its "will to suffering," [15] they form a peculiarly suitable soil for National Socialist ideas. He tries as long as possible to see this combination of characteristics as

7. "From: *Diaries* (1933–34)," tr. R. Winston, pp. 45–46.
8. *Leiden an Deutschland*, p. 5.
9. *Ibid.*, p. 16. See the letter of the same year (*Briefe* 1:329) in which Mann writes to his Italian translator, Lavinia Mazzucchetti: "I am much too good a German, far too closely linked with the cultural traditions and the language of my country, for the thought of an exile lasting years, if not a lifetime, not to have a grave, a fateful significance to me. Nevertheless, we have perforce begun to look around for a new base, if possible in the German language area. At the age of fifty-seven *such* a loss of settled life and livelihood, to which I had become adjusted and in which I was already growing a bit stiff, is no small matter." [Translated by Richard and Clara Winston.]
10. *Diaries*, pp. 45, 47.
11. *Ibid.*, p. 43.
12. *Leiden an Deutschland*, p. 7.
13. *Ibid.*, p. 17.
14. *Diaries*, p. 49.
15. *Leiden an Deutschland*, p. 55.

something noble that has regrettably fallen prey to Hitler's lies and nationalistic propaganda.[16] In politics, the German people resembles "the aristocrat who decides to play the businessman," says Mann,[17] and again and again he stresses the vulgar, plebeian quality of National Socialism. A passage written in the summer of 1934 reads:

And it would be a real irony of history if this most spiritual and "inward" people should be destroyed by what was originally an aristocratic and worthy clumsiness in matters of the external, actual world.[18]

Behind such a statement lies the notion of good qualities seduced or perverted, a notion that will play an important part in *Doctor Faustus*. He speaks of his unhappy fellow countrymen "led by savage and stupid adventurers, whom they think legendary heroes," [19] and later such words occur as "sell," "contagion," "seduction." [20]

The journal does not contain a systematic attempt to work out the historical genesis of National Socialism, but we can spot ideas destined to be worked out later. Significant in connection with *Doctor Faustus* is Mann's suggestion that the Nazi movement represents a sort of mythical recapitulation of Luther:

There really is such a thing as "recurrence," insofar as the tumultous and bloody role of Lutheranism is now being recreated by nationalism, with its antirational and inhumane tendencies, its obsession with blood and tragedy.[21]

Mann notes the ease with which the Nazis make Luther one of their own. The historical parallel "is doing the enemy's dirty work, for who could fail to recognize the resemblance [of Luther] to Hitler?" [22] Mann continues that the similarity to Wagner may be greater still: "Hitler embodies to the letter the unpleasant side of Wagner, though only that much." [23]

Despite the lack of a comprehensive historical survey, the diary notes show Mann considering Hitlerism as a historical phenomenon. He feels that Nazi ideology had its forerunners — though on a higher intellectual plane — in such figures as

16. *Ibid.*, p. 54.
17. *Diaries*, p. 49.
18. *Leiden an Deutschland*, pp. 87–88.
19. *Diaries*, p. 43.
20. *Leiden an Deutschland*, pp. 86, 87.
21. *Ibid.*, p. 73.
22. *Diaries*, p. 47.
23. *Leiden an Deutschland*, p. 43.

Nietzsche, Klages, and George.[24] He says that he early recognized what was coming and dissociated himself from the train of developments:

To repeat: I sensed early and felt deeply what was coming: I suffered from it and opposed the conscienceless, spreading mischief; I incurred, as I expected, the reproach that I incline to sterile rationalism. I was aware of the culpability of the spirit, of its irresponsibility toward reality, which arose from an essentially unpolitical attitude and a narcissistic admiration of its own daring.[25]

In addition to the above poets and philosophers, Mann names a whole series of fairly well known scholars who helped pave the way for National Socialism: Spranger, A. Messer, Bäumler, Goldberg.[26] But according to Mann, many other, less prominent intellectuals and "Blood and Soil" literati also contributed, as did the young people, who, inflammable and easily steered, mistook the Nazi movement for the embodiment of their ideals.[27] As we have shown, many of these forerunners of Nazism appear under various guises in *Doctor Faustus.*

A certain cautious optimism emerges from Mann's repeatedly stated conviction that evil must come to an end, that Hitler and his movement are doomed. Mixed with the optimism, however, is grave uneasiness as to what the future holds for the German people:

One knows in one's heart that these idiots and bloody bunglers will be smashed. And what then? What will become of the unfortunate German people, which is now reeling with illusory happiness? . . . It faces an awakening ten times more terrible than the awakening of 1918.[28]

In the course of the years, as the Nazi atrocities increased, Mann's uneasiness became even more grave and his optimism less evident, although, as we shall see, he struggled to maintain his conviction that the good will win out and make possible a new humanism.[29]

24. *Diaries,* p. 41.
25. *Ibid.,* p. 42 and *Leiden an Deutschland,* p. 11.
26. *Leiden an Deutschland,* pp. 12, 57.
27. *Ibid.,* p. 62.
28. *Ibid.,* p. 6.
29. Letters written in the first half of the thirties also testify to Mann's basic optimism. In June, 1930 he writes: "The best things of the past have been dragged through the mud; humanism is debased or dead. The result: *a new humanism must be founded.*" (*Briefe* 1:301). A few years later, in April, 1935 he says: "Au fond and à la longue I am optimistic. Compulsively and even against their own better judgement and intentions these people

THOMAS MANN WARNS AND EXHORTS THE GERMAN PEOPLE

On February 3, 1936 Mann stepped into the public arena with a letter to Eduard Korrodi, the Swiss literary critic and editor of the literary supplement of the *Neue Zürcher Zeitung*.[30] Although the letter ostensibly states Mann's position on the literature of the emigrants, it actually sets forth in no uncertain terms his attitude to the German regime. A few days later, in a letter written to Hermann Hesse, Mann explains that he has long felt that such a show of colors was necessary.[31] Apparently he hoped that the National Socialists would not make drastic reprisals for his statement. He was mistaken, for in December of that year he lost both his citizenship and his honorary doctorate from the University at Bonn.[32]

The result of these events was the "Exchange of Letters" early in 1937 in which Mann expresses even more plainly his disgust at the regime that had needed only a few short years to bring Germany to the edge of the abyss.[33] He describes himself as a representative of the German cultural tradition: his works are written for Germans, and no bureaucratic decision can deprive him of his fundamental German citizenship.[34] He is convinced that war is simply impossible. Germany would never be able to survive such a test; war would mean the end of the German people. The letter closes with a prayer which reëchoes in the closing words of *Doctor Faustus*:

The pressure was great. And as a man who out of diffidence in religious matters will seldom or never either by tongue or pen let the name of the Deity escape him, yet in moments of deep emotion cannot refrain, let me — since after all one cannot say everything — close this letter with a brief and fervent prayer: *God help our darkened*

are committing every error (not to mention crime) that can possibly lead to their destruction" (*ibid.*, 387). As late as 1938 Mann tried to maintain this faith, in spite of all that had happened. He ends "This Peace" (*Order of the Day*, p. 185) as follows: "We must have no fear. Peace and truth may suffer apparent eclipse. But in us, in our hearts, they are eternally free. And looking down from the bright regions of art, the spirit may laugh at the triumphant folly of the hours."

30. *Briefe* 1:409 ff., 532.

31. In a letter of February 9, 1936 he writes: "Sooner or later I had to declare myself in clear language: for the sake of the world, in which a good many highly ambiguous, half-and-half notions of my relationship to the Third Reich prevail, and for my own sake as well. Something of the sort has long been a psychic necessity for me." [Translated by Richard and Clara Winston.] (*Briefe* 1:414. See also the letter to R. Schickele, February 19, 1936, *ibid.*, 415.)

32. See *Briefe* 1:532.

33. "An Exchange of Letters," *Order of the Day*, pp. 105–13.

34. See above, "Introduction," n. 36.

and desecrated country and teach it to make peace with the world and with itself![36]

The essay "Europe, Beware!" written in 1938, reiterates ideas we have encountered in earlier statements: the brutish Nazis are using mendacious quasi-philosophy, collectivization, and mass psychology to seduce the Germans. The roots of Nationalism lie in the doctrines of violence, racial superiority, Blood and Soil, and so on. Germany will be rescued from an annihilating war by a new fighting humanism, which will offer sufficient resistance to the forces of barbarism.[36] Among all these unvarnished denunciations of Hitler and the Nazi "trimmings of shame," [37] we come upon an essay with the ironic title "A Brother" (1938). Mann claims in this essay that one must recognize Hitler as "an artist-phenomenon," [38] and he spins out the idea of a kinship:

A brother — a rather unpleasant and mortifying brother. He makes me nervous, the relationship is painful to a degree. But I will not disclaim it. For I repeat: better, more productive, more honest, more constructive than hatred is recognition, acceptance, the readiness to make oneself one with what is deserving of our hate.[39]

It is not altogether surprising to find Mann "fraternizing" with the hated dictator; much in his earlier works points in the same

---

35. "Exchange of Letters," p. 113.
36. *Order of the Day*, pp. 81, 74–77, 82. The collection includes the above-mentioned "Appeal to Reason," in addition the "Exchange of Letters" and the introduction to the newspaper *Mass und Wert* founded by Mann and Konrad Falke. (The paper appeared for the first time in September/October, 1937.) The collection also contains "The Coming Victory of Democracy," a lecture delivered in the spring of 1938 in fifteen American cities. The last two essays mentioned deal with more general problems such as what constitutes real democracy; they do not need to be discussed here. Wherever Mann's political thinking becomes abstract, it tends to merge with his personal concerns; see in this connection Olle Holmberg, *TM och det tredje riket*, p. 79 and Max Rychner, "Thomas Mann und die Politik," p. 599. A somewhat dubious attempt at saving Mann's honor as a political thinker is M. Flinker's *Thomas Manns politische Betrachtungen im Lichte der heutigen Zeit* (The Hague, 1959). He maintains in contradiction to all other scholars and to Mann himself that Mann's writings, including the *Betrachtungen*, give us "the voice of one of the most powerful and lucid political thinkers. And of a prophet" (p. 21). On the idea of a fighting humanism see Ilse Metzler, *Dämonie und Humanismus*, p. 65. Zeitblom appears here as a representative of the weak brand of humanism that is incapable of resistance. Another treatment of Mann's politics can be found in K. Sontheimer. *Thomas Mann und die Deutschen* (Munich, 1961).
37. *Briefe* 1:372.
38. "A Brother," *Order of the Day*, p. 156.
39. *Ibid.*, p. 157.

direction. From his youth Mann was fascinated with the ambiguousness of art and the artist, their suspicious proximity to a morbid and even criminal realm. *Tonio Kröger* (1903) contains numerous illustrations of this idea, for instance in the episode of the banker who suddenly begins to write stories after a period of imprisonment, or in Tonio's being arrested in his native city.[40] We encounter the same theme on a larger scale in *The Confessions of Felix Krull*, which Mann began in 1910; the underlying idea is the kinship of the artist with the swindler, the criminal.[41] A variation turns up in the *Betrachtungen*:

The artist, I would suggest, remains until his dying breath an emotional and spiritual adventurer, always disposed toward perversity and chaos, open to all that is perilous and pernicious.[42]

The following passage is even more interesting with reference to Hitler:

Art will never be moral in the political sense, never virtuous; art will never insure progress. Art's basic character is unreliable, treacherous; one cannot eradicate its delight in scandalous a-rationality, its penchant for beauty born of barbarity; even if one denounces this leaning as hysterical, inimical to the spirit, immoral to the point of imperiling the world, it remains an immutable fact.[43]

In all his statements on Hitler, Mann emphasizes the features of the adventurer and swindler. In the diaries for 1933–34 he calls Hitler a "hysterical swindler," "hysterical deceiver," "power swindler," and the members of the Nazi regime become "adventurers" and "hysterical charlatans." [44] In short, Mann has not made a striking discovery in the essay "A Brother"; he is merely summing up what he has felt all along. He acknowledges traits common to his character and Hitler's, but he refrains from examining the use — or misuse — of these traits.[45]

At the beginning of the essay he describes the only feeling

40. Mann writes of the banker, "One might be rash enough to conclude that a man has to be at home in some kind of jail in order to become a poet" (*Stories of Three Decades*, p. 105).
41. *Briefe* 1:456.
42. *Betrachtungen eines Unpolitischen*, p. 403.
43. *Ibid.*, p. 396.
44. *Leiden an Deutschland*, pp. 5, 60, 33, 41.
45. Mann justifies linking the creative artist with the political demagogue when he demonstrates that Wagner and Hitler share certain basic traits. We find this thought in the 1933 address on Wagner, and in the essay on Hitler he writes, "The whole thing is a distorted phase of Wagnerism" (p. 156). In 1944 Mann expresses the same idea in an article: "The Wagnerian art revolution, though on an incomparably higher plane, was a phenomenon related to the National Socialist revolution" ("What is German"? 80).

or manner of conduct that can overcome hatred and disgust: "Love and hatred are great emotions; yet it is strange how prone people are to underestimate, precisely as emotion, that attitude in which they both unite: I mean *interest*." [46] Interest is also the emotion that Adrian Leverkühn declares to be stronger than love.[47]

The essay reiterates several other themes familiar to us from Mann's earlier writings. The qualities that he attributes in the diaries to the German people — arrogance and the need to compensate for a sense of inferiority — are here attributed to the individual Hitler.[48] Mann also discusses the "primitivization" in Europe which has helped lay the foundation for National Socialism. Mann admits that he had contact with the circles responsible for this process, though he gradually dissociated himself from the prevailing tendencies:

Who can wonder, then, that I paid no attention when they degenerated into the political sphere and wreaked their violence on a plane where professors enamored of the primitive and literary lackeys of the anti-intellectual pose were the only ones who did not fear to tread.[49]

The following year (1939) Mann gives serious consideration to the catastrophic results for Germany of aristocratic scorn for politics; in his essay "Culture and Politics" Mann explains that he himself once committed the fatal and typically German error of despising democracy and making a sharp distinction between the mind and politics. Later, he says, he came to realize that "the unhappy course of German history, which has issued in the cultural catastrophe of National Socialism, is in truth very much bound up with that unpolitical cast of the bourgeois mind." [50] The outcome of this attitude could escape no one. Germany had become an "Enemy of Humankind! To this has the German spirit come with its anti-democratic cultural pride." [51]

Mann tries to find comfort in the idea that the Nazi catastrophe will prove a harsh but valuable lesson for the German bourgeoisie, provided the bourgeoisie works its way through to a new, politically aware humanism. But there is some doubt,

46. "A Brother," p. 154.
47. See *Doktor Faustus*, p. 69.
48. "A Brother," pp. 154, 155.
49. *Ibid.*, p. 159.
50. "Culture and Politics," p. 150.
51. *Ibid.*, p. 151.

he remarks resignedly, "whether the bourgeois intellectual of Germany will be able to profit by his hard experience." [52] According to Mann's concluding words, newly won faith in the good, in freedom, truth, and justice will be the only weapon with which to defy the enemies of mankind, "as the medieval monk held out the crucifix before Satan." The new humanist will take on "the role of David against Goliath, of Saint George against the old dragon of violence and lies." [53]

A useful source for Mann's attitude toward Germany after the outbreak of war and at the time of his emigration to America is the collection of radio addresses, *Deutsche Hörer!* broadcast in the years 1940–45. [The English translation, *Listen, Germany!*, only covers the first two and one-half years.] These talks were beamed from New York and London "into the night," in the hope that they would somehow reach the German people; they bombard the misguided country with despairing outbursts of emotion and passionate appeals. Mann knew what was expected of him and was well aware that his words had to reach out to a very broad public. It is impossible to decide what is rhetorical effect and what is genuine emotion. But his intense involvement and the honest desire to warn and exhort the German people are unmistakable. A close examination of the ideas and the wording reveals close correspondences between the public radio addresses and the private diaries for 1933 and 1934.

To a great extent the addresses simply furnish information. Mann thought it important to confront the Germans with the cold facts about what was really going on in Germany, to report on executions and mass murder, to give statistics on innocent persons killed or exiled, to cast light on all matters concealed from the people. [54] But to an even greater extent the addresses contain denunciations of the Nazi regime and of Hitler, coupled with pleas that the German people come to its senses while there is still time, emerge from its delusions and rid itself of National Socialism.

52. *Ibid.*
53. *Ibid.* The final words of the essay are identical with those of the lecture Mann was to have held at the International PEN Congress in Stockholm in Sept. 1939. As a result of the events in Europe the Congress was canceled. See G. Lundgren, *Thomas Mann*, p. 54. This lecture includes most of the ideas on the essence and future of democracy that Mann had expressed elsewhere. See above, n. 36 of this chapter.
54. The Thomas Mann Archives in Zurich possess various newspaper clippings from the war years in which Mann underlined just such statistics.

Mann does not shrink from invective when he characterizes Hitler and his henchmen. In July, 1941 he says:

Look at the collection of its representatives, these Ribbentrops, Himmlers, Streichers, Leys, this Goebbels, the loud-mouthed liar, the Führer himself with his evil inspirations and his fat, pompous Great-Arch- and Reichs-Marshal of the Greater German Great-space Reich! What a menagerie! [55]

In April of the same year Mann expresses his conviction

that Hitler the individual, with his fathomless mendacity, his shabby cruelty and vindictiveness, his incessant shouts of hatred, his degradation of the German language, his inferior fanaticism, his cowardly asceticism and paltry unnature, his whole defective being, which is void of the slightest trace of magnanimity or higher life, that this individual is the most disgusting figure upon whom history has ever cast its light.[56]

However, Mann's talks do not contain only reproaches and condemnations; they are also intended to enunciate the positive message that beyond defeat exists the possibility of attaining peace and freedom. Mann here reiterates his hope that good will finally triumph over evil, or, in more concrete terms, that Nazism will fall and the "good" Germany be resurrected. In the foreword to the edition of the first twenty-five addresses (1942), Mann says,

What I believe unshakably is that Hitler cannot win his war — this is a belief based much more on metaphysical and moral reasons than on military ones.[57]

In the diaries Mann's hope seems to be based mainly on *Realpolitik*; here we see it transformed into a metaphysical expectation. Nor is Mann merely convinced that Germany will be defeated; he prays for defeat. The diabolic powers must be defeated for Germany's sake. And yet Mann cannot hide his growing anxiety over the future of his country. In his September, 1943 address he asks, "What is to become of Germany?" and continues,

One has no right to ask this, after all that has been done to Europe, and yet, with a wrench of the heart one does ask, for Germany was once home.[58]

55. *Listen, Germany!* p. 40.
56. *Ibid.*, pp. 27–28.
57. *Ibid.*, p. viii.
58. *Deutsche Hörer!* p. 98. [Not included in the English translation.]

And when Mann's wish is fulfilled and Germany has been delivered from the Nazis, he is anything but happy. The last radio talk, delivered May 10, 1945, clearly reveals his inner conflict; it begins: "How bitter it is when the world is rejoicing over the defeat, the deepest humiliation of one's own country!"[59]

On the whole, Mann's opinions show little change from the 1933–34 diaries to the radio talks. The general tone becomes somewhat more bitter, the optimism recedes, and Mann's uneasiness and despondency deepen under the crushing impressions of the war years. As his concern for the future of Germany intensifies, the question of culpability becomes more and more pressing. To be sure, the problem is already present in the diaries. In August, 1934 he writes, "What has been committed in the way of crimes, lies, irreparable atrocities and unbearable baseness cannot be allowed to end with reconciliation and total exoneration. That would violate every dictate of morality."[60] But just as Mann's optimistic trust in the eventual victory of the good gradually becomes a vaguer, more religiously tinged aspiration, the whole question of culpability takes on increasingly metaphysical dimensions.

Mann's awareness of Germany's guilt finds unmistakable expression in some of the radio talks of late 1941 and early 1942. In his Christmas Eve address he asks rhetorically:

Is my guess right that shame and infinite longing fill you tonight, longing for innocence, for a way out of the enmeshment in insane guilt in which you are writhing; that shame, burning shame fills you in the face of the loving spirit of this festival? Look around you; what have you done? In Greece two hundred human beings starve to death every day — that is only one example of the indescribable misery, the death of peoples, the rape of human beings, the agonies of bodies and souls all around you, which your seductible nature, your terrible obedience have caused.[61]

And in January, 1942:

The longer the war lasts, the more desperately this nation entangles itself in guilt.[62]

But Mann does not rely solely on the ethical categories of guilt and retribution. Occasionally we encounter another explana-

---

59. *Ibid.*, p. 131.
60. *Leiden an Deutschland*, p. 78 f.
61. *Listen, Germany!* p. 64.
62. *Ibid.*, p. 72.

tion: the catastrophic developments in Germany can be seen as a terrible mistake, "half culpability, half calamity," as he says in a radio address of 1945.[63] Germany labors under a curse which all the powers of good are powerless to dispel. Later he puts the case even more clearly:

We will not raise the issue of culpability. That is no word for this fateful chain of events resulting from an unfortunate history; and if it be culpability after all, the world has a great share in it.[64]

It might seem that Mann, living in relative tranquillity as an emigrant, was unwilling to blame his unlucky fellow Germans for unbearable crimes and brutality and instead wished to ascribe their offenses to an unmerciful fate. But much suggests that Mann's motivation was more complex. Our quotations indicate that he by no means hesitates to put his finger on Germany's fault. Mann seems rather to be testing out various interpretations. Morally the Germans cannot be absolved of their guilt toward humanity, but on a higher, metaphysical plane, Mann visualizes this moral guilt as something inevitably imposed by destiny. As we shall see, this dual explanation forms the structural core of *Doctor Fasutus.*

Mann voices the same attitude toward the problem of guilt in the article "What is German?" (1944):

We cannot deny their [the Germans'] responsibility, for somehow man is responsible for his being and doing; but we are inclined to speak of a historic course, a dark destiny and aberration, rather than of crime and guilt.[65]

Mann's talk of a "dark destiny" implies a notion he seems unwilling to formulate clearly but which is central to his whole view of history: Germany forms an exception among the peoples; it is destined to undergo exceptional sufferings and therefore also to attain exceptional greatness.[66] If there is anything comparable, it is the fate of the Jews, whom the Germans subject to terrible persecution precisely because of the similarity.[67] In *Doctor Faustus* we find this same parallelism between

63. *Deutsche Hörer!* p. 119.
64. *Ibid.*, p. 120.
65. "What is German?" p. 80.
66. In an otherwise excessively Marxist essay E. Fischer makes the incontrovertible point that in *Doctor Faustus* Mann pays tribute to a sort of "myth of destiny," despite his critical attitude toward National Socialism; see "*Doktor Faustus* und die deutsche Katastrophe," *Kunst und Menschheit*: Essays, pp. 37–97.
67. In "Germany and the Germans" (p. 65) Mann cites Goethe as a witness: "In oral conversation, at least, Goethe went so far as to wish for a

the two peoples suggested by the Jewish impresario Saul Fitelberg.

THOMAS MANN AS APOLOGIST

While Mann held fast to the idea that Germany was cursed by fate, he was also seeking a more concrete explanation for the way events had developed. The lecture "Germany and the Germans," delivered in Washington on June 6, 1945, Mann's seventieth birthday, represents an attempted explanation. The speech consists primarily of an analysis of the circumstances that set Germany on its fateful course. If Mann speaks in his radio addresses as a fellow countryman who warns and exhorts his people from a safe distance, he here speaks as a refugee who still identifies with his native land and therefore assumes the role of apologist.

"Germany and the Germans" does not present any ideas we have not already encountered. Mann's characterization of the German spirit accords fully with what he has said earlier about the Germans and Hitler. What distinguishes this talk from earlier statements is that Mann here constructs a thoroughgoing psychological explanation for the degeneration of the German spirit and describes this degeneration as a historical process. The lecture is especially interesting in connection with *Doctor Faustus*, since it was written during a monthlong interruption of work on the novel, in February and March of 1945.[68]

In Mann's own words, "Germany and the Germans" tells the saddening story of German 'inwardness.' "[69] One of its striking features is Mann's indulgence of his familiar inclination to personify Germany and ascribe to it certain typical character traits. The lecture provides evidence that he is still anchored in the tradition of German romanticism, with its conception of the "soul of the people" ("Volksseele"); at the same time the lecture results from Mann's very personal sense of identification with Germany. Under these circumstances, a review of Germany's plight becomes a self-interrogation: "The truths that one tries to utter about one's people can only be a product of self-examination."[70]

German Diaspora. 'Like the Jews,' he said, 'the Germans must be transplanted and scattered over the world!' And he added: '. . . in order to develop the good that lies in them fully and to the benefit of the nations.' "
68. *Story of a Novel*, p. 109.
69. "Germany and the Germans," p. 64.
70. *Ibid.*, p. 49.

The characteristic described in "Germany and the Germans" as typically German is "inwardness," a difficult concept which Mann attempts to define by means of other, equally difficult concepts. According to Mann, the concept embraces depth of feeling, otherworldly speculation, a sense of the mysterious, demonic side of existence; inwardness finds its best expression in music. Although "inwardness" centers the Germans' attention on their own egos, they long for human contact. But here an unfortunate conflict arises: the Germans are basically lone wolves, completely lacking in political experience; both as individuals and as a nation they have a dangerous tendency toward isolation. Yet they dream of friendship and a place in the community of peoples. Their isolation gives rise to a certain intolerance, which, combined with their arrogance and misanthropy transforms their attempts at contact into aggression. Or, as Mann expresses it in his earlier article, "What is German?"

Translated from political terminology into the psychological, National Socialism means: "I do not want the social at all. I want the folk fairytale." But in the political realm, the fairytale becomes a murderous lie.[71]

Assigning these purely personal attributes to Germany enables Mann to explain its fate in psychological terms, and his wording sometimes sounds almost psychoanalytical. Thus he refers to National Socialism as "an exaggerated over-compensation of the German lack of political talent."[72]

This tendency to personify Germany and to see its historical development as a psychological process reaches its climax in *Doctor Faustus*, where Germany becomes Adrian Leverkühn. But with both the novel and the lecture we must keep in mind that Mann uses psychological terminology as a metaphorical way of portraying historical drama.

71. "What is German?" p. 81.
72. *Ibid.* It is interesting that a professional psychologist had anticipated Mann in his analysis of the German problem. This was C. G. Jung, who influenced Mann in other contexts. His *Essays on Contemporary Events* (London, 1947), express ideas that bear a startling similarity to Mann's. The earlier essays, all of which appeared separately during the 1930's and early 1940's, offer a rather vague diagnosis. But in "After the Catastrophe," originally published in the *Neue Schweizer Rundschau*, NF 13, June, 1945, Jung says unflinchingly: "the history of the last twelve years is the case-sheet of a hysterical subject's illness" (*Essays*, p. 62). Jung sees Faust as a symbol of the hysterical split in the German soul, and the examples he names are Wagner and Nietzsche! So far we have no documentary evidence that Mann was acquainted with Jung's essay.

The picture of Germany's historical evolution that Mann presents in "Germany and the Germans" is highly subjective, traced in bold, sweeping lines. Mann considers that the origin of the present fateful events lies in the "romantic germ of illness and death," which was planted in the period of Germany's transition from the Catholic Middle Ages to the Lutheran Reformation; its deadly fruit was the Second World War.[73] As Mann surveys these four or five hundred years of political, spiritual, and cultural development, he perceives in them not only a triumph of the creative powers of the German mind, but also a long sickness, resulting from the ill-starred inbreeding of all the specifically German qualities.

According to Mann, certain figures in German history personify these peculiarly German qualities, and he attributes to these figures a symbolic meaning above and beyond their recognized achievements. In addition to Faust he mentions Luther and Nietzsche, who in "Germany and the Germans" take the place of historical figures like Dürer and Wagner used by Mann in other contexts. But these figures represent only one side of the German spirit. Along with the olden-time, provincial, unworldly, and isolationist tendencies there exists a more broadminded humanism, exemplified by Erasmus or, in "Germany and the Germans," Tilman Riemenschneider, the gifted carver of Würzburg, who took the side of the rebels during the Peasants' War and upon Luther's suggestion was tortured after the defeat. This humanism claims for its own the classicistic Goethe, who counteracts the Faustian Goethe. Goethe, in fact, is the great figure who succeeds in uniting the two "souls in his breast"; as we know, Thomas Mann follows in his footsteps.

But, Mann notes, these spokesmen for humanism and tolerance did not set Germany's course; that was done by the others, the demonic Faustian types who bore within them the poisons of disease. Mann also uses the metaphor of corruption for Germany's development. In simple terms this corruption consists of nationalistic *hybris,* the growing conviction that Germans are racially and spiritually superior, chosen to rule the world. The beginning of the process also falls in the transition period between Middle Ages and Renaissance, when the concept of the nation-state is just awakening in Europe. Mann sees this transition period mirrored in Martin Luther.

73. "Germany and the Germans," p. 64.

Mann clearly regards the Reformation as a specifically German event. He says of Luther's "antipolitical servility":

> But it is also and chiefly typical in a monumental and defiant manner of the purely German sundering of the national impulse and the ideal of political liberty. For the Reformation, like the later uprising against Napoleon, was a *nationalistic* movement for liberty.[74]

As a result of the Reformation, Germany cut itself off from the European cultural community which had characterized the Middle Ages, and the isolation deepened when German came to replace Latin as the language of the liturgy and of theology. Luther's significance for this development must not be overlooked; Mann considers his efforts on behalf of the German language very important. Luther was the first to try to make German an adequate vehicle for the German spirit. According to Mann this effort is crowned in the works of Goethe and Nietzsche.

The other figure that Mann sees as typical of the transition period is Dürer, although his name does not occur in "Germany and the Germans." Mann formed his idea of Dürer much earlier; in an essay on Dürer written in 1928, he adds him to the familiar list of representative Germans: "Dürer, Goethe, Schopenhauer, Nietzsche, Wagner — there it would all be, . . . the whole fateful complex and galaxy, a whole world, the German world."[75] This artist embodies for Mann the deeply Protestant attitude of hard-working "devotion to his craft" — one need only think of his characteristic portraits of solid burghers — mixed simultaneously with a medieval superstition and mysticism that survived the Reformation and the Enlightenment and maintained its power over the German popular imagination deep into the romantic age.

An important phase in the ill-omened German development from Reformation to National Socialism is romanticism. In "Germany and the Germans" Thomas Mann gives a penetrating definition: Romanticism embraces all the good and all the evil that the German spirit has to offer; "German *Roman-*

---

74. *Ibid.*, p. 55. M. Doerne has discussed Mann's concept of Luther and its basis in contemporary German theology. He stresses that Ernst Troeltsch is responsible for the theory that Luther was primarily a product of the Middle Ages. See "Thomas Mann und das protestantische Christentum." W. Kohlschmidt has investigated the connection in Mann's thinking between the Reformation and nationalism: "Musikalität, Reformation und Deutschtum: eine kritische Studie zu Thomas Manns 'Doktor Faustus.' "

75. "Dürer," *Past Masters and Other Papers*, p. 150.

ticism, what is it but an expression of this finest German quality, German inwardness?" [76] German romanticism in the broadest sense, including music as well as literature, is characterized by a certain "antiquarianism of soul" which comes close to the irrational and demonic side of existence and finds its highest expression in mysticism and in music.[77] However, romanticism also harbors a good deal of "pessimism of sincerity" and an inclination to "Machiavellianism," which pass via Bismarck to Hitler.

Wagner and Nietzsche are the principal artistic representatives of romanticism for Mann. What earns Wagner his position is *The Ring of the Nibelungen,* which glorifies Germany's Aryan past and is, in Mann's eyes, the most striking artistic manifestation of the nineteenth-century middle-class spirit in Germany.[78] There are good objective reasons why Mann should attribute such importance to Wagner, but we must also remember the extraordinary influence Wagner had on Mann's personal development as a man and an artist. Nietzsche occupies the place next to Wagner in Mann's intellectual world; and indeed they embody much the same historical tendencies. Although Nietzsche regarded the "German" with skepticism, his doctrine of the superman gave fatal impetus to German nationalism in its drive to realize its dream of greatness, previously rather vague.

Whereas Mann sees good and evil mixed in these representatives of German nationalism, Hitler is an unalloyed product of evil, of the demonic, of total degeneration. The creative geniuses Luther and Nietzsche embody a fascinating contradiction, but Hitler is simply a despicable and all too unambiguous tool in the hands of the barbarous and destructive forces which his great predecessors had held in check.

When Mann personifies Germany or sees it reflected in certain typical figures, he is apparently seeking an intelligible explanation for his country's misfortunes; psychological char-

76. "Germany and the Germans," p. 61.
77. *Ibid.*
78. Along with such typical representatives of the "monumental art" of the nineteenth century as Dickens, Thackeray, Tolstoy, Dostoevsky, Balzac, and Zola, Mann names Richard Wagner, "whose work certainly has much to do with the epic but is really musical drama. Germany's contribution to the monumental art of the nineteenth century is not literary but — very characteristically — musical." See "Die Kunst des Romans," *Altes und Neues,* p. 400. Cf. "Sufferings and Greatness of Richard Wagner," *Essays of Three Decades,* p. 308.

acteristics and their development are easier to grasp in an individual than in an entire people. But Mann so greatly expands the symbolic significance of the individual that he arrives at the romantic identification of the individual with the race. And psychology is only a metaphor: the products of the German spirit must also be viewed from an ethical and metaphysical perspective, the perspective that in fact poses the central issue of *Doctor Faustus* and imparts form to Adrian Leverkühn's pact with the devil. It is not by accident that Mann discusses this very problem in a magazine article written in 1945 and 1946. There he puts aside poetic disguises and speaks openly of the Germany that "made a pact with the devil." [79]

The concept of a devil's pact presupposes the notions of freedom and responsibility, and Mann's psychological and historical explanations merge with the ethical categories of guilt and retribution. At the same time Mann cannot dismiss the suspicion that Germany's entire guilt-ridden situation is somehow imposed by fate. Such a view is by implication teleological. To suggest that fate establishes a definite goal, or to speak of guilt and retribution, presupposes the existence of some higher power. But does Mann actually commit himself in this respect? Is one entitled to discuss *Doctor Faustus* as a religious work? This is one of the most debated issues in Mann criticism. "Germany and the German" and other works of this period do not give a definitive answer. The novel itself will have to provide a clue.

We have now traced Mann's attitude toward the German tragedy up to and including the *Doctor Faustus* period. In his speeches to the German people Mann surrenders his usual ironic tone; critical reflection largely disappears, and he gives vent to his personal feelings as never before. The events in Germany seem to absorb his whole attention and hamper his efforts to achieve artistic form. The radio talks, or "conjurations" as he called them, offer him the best possible framework for expressing what fills his mind:

The fifty radio messages to Germany (or were there more?), which are now being printed in Sweden, these conjurations which constantly repeat themselves will testify that often enough something was more vital to me than "art." [80]

79. "Warum ich nicht nach Deutschland zurückgehe," p. 364.
80. *Ibid.*, p. 363.

Mann sees art as necessarily containing an element of ironic distance and playfulness. And he says in *Doctor Faustus*, "when it becomes serious, then one rejects art and is not capable of it" (176). Mann could not dream of trying to create a literary work out of the raw material of his immediate emotions and thoughts. But he could no longer countenance hiding from the burning issues of the present in the realm of myth and history, as he had done with the *Joseph* novels and *The Beloved Returns*. After a lifetime of identifying with and defending his country he had to step back and view it objectively, as an artistic subject. His brother Heinrich, who had early come to regard his country's evolution with profound skepticism, describes the great sorrow Mann endured when he was forced to accept alienation from his country:

Previously he had stood up for the existing Germany against the rage of the world and against his own doubts. He had a long and hard struggle with his conscience before he decided to contradict his country. . . .

It was fated that Germany would deal a harsher blow to him than to most other Germans. He was all the more heartsick at Germany's transformation because it was so late in the day that Germany became an enemy of reason, of thought, and of man, an anathema. He felt betrayed.[81]

Mann now faced the apparently impossible task of finding artistic expression for contemporary events, shaping Germany's tragic story into a work of art. The novel *Doctor Faustus* originates in the paradox of overcoming the impossible. It deals with real and recent happenings in a way that Mann would earlier have believed incompatible with true art. *The Story of a Novel* records Mann's constant doubts whether he would be able to complete his enterprise. In a letter written in 1945 he calls it "the perhaps impossible novel I have been rolling before me since 1943." [82]

To be able to write *Doctor Faustus* Mann had to revise his idea of how a work of art is created, if not his idea of art itself. He had never created his works out of thin air without reference to reality, but he had allowed his poetic imagination free rein with themes placed at a safe distance. But in *Doctor Faustus* he had to impose artistic form on a reality that

81. H. Mann, "Mein Bruder," *Ein Zeitalter wird besichtigt*, p. 213. Cf. A. Kantorowicz, *Heinrich und Thomas Mann: die personlichen, literarischen und weltanschaulichen Beziehungen der Brüder*, p. 47.
82. *Gespräch in Briefen*, p. 123.

threatened to overwhelm him. Thus Mann of necessity resorted to compositional methods and principles, of which we can find only slight traces in his earlier works. The emphasis now shifted from transforming the material to arranging it into a meaningful whole. Faithfulness to reality, ruthless self-revelation and searing pertinence to contemporary events: these were the elements demanded of a work which was to be written when art itself was in jeopardy.

4

Doctor Faustus as a "Historical" Novel

A characteristic of *Doctor Faustus* is the multiple time-structure. Zeitblom is fascinated by his double time-reckoning: "both the personal and the objective, the time in which the narrator moves and that in which the narrative does so" (252). The "personal" time comprises the period from May, 1943, when Zeitblom begins the biography (3), to the final collapse of Nazi Germany in May, 1945; the "objective" time, which Zeitblom also calls "historical," covers Adrian's life from 1885 to 1940. Zeitblom adds a third time level to these two, that of the future reader (252). In addition to the levels apparent to the fictitious biographer Zeitblom, there is another which the real narrator, Mann, carefully avoids mentioning; it is, however, even more deserving of the designation "historical." It has been widely recognized in *Faustus* criticism that the book is a novel based on the history of Germany.[1] We can thus pick out three time levels that exist independently but mutually influence each other. The "objective" time level, Adrian's life, contains the sum of all previous German history or is a symbol of it; at the same time it anticipates the events taking place while Zeitblom tells his story.

The numerous surveys of history and historical allusions support our contention that *Doctor Faustus* may be considered a "historical" novel. Analysis of Mann's sources reveals how he superimposed several time levels; for example, the Reformation period, the turn of the century, and the Nazi period

1. Hans Mayer distinguishes three time levels: Adrian's life, the present of the narrator Zeitblom, and the present of the narrator Mann, which often deviates from Zeitblom's and thus puts the events of the novel in greater relief: "One experiences simultaneously Leverkühn's life, the interpretation of it, and the interpretation of the interpretation" (*Von Lessing bis Thomas Mann*, p. 386). Krey ("Die gesellschaftliche Bedeutung der Musik im Werk von Thomas Mann," p. 329), on the other hand, sees the time of Luther as the third level, the first two being Adrian's life and Zeitblom's present.

coalesce in Mann's description of the Winfried Society and the Kridwiss circle. Mann's copious musical material covers all the important eras. But not until we have exhausted the historical content of *Doctor Faustus* will we see how Mann integrates into his novel the political views analyzed in our previous chapter.

The historical periods prior to Adrian's appearance on the scene are portrayed for the most part symbolically. We have seen that Adrian is a composite of several well-known German personalities, and that his personal fate symbolizes that of his country in various ways. The symbolic traits in Adrian seem to have been combined according to the musical analogy of the chord.

As a schoolboy Adrian is fascinated by the chord, and the terms in which he talks to Zeitblom about the mysteries of harmony apply symbolically to himself. He speaks

of the transformation of the horizontal interval into the chord, which occupied him as nothing else did; that is, of the horizontal into the vertical, the successive into the simultaneous. Simultaneity, he asserted, was here the primary element; for the note, with its more immediate and more distant harmonics, was a chord in itself, and the scale only the analytical unfolding of the chord into the horizontal row. [73–74]

The historical events treated in *Doctor Faustus* present a horizontal chronology which unrolls in the dimension of time like the succession of notes in a scale or a melody. Mann compresses five centuries of horizontal historical time into one short human life, and in so doing he transforms the horizontal into the vertical, succession into simultaneity; Adrian thus functions as a chord. He sums up an entire process of historical evolution as a chord sums up a series of notes. But Adrian states that simultaneity is the primary element; thus Adrian, the chord, would be primary with regard to the historical development of Germany. Formulated differently, this paradox becomes more plausible: a certain complex of natural endowments and qualities is primary, while historical developments represent the (secondary) application or demonstration of the possibilities inherent in these endowments and qualities. The primary combination is in this case nothing more nor less than the essence of Germany, for which Adrian is a symbol.

Since Adrian functions as a chord, his personal evolution deviates somewhat from the ordinary. In the course of his life he does not leave each stage behind as he transcends it; rather, all the stages of his development are present simultaneously, like notes sounded together. Luther, Faust, Beethoven, Hugo Wolf, Nietzsche, and all the other "models" are summarized in Adrian. As "representative" Germans they all share certain features that provide a constant in the evolution of the German spirit.

This constant also appears more concretely in the novel: Kaisersaschern is the geographical and sociological symbol of the atmosphere "of Faust and Dürer" that always surrounds Adrian. This city embodies the essence of the German mentality; along with its bourgeois, Protestant aspect exist traces of "a morbid excitement, a metaphysical epidemic latent since the last years of the Middle Ages" (36). Mann devotes particular attention to the architecture: to the castle and the cathedral, to the "faithfully preserved dwelling-houses and warehouses," to the "Town Hall of mixed Gothic and Renaissance architecture" (35–36). Adrian looks out on a similar city from his student's lodgings in Halle: "He had a view of the square, the medieval City Hall, the Gothic Marienkirche" (92). And in Leipzig Adrian encounters similar medieval features (141). He then flees modern Munich for the peaceful atmosphere of the abbot's chamber at Pfeiffering, which is reminiscent of an interior by Dürer although the building dates from the seventeenth century (205 ff).

Mann further adds to the symbolic import of Kaisersaschern by allusions to other German cities rich in associations.[2] By placing Adrian within this milieu, Mann underlines an atmospheric continuity in the history of the German spirit. The novel leaves no doubt that Kaisersaschern should be taken as a symbol. At one point the devil says to Adrian, "If you had the courage to say unto yourself: 'Where I am, there is Kaisersaschern' — well and good, the thing would be in frame." (226). Adrian shares the sense of being spokesman for an entire cultural milieu and heritage with his creator, Thomas Mann, who, we recall, said, "Where I am, there is German culture."[3] Both Mann and Adrian are "representative" Germans, although Mann represents a different, more humanistically oriented Germany.[4]

2. See above, p. 14.
3. H. Mann, *Ein Zeitalter wird besichtigt*, p. 208.
4. In the *Joseph* novels Mann had already developed the concept of the

Another aspect of Adrian's functioning as a chord is that the stages of his life correspond to various phases of German history. One should not insist on exact equivalents, but much would indicate that Mann intends these echoes. Adrian's childhood in the shadow of the old linden in the Buchel courtyard (11) suggests an ancient Germanic way of life. As the typical old German city, Kaisersaschern combines features of the Middle Ages and of the Reformation period; Adrian occupies a sixteenth century burgher's "dwelling-house" (39). The chapters on Halle recapitulate the development of German theology from the Reformation to the beginning of the twentieth century, but the seventeenth century, the age of Francke, "the patron saint of the town" (86), receives considerable emphasis. When Adrian moves to Leipzig, he observes that he has come to a modern city: "On the Pleisse, the Parthe, and the Elster existence and pulse are manifestly other than on the Saale; for here many people be gathered togyder, more than seven hundred thousand" (139). And the move to Munich is the final stage in the progression from an ancient rural way of life to the bustle of the modern metropolis.

In the description of Adrian's years in Munich (1910–30), the historical level and the biographical level often coincide. Adrian experiences the First World War and the subsequent upheavals; this period anticipates symbolically the time level that Zeitblom considers his "personal" level, that is, the period of the Second World War, of which he gives a blow-by-blow political and even military account.

There is ample reason for connecting Adrian's personal fate with the national catastrophe.[5] In both cases the final collapse

representative individual. Sørensen ("Thomas Manns 'Doktor Faustus,' " p. 84–85) suspects that as early as the middle 1930's Mann was planning a mythic work like the *Joseph* novels but one that dealt with "national, that is, German, myth." Sørensen also cites a letter from Kerényi to Mann written in 1934 (*Gespräch in Briefen*, p. 60) in which Kerényi suggests that there is a symbolic parallel between Nietzsche's insanity and the approaching German catastrophe. Sørensen further says that the Nietzsche biography of Ernst Bertram, which Mann so greatly admired, presents "Nietzsche as the myth of the Germanic and as the reincarnation of the musical and theological time of Luther, Dürer and thereby also of Faust." It may be too much to claim that the Faust novel was conceived in the 1930's, but we must keep in mind the connection between Mann's mythological speculations and the version of history he presents in *Doctor Faustus* (hereafter cited as *DF*).

5. See W. Seiferth, "Das deutsche Schicksal in Thomas Manns *Doktor Faustus*," and H. Hatfield, *Thomas Mann*, pp. 124–25. H. M. Wolff argues that Mann considered the symbolic identity of Adrian with the Germany

is preceded by dire omens; Germany's retreats and terrible losses correspond to the illnesses and deaths that cut a wide swath through Adrian's circle. Zeitblom himself draws the parallel. When he tries to enunciate what the war means, his words could equally well apply to Adrian (for example, 173). And when Zeitblom discusses Adrian's illness, he is compelled to admit that Adrian and Germany are identical:

> Little as it was possible to connect his worsening health in any temperamental way with the national misfortune, yet my tendency to see the one in the light of the other and find symbolic parallels in them, this inclination, which after all might be due simply to the fact that they were happening at the same time, was not diminished by his remoteness from outward things, however much I might conceal the thought and refrain from bringing it up even indirectly. [342]

Toward the end of the novel Zeitblom states in no uncertain terms that Adrian's downfall and that of Hitler's Germany have one and the same cause, insanity (482), and the final page of the book completes the identification; Germany is described as having pacted with the devil, and Zeitblom's prayer names the double protagonist in one breath: "my friend, my Fatherland" (510).

THE CONSTRUCT OF MUSIC HISTORY

Doctor Faustus thus covers German history from the late Middle Ages to the end of the Second World War, and Adrian Leverkühn incarnates the spirit of Germany. But since Mann holds that the German spirit and German genius are characterized by musicality, *Doctor Faustus* also takes in the history of German music. We have already seen that Mann includes a sizable number of musicians and musical instruments; and among the sources we traced, the musical ones occupy a prominent position. The numerous and extensive discussions of musical matters are altogether appropriate for the biography of a musician. But Mann includes the musical material for the same reason that he chooses the biography of a musician as a vehicle for a spiritual history of Germany: Mann sees music, the evolution and central issues of music as paradigmatic for Germany's artistic, cultural, political, and spiritual problems in general. What the novel therefore says about music has multiple

of the Second World War so important that he intentionally manipulated the dates of Nietzsche's life to make them coincide with events of the war (*Thomas Mann*, p. 120).

symbolic significance, and Mann's version of music history is a fundamental element of the novel.

We have just seen that important moments in Adrian's childhood and youth coincide with important stages in the historical development of Germany. An exact chronological version would have proved tedious and pedantic; instead Mann lets the historical allusions appear as if by accident, suggested by associations. Thus, facts of musical history are introduced for their bearing on Adrian Leverkühn's immediate concerns.

The development of medieval polyphony out of its origins in the liturgy to secular instrumental music is touched on when the names of Perotinus Magnus and Palestrina occur in a discussion of polyphony (372, 281). Masters of Renaissance music are mentioned (61, 281), and there is a full discussion of the musical achievements of the Baroque, among them the birth of opera in Italy with Monteverdi and Scarlatti (177, 488; 72, 420). Then we find the beginnings of the oratorio and the history of its perfection suggested by the names of Carissimi and Schütz, Bach and Handel (177–78, 63, 372); then the refinements in instrumental music at the time of Vivaldi and Tartini (199, 348, 410). The latter were primarily masters of the violin, and indeed an improportionately large number of the composers mentioned in the novel wrote for the violin: Paganini (160), Spohr (199), Bériot (410), Vieuxtemps (199, 410), and various others. But this preponderance can be explained by the fact that Adrian studies most of these composers as preparation for his own concerto for violin, an instrument traditionally linked with the demonic.

The names cited thus far belong to the musical history of Europe; Mann's horizon narrows when he reaches the eighteenth century and concentrates on German music. Thus Rossini is never mentioned, whereas Mann devotes long sections to his contemporary, Beethoven. From the Viennese classical period on, German and Austrian music took the lead in European musical life, and Beethoven's life coincided with the rise of German nationalism occasioned by the Napoleonic wars. This may be an additional reason for Mann's giving Beethoven such as important place in his Faust novel. The discussions of Beethoven's music clearly show Mann's conception of music as a paradigm.[6] Since Beethoven strikes Mann as the typically

6. Engländer has pointed out that the primacy of Beethoven in *DF* must be seen in the context of the lively controversy that raged in the 1920's over the content and meaning of Beethoven's music. There were two

German genius, he portrays him as one of Adrian Leverkühn's immediate predecessors.

According to Mann, two forces are fighting for mastery in Beethoven's music — the two souls of Faust, as it were. One is the principle of homophonic harmony, which romanticism inherited from classical music; the other is the principle of contrapuntal polyphony, which had been the starting point of classical music. Kretschmar sets up an important equation: harmonic homophony equals subjectivity, contrapuntal polyphony equals objectivity. Mann occasionally uses the term "expression" as a synonym for subjectivity (53). From the technical point of view, objectivity consists in applying strict rules, accepting what Kretschmar calls the "conventions" of music (53). Subjectivity protests against established rules, favoring instead improvisation and individual impulse. Beethoven brings about a confrontation in the sonata between the two principles. In contrast to earlier composers, he transforms the development section into the essential part of the movement, thus violating the traditional rules and surrendering to subjectivity (190–91). It is easy to understand how this subjectivity unites with personal expression, for Beethoven is, after all, the very type of the romantic genius, openly defying the social and artistic conventions. Yet Beethoven's surrender to personal expression was neither spontaneous nor naïve; all his life he struggled pathetically to master the most difficult of all contrapuntal forms, the fugue (56–57).

The concept of "breakthrough" furnishes one of the keys to an understanding of Mann's Beethoven and of the entire novel. It can apply to an individual, a nation, or an art form (307–8). According to Kretschmar and his pupil Adrian, the history of music from the Renaissance to Beethoven takes its character from a process wherein the musical forms gradually liberate themselves from the formulas of religious ritual. This secularization of music is seen as both regrettable and dangerous, because it leads to isolation (59, 82). Beethoven's struggle with the fugue represents the secularized artist's

opposing interpretations: the romantic, metaphysical interpretation based on Hermann Kretzschmar, versus the formalistic interpretation ("Thomas Mann's Faustroman som musikalisk spegelbild," p. 4 ff.). An essay written by Engländer for the 1927 Beethoven Jubilee gives a survey of the different schools of thought on Beethoven analysis "Grundzüge der Beethoven-Literatur." In such a contest Wendell Kretschmar's poeticizing interpretation of Beethoven appears as a parodistic exaggeration of Hermann Kretzschmar's method.

battle to emerge from isolation into a sort of religious community. Beethoven fails in the area of church music but achieves his breakthrough in the joyful chorus of the *Ninth Symphony* with its tidings of all-embracing brotherly love. Yet the principle of subjectivity and vivid expression of feeling that Beethoven passes on to the romantics gradually loses so much of its original impetus that a new breakthrough becomes necessary; this new breakthrough is Adrian's life goal (321–22).

To Mann, Beethoven is not so much the perfecter of classical music as the figure who stands at the gateway to Romanticism, and the different currents in this period — nationalistic Romanticism, program music, and Impressionism — are well accounted for in *Doctor Faustus*. Adrian submits that in Romanticism music becomes impoverished and shallow as the result of excessive subjectivity. We are then confronted with an important stage in the progression of music toward its crisis: with Wagnerianism. Mann mentions Richard Wagner only a few times, and then almost in an aside; this may seem surprising in view of the veritable cult of Wagner in Mann's earlier works. In *Buddenbrooks, Tristan,* and *The Sufferings and Greatness of Richard Wagner* Mann discusses Wagner not only as his favorite composer but also as an outstanding figure in the intellectual and musical history of Germany, and there is no reason to suspect that Mann's opinion changed appreciably.[7]

The Wagner Mann loves is the composer of *Tristan*, in which the erotic intoxication of the senses enters into a "demonic" alliance with death.[8] We have already mentioned that in "Germany and the Germans" Mann points out the dangers inherent in German romanticism, among them the "priority over the rational which it grants to the emotional, even in its arcane

7. In *The Story of a Novel* (p. 95) Mann quotes in his diary from 1944: "The triad world of the *Ring* is at bottom my musical homeland." M. Gregor discusses the significance of Wagner for *DF* in *Wagner und kein Ende*. Gregor says that it is to be expected that Wagner would play an important part in a Nietzsche novel, but he adds, "Leverkühn's problems are not restricted to those Wagner faced. His interest is aroused when he discovers the elemental in music, which is what he first wants to recapture; on this the novel contains many intelligent comments, partly in connection with the *Nibelungen* music. Leverkühn has passed beyond Wagner; the chord no longer provides him with "harmonic means of gratification," for he is concerned with the polyphonic dignity of single voices. Yet music has retained its role as seductress" (p. 31). Also see W. Blissett, "Thomas Mann: the Last Wagnerite."

8. See *Die Forderung des Tages* (Berlin, 1930), p. 398, and *Story of a Novel,* p. 94.

forms of mystic ecstasy and Dionysiac intoxication." [9] This formulation would certainly be appropriate for *Tristan und Isolde*. Mann speaks of the "germ of morbidity" that romanticism contains "as the rose bears the worm," and he maintains that "its innermost character is seduction, seduction to death." [10] We saw above how Mann links Wagner with Hitler and National Socialism, implying that the latter represent the final stage in the degeneration that set in with romanticism. Mann does not, however, consider Wagner a founder of Nazism, emphasizing rather the "innocence of the artist." [11] Would it be going too far to interpret the action of the novel as an analogue to the historical process? After all, Hetaera esmeralda infects Adrian with a "germ of morbidity," and the infection occurs by seduction, to be precise, "seduction to death." [12] The infection that Wagner transmitted to Germany spread and reached its climax in the 1930's, when the Nazis chose *The Ring of the Nibelungen* as the perfect artistic expression of their version of German mythology.

Doctor Faustus contains only brief mention of the music written by Wagner's immediate successors, who developed the homophonic harmonic style to the point of self-destruction (151–52, 239 ff.). The harmonic subtleties of the impressionists and the overripe sounds in the works of Richard Strauss do not admit of further refinement. The generation to which Adrian Leverkühn belongs cannot continue in the old paths. Something radically new has to be created, or, what might come to the same thing, a past epoch has to be resurrected. This is where music stands when Adrian Leverkühn begins to compose.

THE CONSTRUCT OF THEOLOGICAL HISTORY

Adrian's studies and his basic orientation make it inevitable that music and theology should be intimately connected in *Doctor Faustus*, and Mann is explicit about their interpenetra-

9. "Germany and the Germans," p. 63.
10. *Ibid.*
11. See above, p. 3.
12. In this connection Nietzsche's view of Wagner in *The Case of Wagner* proves significant: "He has made music sick," "Wagner est une névrose," "Wagner is a seducer on a grand scale" (*Complete Works* [New York, 1924] 8:11, 13, 39). There is a detail in *DF* that seems more than accidental: both Adrian and Nietzsche move to Leipzig; there Nietzsche first encounters Wagner, Adrian the Hetaera esmeralda.

tion. Thus on one occasion Adrian explains that "through liturgy and her history music plays very strongly into the theological" (82), and later he justifies changing his field of study by saying, "My Lutheranism . . . sees in theology and music neighboring spheres and close of kin" (131). The devil states more provocatively, "A highly theological business, music — the way sin is, the way I am" (242). Logically enough, Mann sets up his history of German theology as a parallel to the history of music; in *Doctor Faustus* the two realms complement each other. Mann does not devote nearly so much space to theology and church history as to music, but he does review the more important periods, from the Reformers' rebellion against medieval Scholasticism down through the emergence of critical theology in the early twentieth century.

The history of music is plotted in terms of the tension between two opposing principles — adherence to strict form on the one hand, the will to personal expression on the other — each prevailing at various times. Mann also sees this tension in theological history; he sets personal religious feeling in opposition to the rigid forms imposed by orthodoxy and the organized Church (119). Catholic Scholasticism, against which Luther rebelled, is represented, in the novel, by Thomas Aquinas (103, 498) and Albertus Magnus (132).

The chief exponent of the Reformation and the Beethoven of theology (88) is Luther, present in the novel both as himself and as a caricature-reincarnation, Professor Ehrenfried Kumpf of Halle. The two are so nearly identical that even the devil has difficulty telling them apart (231); they are identical in the same mythical, representative way as Beethoven and Adrian. Around the Reformer, Mann has grouped a goodly number of contemporaries, both supporters and opponents, among them the Catholic canon Crotus Rubianus and the first Lutheran superintendent, Justus Jonas, both of Halle (87). Of the humanists who took part in the struggles for or against the Reformation he mentions Erasmus, Melanchthon, and Hutten (87–88) as well as Dr. Eck (141) and Dürer's friend Willibald Pirkheimer (173). We should add to this list all the fictional characters who bear the names of Luther's friends and contemporaries.

Kumpf revives Luther's personality, but it is Adrian Leverkühn who takes up his historical role as a revolutionary and innovator; sometimes he adopts Luther's very words. Adrian simultaneously incarnates the Reformer and symbolically anticipates Nazism, linking the Reformation with the Hitler era. Thus Mann conveys the suggestion that the two periods have a direct bearing on each other, a suggestion that he develops in "Germany and the Germans," [13] when he explains that the Reformation planted the seed that held such grave implications for Germany. Adrian likewise succumbs to a germ implanted early in his life. In the novel Mann contrasts the fanatical aspect of Lutheranism, which was to develop into rigid orthodoxy and religious intolerance, with the somewhat skeptical broadmindedness of Northern humanism, represented by the Catholic Zeitblom. Since he lacks the qualities that go with Lutheran nationalism, Zeitblom can divorce himself from the insanity taking its toll all around while he writes the biography of his friend; but his aloofness is passive and unobtrusive. Here Mann passes judgment on a humanist tradition that has become so emasculated that it can no longer muster the strength to defend the basic human values.[14]

Mann's version of theological history continues as follows: the revolt of subjectivity against absolute norms, the central accomplishment of the Reformation, is suppressed by orthodox Lutheranism, and the moment comes for a new revolt — Pietism. Mann explicitly designates the two movements as one of a kind (88). The representative of Pietism in the novel is Francke (86), responsible for making Halle the center of the movement. Christian Wolff (89) belongs to a somewhat later phase in the history of theology; he is a theologian of the Enlightenment, a tendency opposed by the Pietists. Subjective feeling plays an even more prominent part in Pietism than in the Reformation, and in that sense Pietism anticipates — both historically and in the world of the novel — the romantic search for personal expression that is associated in music with the name of Beethoven.

When Zeitblom reflects on the history of religion in connection with Adrian's interest in theology, he gives only the briefest mention to romantic theology. Schleiermacher, for a time at Halle, is mentioned in passing (88). According to Zeitblom, German theology divides at the beginning of the eighteenth century into emotional, subjective religiosity and the skeptical, relativistic theology of the Enlightenment, later called "liberal"

13. "Germany and the Germans," p. 54.
14. This side of Zeitblom's nature is discussed by Metzler (p. 65).

theology. In the course of the nineteenth century both currents lose so much of their original vigor and character that a renewal is again obviously necessary. Toward the beginning of the twentieth century, Protestant theology seeks to draw new strength and vitality from orthodox Neo-Thomism (90).

These are the essential features of German Protestant theology as outlined in *Doctor Faustus*. The picture is sketchier than for music because Adrian is primarily a musician. Sometimes Mann creates a parallel between musical and theological developments; thus the nineteenth century is characterized as a time of liberalization and sentimentalization. For the earlier periods the two disciplines are made to complement one another: the decisive reversal introduced into music by Beethoven and the romantics turns out to have been anticipated twice in theology. But in the twentieth century Adrian Leverkühn finds both fields in a similar situation, and when he reverts to medieval polyphony he is performing an act equivalent to that of the theologians who revive Neo-Thomism.

Since the situation Adrian confronts in music has theological implications, it should come as no surprise that what he composes in his new style has religious import. We shall return to this subject in our closing chapter.

PHILOSOPHIES OF HISTORY

If *Doctor Faustus* is a "historical novel," Mann seems as a historian less interested in "how things actually were" than in the hidden meaning of events. The description of Jonathan Leverkühn's "visible music" indicates symbolically what Mann intended with his novel:

To the small amount of physical apparatus which Adrian's father had at his command belonged a round glass plate, resting only on a peg in the center and revolving freely. On this glass plate the miracle took place. It was strewn with fine sand, and Jonathan, by means of an old cello bow which he drew up and down the edge from top to bottom made it vibrate, and according to its motion the excited sand grouped and arranged itself in astonishingly precise and varied figures and arabesques. This visible acoustic, wherein the simple and the mysterious, law and miracle, so charmingly mingled, pleased us lads exceedingly; we often asked to see it, and not least to give the experimenter pleasure. [17–18]

Another natural phenomenon captures Jonathan Leverkühn's imagination: the mysterious hieroglyph-like traceries on certain

New Caledonian shells (16). Here again a pattern of great artistry awakens Jonathan's Faustian urge to break nature's code. For he has no doubt that these patterns mean something, even if it cannot be formulated: ". . . that Nature painted these ciphers, to which we lack the key, merely for ornament on the shell of her creature, nobody can persuade me" (17).

What is extraordinary and mysterious about these phenomena is that lifeless materials seemingly arrange themselves into sophisticated patterns. The existence of these patterns suggests some higher power; it encourages human beings to seek a deeper meaning in nature. The fate of Adrian Leverkühn, that is, the historical fate of the German nation, likewise forms a complicated but consistent pattern. But does this consistency result from chance; or do hidden forces and principles direct the course of history? There can be no doubt that Mann gave very serious consideration to this question when writing *Doctor Faustus*, but it is difficult to determine how he pictured these forces or principles to himself. For Mann seems to work with several theories at once; for one and the same event or phenomenon in the novel or in historical reality Mann furnishes various explanations. Both in the discussion of historical questions and in the portrayal of Adrian's personal evolution we find elements of a philosophy of history. Since Adrian symbolizes Germany, it is safe to assume that factors affecting his development apply *mutatis mutandis* to the development of the nation.

Mann takes extraordinary care to indicate the background of every event connected with Adrian. In some respects *Doctor Faustus* is an exemplary naturalistic novel, not only because of the scientific exactitude of external detail and the wealth of precise description, but also because of the emphasis on determinism. Heredity and milieu determine Adrian's life as much as the lives of the French naturalists' heroes. His bluish-greyish-greenish eyes are explained as a mixture of his parents' blue and black eyes (22); Mann obviously intended an allusion to the mixture of blond Nordic stock and dark Alpine stock that forms the German national physiognomy. Adrian's migraine headaches and his penchant for speculation are inherited from his father (12–13); since the romantics, melancholy pondering has been designated a Nordic trait. Adrian's musical talent comes from his mother (22); Mann thus portrays musicality as the South's contribution to the German soul.

147

Determinism manifests itself most clearly in the course of the illness that leads to Adrian's collapse. Following the visit to Hetaera, the physiological aspect of Adrian's life is determined — precise medical explanations establish this beyond a doubt — but the predisposition to disease has been present from the beginning. Adrian seeks out the kind of love that Hetaera can offer because he is basically cold (6) and thus excluded from normal human relationships. Yet this coldness tends to produce its opposite; Adrian is disgusted by sensuality but cannot escape its lure. The two poles in Adrian's nature, sensuality and abstract idealism, and characteristic of German romanticism, and romanticism, according to "Germany and the Germans," anticipated much of National Socialism. Because the German spirit lacked equilibrium it was susceptible to seduction, to the Wagnerian infection.

Adrian's inner development likewise follows rigidly deterministic lines. Here Mann seems to have made almost exclusive use of Freudian categories. Freud particularly emphasizes that psychological development can be explained in strictly causal terms.[15] Adrian displays several neurotic symptoms: excessive unsociability, the belief that he brings death to those around him, and so forth. A psychoanalytical search for childhood causes of his neurosis uncovers ample material. Thus Adrian's attachment to a certain kind of milieu can be seen as a bond with his mother; Adrian in fact always finds his way to typical mother-figures. His two favorite spots in Buchel and Pfeiffering are the hill and the pond, both Freudian symbols for the mother. The psychoanalyst would explain Adrian's attempt to drown himself in the pond as regression or infantilism. In this episode Adrian's symbolic function is unmistakable: German life in the period Mann is treating was characterized by regression to the primitive and archaic in the cult of Wotan and the mysteries of "Blood and Soil."

Mann offers what seems to be a psychoanalytical interpretation of yet another factor in Adrian's life. Many of Adrian's neurotic symptoms can be traced back to a psychic trauma destined to determine his whole further development: to the meeting with Hetaera. We can find considerable evidence that this was how Mann wished the borrowed Nietzsche episode

15. It is well known that Mann was acquainted with Freud and the psychoanalytic approach. See F. J. Hoffman, *Freudianism and the Literary Mind* (Louisiana, 1945), pp. 209–29, and W. F. Michael, "Mann auf dem Wege zu Freud."

understood. In his essay on Nietzsche (1947), Mann gives the following analysis of Nietzsche's reaction to his experience in the brothel:

But it had been nothing more nor less than what psychologists call a "trauma," a shock whose steadily accumulating after-effects — from which his imagination never recovered — testify to the saint's receptivity to sin.[16]

If Adrian's life symbolizes Germany's historical development, the deterministic explanation of his life represents a deterministic explanation of German history. Mann unquestionably regards the German catastrophe as the last link in an iron chain of causal factors. Yet purely causal explanations are incapable of evoking by themselves that strange pattern, "wherein the simple and the mysterious, law and miracle, so charmingly" mingle (18).

Mann's very first writings give substantial proof that he is anchored in the German dialectical tradition; two constants in his work are the antitheses between the burgher and the artist, between nature and the spirit. With this foundation Mann might be expected to lean toward a dialectical interpretation of history. We have already seen that Mann sets up a dialectical structure for the history of theology and music; periods of "subjectivity" and license alternate with periods of orthodoxy, classicism or "objectivity." Adrian articulates this principle for art and music, but his words hold true for intellectual development as a whole:

But freedom is of course another word for subjectivity, and some fine day she does not hold out any longer, some time or other she despairs of the possibility of being creative out of herself and seeks shelter and security in the objective. Freedom always inclines to dialectical reversals. She realizes herself very soon in constraint, fulfils herself in the subordination to law, rule, coercion, system — but to fulfil herself therein does not mean she therefore ceases to be freedom. [190]

Brahms' treatment of Beethoven's sonata form is cited as an illustration (191), but even earlier Zeitblom uses similar categories to describe the transformation of the original Reformation into Lutheran orthodoxy.

Although history in *Doctor Faustus* moves in pendulum swings, one can hardly speak of a dialectical interpretation of

16. *Last Essays*, p. 145. The word also occurs in *DF*. Zeitblom says of the experience in the brothel, "His intellectual pride had suffered the trauma of contact with soulless instinct" (148).

history in the Hegelian sense, for it is doubtful whether the antitheses in the novel ever come to rest in a synthesis. Marxist critics tend to overlook this fact and interpret *Doctor Faustus* in terms of the class struggle, as a novel of the decay and decline of the bourgeoisie.[17] Such an interpretation distorts Mann's central concerns. *Doctor Faustus* nowhere offers anything like a synthesis; certainly we find no suggestion of a potential communist paradise; the novel suggests instead that any *rapprochement* between the two poles of "subjectivity" and "objectivity" invokes the demonic. Music again serves as a symbol in the following response by Zeitblom to the contrasts in Adrian's work:

. . . the *espressivo* takes hold of the strict counterpoint, the objective blushes with feeling. One gets the impression of a glowing mould; this, like nothing else, has brought home to me the idea of the daemonic. [178]

Can such a mechanism be observed in history? We shall indeed see later that Mann considers Germany's evolution a sort of "demonization" process. But first we must discuss another interpretation that Thomas Mann offers for the historical events that play into *Doctor Faustus*.

Mann perceives a tendency to repetition in the structure of Germany's intellectual development. The pattern of rebellion against objective form by subjective feeling fits several periods in musical and theological history, and since Mann uses these periods as the basis of his version of history, one may justifiably speak of a sort of cyclical interpretation of history. The novel suggests in several ways that the intellectual and political upheavals in twentieth-century Germany simply recapitulate what occurred in the time of Luther. The section on Adrian's fellow theologians in Halle illustrates this theme: in their life style and their opinions the students and professors participate in modern conditions and tendencies, while their names link them to Reformation times.

But repetition manifests itself even more concretely. Adrian's life falls into three periods all spent in very similar surroundings. The farm at Buchel scarcely differs from the Pfeiffering estate near Munich where he lives during most of his adult creative life, and after his collapse he returns to spend his last ten years at home. Before settling in Pfeiffering he passes more

17. I. Diersen, *Untersuchungen zu Thomas Mann*, e.g., p. 303; G. Lukács, *Thomas Mann*, e.g., pp. 112–13.

than a year in the Italian village of Palestrina, which in several respects bears a striking resemblance to Pfeiffering.

The similarities between the Buchel and Pfeiffering farms and their occupants are as great as would be compatible with the novel's claim to realism. Zeitblom himself draws attention to the curious parallelism (25, 204); when describing Adrian's home he points out correspondences between Buchel and Pfeiffering as "an extraordinary likeness and reproduction" (25). Buchel's layout, with the hill and the cold pond, is repeated in Pfeiffering's Rohmbühel and Klammerweiher, and the Leverkühns' great linden becomes the Schweigestills' elm (26). Adrian's brother resembles Gereon Schweigestill, and Ursula resembles Clementine Schweigestill. The Pfeiffering family does not have a second son, "which rather strengthened the case than otherwise, for who would this second son have been" (26). The watchdog Suso reappears as Pfeiffering's Kaschperl, and the milk maid Hanne's place is taken by Waltpurgis in Pfeiffering (26–27). Father Leverkühn has much in common with Max Schweigestill, including the tendency to brood and a disposition to migraine. Both are reflective smokers who exude a pleasant smell of pipe tobacco (26).

The correspondences between the mother figures are even more striking. Of Elsbeth Leverkühn Zeitblom says: "The hair half covered the ears . . . it was drawn tightly back, as smooth as glass, and the parting above the brow laid bare the whiteness of the skin beneath" (21), and he particularly mentions "the capable brown hands with the wedding ring on the right one . . . neither coarse nor fastidiously cared for" (22). He singles out the same features in Else Schweigestill: "her brown hair, only touched with grey, drawn smoothly away from the parting, so that you saw the white skin," "her well-shaped capable little hands with the plain wedding ring" (206). And he says of Peronella Manardi, "hair . . . with at most a faint silver network on the smooth head," "small, work-hardened hands, the double widow's ring on the right one" (212).

Palestrina is not strictly speaking an "imitation" of Adrian's other milieus, but certain features clearly suggest Buchel and Pfeiffering. Zeitblom describes the top of the mountain above Palestrina as a spot dear to himself and his wife (211), and the cloisterlike atmosphere of Pfeiffering (205) is recreated in Palestrina by the monastery garden Adrian frequents (215). Zeitblom confirms that these features form part of a pattern in

Adrian's life when he says of Adrian's winter headquarters in Rome, "The role of the cloister garden of Palestrina was played in Rome by the Villa Doria Panfili" (218).

Although we thus have sufficient evidence for a principle of repetition in the structure of the novel, Mann's habit of operating with parallel explanations for one and the same phenomenon prevents us from ascertaining whether he subscribes to one unqualified philosophy of history. We are, however, entitled to recall that the *Joseph* novels and *The Beloved Returns* are permeated with the idea of recurrence,[18] which forms the core of the "mythic method" as used in the twentieth century. Joyce's *Ulysses*, the prime example of the contemporary mythic novel and considered by Mann to be related to his *Doctor Faustus*,[19] is deeply indebted to Vico's cyclical concept of history.[20]

Mann's portrayal of history in the *Joseph* novels plays on mythic man's conception of time as an eternal cycle. The mythic pattern constantly repeats itself, reincarnated in different human beings, who play their parts according to timeless rules. Thus Joseph calmly and proudly accepts the three-day torture in the spring, aware that it is part of his role as a chosen one; for Joseph is an incarnation of the god Tammuz-Adonis who is buried and passes to the Underworld to wait for resurrection.[21] This myth can be linked to history, the symbol of the grave foreshadowing the historical Christ. Joseph can likewise be seen as a reincarnation or repetition of earlier figures, some of them legendary. In *Doctor Faustus* we find this very form of recurrence; the concept of "Faustian" man plays the same part as the myth of Tammuz-Adonis in *Joseph and his Brothers*. Beethoven, Nietzsche, and Adrian all reincarnate or reënact the Faust myth as Mann interprets it.

Mann's interest in the recurrence theory dates back to before his systematic studies of mythology. An interesting comment of 1926 tells us:

German heads, and not only professorial heads, harbor a strong belief in historical recurrence, and especially recurrence in the history of ideas. Thus historical interest at present centers on the German romantic revolution of the early nineteenth century against the En-

---

18. Cf. on the *Joseph* novels, R. Thieberger, *Der Begriff der Zeit bei Thomas Mann*, pp. 83 ff. E. Eiffert also discusses this question in an unpublished dissertation, "Das Erlebnis der Zeit im Werke Thomas Manns."
19. *Story of a Novel*, p. 91.
20. See H. Levin, *James Joyce*, pp. 101 ff.
21. See "Freud and the Future," *Essays of Three Decades*, pp. 421 ff.

lightenment, idealism and classicism of the eighteenth century, that is, on the antithesis between belief in humanity and belief in nationality.[22]

Mann avoids mentioning his own stand on the matter, but one may assume from his long admiration for Nietzsche and Schopenhauer and profound knowledge of their works that he largely shares the romantics' view.

Nietzsche's concept of "eternal recurrence" stems from Schopenhauer, who rejects causality as a regulative principle in historical and individual affairs. Schopenhauer treats the problem in his essay *On the Four-Fold Foot of the Principle of Sufficient Reason*, in which he draws a parallel between causality and temporality, regarding them both as functions of the human intellect, as Kantian categories. As a disciple of the Indian philosophers, Schopenhauer contends that the veil of Maya prevents us from seeing reality without illusion.[23] In his Schopenhauer essay, written in 1938, only five years before he started work on his *Doctor Faustus*, Mann chooses for discussion precisely this idea of Schopenhauer's.[24]

Following in Schopenhauer's footsteps, Nietzsche cannot consider time, space, and causality anything but illusions. In the section "Against Causality"[25] of his *Will to Power*, Nietzsche develops this theme: time and space do not exist "for themselves." Changes are nothing but phenomena of our own representation. Seeing causal links in a succession of events is a mistake: *"There is no such thing as a cause or an effect."*[26] The fact that we can predict the course of an event with fair accuracy is based not on the law of cause and effect but on *"the recurrence of 'identical cases.'"*[27]

In his Nietzsche essay of 1947 Mann echoes this criticism of over-emphasis of causal connections. The example he chooses is significant for our discussion of *Doctor Faustus*: he attacks those who would see Fascism as a direct result of Nietzsche's pronouncements. According to Mann, more is at issue than a simple causal reaction. Fascism seized upon and put into practice ideas that were in the air; Nietzsche had simply acted as an extremely sensitive instrument, registering the spirit of a new age before

22. *Pariser Rechenschaft*, pp. 58–59.
23. *Two Essays by Arthur Schopenhauer*, tr. Mme Karl Hillebrand.
24. "Schopenhauer," *Essays of Three Decades*, pp. 388 ff.
25. Nietzsche, *Complete Works*, vol. 15, secs. 3/4, pp. 53 ff.
26. *Ibid.*, p. 57.
27. *Ibid.*

it became patent.[28] Mann further remarks that the modern skepticism of science toward all laws of causality corroborates Nietzsche's claims.[29] And when in his novels Mann uses the concept of "recurrence of identical cases,"[30] he is at once holding faith with his philosophical mentor Nietzsche and concurring in a belief that influenced many of his contemporaries.

Another philosopher of history who must be mentioned is Oswald Spengler, whose famous *Decline of the West* (1918) has many external features in common with Mann's historical thinking. Spengler sees cultures as organisms that undergo a recurrent cycle of birth, flowering and death. Such concept pairs as culture-civilization and soul-intellect remind one of the *Betrachtungen eines Unpolitischen*, which appeared the same year as Spengler's work.[31] In view of these similarities, it may seem strange that Mann expresses open hostility to Spengler. In his short essay "On the Theory of Spengler" (1924),[32] he speaks of Spengler's "hyena-like gift of prophecy." Bitter polemics alternate with biting irony. Of his more objective arguments, the following deserves our interest:

Intellectualism, rationalism, relativism, cult of causality, of the "natural law" — with all that his theory is saturated; and against that leaden historical materialism the materialism of a Marx is sheer blue-sky idealism.[33]

One of Mann's reasons for rejecting Spengler's philosophy of history is that it overemphasizes causality; Mann thus takes his place beside Nietzsche in the battle against the materialistic view of history. Many of his contemporaries share this attitude, particularly the expressionists. In 1925 Albert Soergel's monumental survey of modern German literature summarized the

28. *Last Essays*, p. 167.
29. *Ibid.*, p. 171.
30. The concept of "eternal recurrence" is a difficult aspect of Nietzsche's philosophy. It is discussed in a book by J. Stambauch, *Untersuchungen zum Problem der Zeit bei Nietzsche*, pp. 193 ff.
31. As early as 1925 R. H. Grützmacher pointed out similarities between the philosophies of history of Mann and Spengler. He maintains that *Buddenbrooks* corresponds as microcosm to macrocosm to Spengler's version of the decline of the entire Occident. He thinks that awareness of their similarities explains Mann's critical attitude: "In Spengler Mann encounters the ghost of his *own* earlier development, for which reason he is especially alarmed and anxious to keep him at bay" ("Spengler, Keyserlingk und Thomas Mann").
32. "On the Theory of Spengler," *Past Masters and other Papers*, p. 217–27.
33. *Ibid.*, p. 226.

expressionists' program as follows: "Down with the tyranny of the law of causality in literature!" [34]

Among the modern researchers who directly or indirectly influenced Mann's speculations on mythology is C. G. Jung.[35] Jung, to be sure, does not hold a cyclical view of history, but his doctrine of archetypes, "lived vita" as Mann calls them in an essay of 1936,[36] is a clear reaction against causal determinism. It is symptomatic that one of the fundamental points of difference between Freud and Jung was precisely the concept of causality.[37] We have already pointed out that the naturalistic and deterministic features of *Doctor Faustus* contain echoes of Freud, and we suggested that Adrian's psychic abnormality might be interpreted as a traumatic neurosis. In Jung's terminology, Adrian's life becomes a role played in imitation of an archetypal model. Here we have a striking example of the manifold structure of meaning in the novel; as one can analyze it using the categories of causal determinism on the one hand and of myth and type on the other, one can adopt the terminology of either Freud or Jung. As a matter of fact, several years before *Doctor Faustus* Mann had already linked the two systems in a manner that proves of interest for our discussion of *Doctor Faustus*. In "Freud and the Future" he writes:

Infantilism — in other words, regression to childhood — what a role this genuinely psychoanalytic element plays in all our lives! What a large share it has in shaping the life of a human being; operating, indeed, in just the way I have described: as mythical identification, as survival, as a treading in footprints already made! [38]

Here neurotic bonds are identified with mythic recurrence, and both explanations are relevant for Adrian's fate.

34. A. Soergel, *Dichtung und Dichter der Zeit. N.F.* "Im Banne des Expressionismus," p. 2. Similarly F. Gundolf attacks the conception of man as "a bundle of historical causalities" (*Stefan George in unserer Zeit*, p. 5). K. Edschmid also dissociates himself from the "trivial, meaningless logic, the humiliating morality and causality" (*Über den Expressionismus in der Literatur und die neue Dichtung*, p. 58).

35. We have already mentioned Jung's description of the German catastrophe as a neurotic phenomenon (chap. 3, n. 72 above).

36. "Freud and the Future," *Essays of Three Decades*, pp. 421 ff.

37. E. A. Bennet, *C. G. Jung* (London, 1961), pp. 104 ff.

38. *Essays of Three Decades*, p. 426. Peter Heller in "Thomas Mann's Conception of the Creative Writer," pp. 792–93, remarks upon Adrian Leverkühn's pathological "wish for recurrence" which finds fulfillment in "the second infancy of insanity." He also suggests that this drive to return to earlier stages corresponds to a similar mechanism in Mann, as, for example, when he returns in his Faust novel to the archaic conditions that prevailed in Germany long before *Buddenbrooks*.

Wherever we find the idea of recurrence in Mann's works, it is associated with evolution. This combination is present to some extent in *Tonio Kröger* and becomes a major theme in the *Joseph* novels and *The Beloved Returns*. One critic uses the fitting simile of spiral motion for this modified version of recurrence.[39] Joseph's life repeats the lives of earlier mythic figures, but within the repetition he is allowed a certain amount of freedom and thus given the possibility of becoming a responsible "provider." In his Goethe novel Mann sums up this idea in the formula "recurrence enhanced by awareness."

In *Doctor Faustus*, too, the idea of recurrence appears in alliance with the idea of evolution, but a decisive change has occurred. In Mann's earlier works the spiral moved upward into higher realms of the spirit; in *Doctor Faustus* it moves downward into the realm of darkness and the demonic.

HISTORY MADE "DEMONIC"

We have already seen that "Germany and the Germans" tries to trace Germany's downward path to the demonic and destruction. Mann seeks to explain the nation's plunge into a catastrophic war by its intellectual history; he sets himself the riddle to solve of "why their good, in particular, so often turns to evil, becomes evil in their hands."[40] For one of Mann's fundamental contentions is that Germany's originally good and praiseworthy qualities have become corrupted. "Inwardness," the source of German metaphysics, music, the Reformation, and romanticism,[41] produces, according to Mann, "melancholy" — rather than tragic — results: "Wicked Germany is merely good Germany gone astray, good Germany in misfortune, in guilt, and ruin."[42]

How does Mann portray this "demonization" in *Doctor Faustus*? Instances of inwardness make their appearance early in the novel, bearing the characteristics that Mann designates as the root of the evil: intimacy with the irrational and demonic forces of life, an inclination toward profundity and mysticism.[43] The evolution of some of the names that figure in

39. Eiffert, "Das Erlebnis der Zeit," p. 81.
40. "Germany and the Germans," p. 60. Cf. *Leiden an Deutschland*, pp. 87–88. and *Listen, Germany!* pp. 107 ff.
41. "Germany and the Germans," pp. 60 ff.
42. *Ibid.*, p. 64.
43. *Ibid.*, p. 61.

Adrian's childhood environment points unmistakably to demonization. The hill near the farm is called Mount Zion, and the watchdog is named after the medieval mystic Heinrich Suso. When these childhood surroundings recur in Pfeiffering, significant changes have taken place in the names: the hill is now called the Rohmbühel, a name taken from the Faust chapbook. The milkmaid's name, Waltpurgis, suggests witchery and magic. The pious mystic has been replaced by Kaschperl, the devil himself. Elsewhere in the novel we encounter the name Kaspar in connection with Weber's *Freischütz*, and Adrian uses the name for the devil (227). Zeitblom dwells on the fact that Adrian and the dog have a mystical bond (26, 256, 258). Suso is said to be "by no means good-natured to strangers." But he is really dangerous when "let free to roam the court at night" (24). This description seems to suggest that the German soul's greatest peril arises from what the romantics called "the nocturnal side of Nature," those aspects that lie outside the control of light and reason.

The deterioration of German inwardness symbolized by the changing names corresponds to the line from romanticism to Hitler plotted in "Germany and the Germans." There we noted that Mann often employs words like "diabolical" and "hell" in connection with Hitler. The word "dog" also occurs frequently. The expression "go to the dogs" is a common one, but Mann's predilection for it is striking. In a radio talk of 1941 he says, for example:

I admit that what is called National Socialism has long roots in German life. It is the virulent perversion of ideas which always harbored the germ of corruption, but which were by no means foreign to the good old Germans of culture and education. There these ideas lived in grand style; they were called "romanticism" and held much fascination for the world. One may well say that they have gone to the dogs and were destined to go to the dogs, as they were destined to go to Hitler.[44]

In a speech given the same year he compares Hitler's voice to the "voice of a raging dog";[45] one thinks immediately of the "yapping of the yard dog" Kasperl in *Doctor Faustus* (256).

Apart from the symbolism of names, Mann has various other ways of presenting the demonic potentialities of German inwardness. At the beginning of the novel Zeitblom asks "whether

44. *Listen, Germany!* p. 44. Cf. *Leiden an Deutschland*, p. 12.
45. *Listen Germany!* p. 65.

a clear and certain line can be drawn between the noble peda-
gogic world of the mind and the world of the spirit which one
approaches only at one's peril," a question which "is very
pertinent to my theme" (9). Shortly thereafter Zeitblom illustrates the difficulty of making a clear distinction. He stresses
Jonathan Leverkühn's contemplativeness and mysticism, as
well as his Faustian "speculation" and experimentation.
Jonathan's innocent and engaging thirst for knowledge and his
interest in research both contain a questionable element, and
Zeitblom approves of the interpretation "that all this had quite
close relations with witchcraft, yes, belonged in that realm and
was itself a work of the 'Tempter'" (17). The Faustian urge
to probe the universe and coax forth nature's secrets can easily
degenerate into diabolical presumption and arrogance.

Adrian's explorations of the ocean depths and the universe
occupy a much later stage in this development — or degeneration. He recounts his adventures to Zeitblom in the evening —
"when Suso, the yard dog, in other words Kaschperl was loosed
from his chain and allowed to range the courtyard" (267).
Adrian's companion, Professor Capercailzie, is an unmistakably
demonic figure. Adrian's urge "to fling himself in the ocean of
the worlds" (266) terrifies the good humanist Zeitblom, who
sees in it an unholy desire for knowledge. It exceeds the limits
of the human and the humane; (266, 269) the proper label for
such undertakings is "devil's juggling" (272).

Adrian's descent into the "virginal night" perhaps symbolizes
a special form of "inwardness," that is, the exploration of the
abysses of the human soul. The sense of shame mentioned in
the following quotation would be as much justified in the case
of the nether regions of the soul as of the sea:

Adrian spoke of the itch one felt to expose the unexposed, to look at
the unlooked-at, the not-to-be and not-expecting-to-be-looked-at.
There was a feeling of indiscretion, even of guilt, bound up with it,
not quite allayed by the feeling that science must be allowed to press
just as far forwards as it is given the intelligence of scientists to go.
The incredible eccentricities, some grisly, some comic, which nature
here achieved, forms and features which seemed to have scarcely any
connection with the upper world but rather to belong to another
planet: these were the product of seclusion, sequestration, of reliance
on being wrapped in eternal darkness. [268]

If one assumes that Mann means here the shocking revelation
of hidden aggressions — "predatory mouths . . . obscene jaws"
(268) — by depth psychology, one must also realize that Mann

did not consider depth psychology a product of moral degeneration; its function in this context is to discover certain human inclinations that were later to be unleashed by National Socialism.

The symbolism of Adrian's fantasies about outer space carries much the same significance. Adrian is fascinated by the theory of a constantly exploding and expanding universe; we are reminded first of the twentieth-century scientific triumphs in which Germany played an important part. But symbolically the theory suggests Germany's dreams of national expansion and world domination. When Zeitblom protests with "religiously tinged humanism" against Adrian's astronomical fantasies, his terminology echoes the speeches with which Mann bombarded Germany in the early 1940's when it was trampling all human values under foot:

What reverence and what civilizing process born of reverence can come from the picture of a vast impropriety like this of the exploding universe? Absolutely none. Piety, reverence, intellectual decency, religious feeling, are only possible about men and through men, and by limitation to the earthly and human. Their fruit should, can, and will be a religiously tinged humanism, conditioned by feeling for the transcendental mystery of man, by the proud consciousness that he is no mere biological being, but with a decisive part of him belongs to an intellectual and spiritual world, that to him the Absolute is given, the ideas of truth, of freedom, of justice; that upon him the duty is laid to approach the consummate. [273]

In "Germany and the Germans" Mann calls the drive for national expansion the expression of another "highly valuable, positive trait," the "inner boundlessness," "universalism and cosmopolitanism" of the Germans. Mann observes that this trait has been perverted into the drive for hegemony in Europe and the world.[46] According to Mann, cosmopolitanism is in fact characteristic of some of the most highly "representative" Germans, among them Goethe and Nietzsche;[47] Adrian Leverkühn, in accordance with his symbolic role, shares this trait. In the student discussions Adrian meets his friends' patriotic arguments with light irony; his principal opponent in the discussions bears the descriptive name of Deutschlin (116–17). Adrian's attention is directed outward toward Europe, an orientation that comes out in his esteem for foreign literatures.

46. "Germany and the Germans," p. 60.
47. *Essays of Three Decades*, pp. 87 ff.; *Last Essays*, p. 170.

He often takes the texts for his compositions from the works of English, French and Italian poets.

Adrian's cosmopolitanism emerges most clearly in the chapter on the impresario Fitelberg, who attempts in vain to lure Adrian and his music into the world (402 ff). Fitelberg praises the curious combination of Germanness and cosmopolitanism in Adrian's work. Zeitblom remarks earlier that Adrian's music is very German, "music of Kaisersaschern" (83), and Fitelberg agrees: "C'est 'boche' dans un degré fascinant" (402). At the same time he praises Adrian's "broadmindedness in the choice of his texts, ce cosmopolitism généreux et versatile" (402). But this admirable attitude of Adrian's is obstructed by his typically German unwillingness to commit himself to the rest of the world. Fitelberg understands and respects this feeling, but he cautions Adrian about it, and appropriately he slips into reflections that apply to the German nation as a whole.

Fitelberg sees Adrian's withdrawl to Pfeiffering, "ce refuge étrange et érémitique" (404), as an expression of the typically German inclination toward isolation that grows out of a sense of being somehow unique:

You do not want to hear about other destinées, only your own, as something quite unique — I know, I understand. . . . You pay tribute to an arrogant personal uniqueness — maybe you have to do that. [404–5]

This tendency seems to Mann one of the sure sources of the German catastrophe.[48] Later Fitelberg continues in the same vein:

You probably do not realize, cher Maître, how German is your répugnance, which, if you will permit me to speak en psychologue, I find characteristically made up of arrogance and a sense of inferiority, of scorn and fear. I might call it the ressentiment of the serious-minded against the salon world. [406]

"Arrogance and a sense of inferiority" — that is the dangerous combination of characteristics that Thomas Mann designates in his 1933–34 diaries as the fertile soil in which Nazi ideology rooted;[49] in "A Brother" he assigns them to Hitler himself.[50] As Fitelberg comes to the end of his remarks, he is no longer talking about Adrian and his music. He openly discusses German nationalism, drawing a parallel to Jewish nationalism;

48. *Leiden an Deutschland*, pp. 7, 54, 55.
49. *Leiden an Deutschland*, p. 17.
50. "A Brother," *Order of the Day*, pp. 154, 156.

any other form of nationalism is "child's play" by comparison (408). In parting he issues a clear warning, the very same warning that Mann had been giving since the beginning of the 1930's:

With their nationalism, their pride, their foible of 'differentness,' their hatred of being put in order and equalized, they will get into trouble. [408]

Mann considers the Germans' theological bent another of the basically admirable traits that can become corrupted, with catastrophic results. Interest in religion and theology is closely related to the German love for speculation and brooding that we see in Jonathan Leverkühn, who pores over both the sacred texts and Luther's commentaries in the old family Bible (13). Adrian displays the same combination of Faustian tendencies and Lutheran Protestantism as his father. Adrian's devout parents are pleased that he begins his academic career as a student of theology in Halle (80). But at the first mention of Adrian's choice of a profession, we are given to suspect that he is not motivated by his father's seemingly innocent piety. Zeitblom is shocked at his friend's choice; he says: "I divined very clearly — that he had made his choice out of arrogance" (80).

The theological instruction offered at the University of Halle proves highly dubious. The demonic features of Professor Kumpf (Luther reincarnated) shrink to insignificance in comparison with the diabolical doctrines of Schleppfuss. When Mann summarizes the bold dialectics of Schleppfuss's lectures, he almost uncannily undermines the entire philosophical and theological thought of the renowned nineteenth century, built on the irresponsible manipulation of abstractions. Mann shows how the dialectical method works to dissolve fixed oppositions, thereby paving the way for the collapse of morality and the destruction of traditional values that took place under Nazism. The following quotation from Schleppfuss illustrates this effect:

For he received, if I may so express myself, dialectically speaking, the blasphemous and offensive into the divine and hell into the empyrean; declared the vicious to be a necessary and inseparable concomitant of the holy, and the holy a constant satanic temptation, an almost irresistible challenge to violation. [100]

What makes theology suspect, however, is less its potential historical implications than its affinity for the demonic. Schleppfuss exemplifies for Zeitblom the idea "that theology by its very nature tends and under given circumstances always will tend to become dæmonology" (99). In his farewell address Adrian describes his study of theology as a step toward his pact with the devil:

So did I feed my arrogance with sugar, studying divinity at Halla Academie, yet not for the service of God but the other, and my study of divinity was secretly already the beginning of the bond and the disguised move not Biblewards, but to him, the great religiosus. [499]

His theology study is also only a preliminary step toward his real career:

For who can hold that will away, and 'twas but a short step from the divinity school over to Leipzig and to music, that I solely and entirely then busied myself with figuris, characteribus, formis conjurationum, and what other so ever are the names of invocations and magic. [499]

"Germany and the Germans" likewise maintains that music and theology are connected and originate in German inwardness. Mann there calls music "Christian art with a negative prefix";[51] the two disciplines share the disposition toward abstract speculation and mysticism that Adrian inherits from his father and expresses emphatically in his compositions. As we have seen, Adrian is fascinated by abstract or magical number relationships and constellations (499).

It is these features that Mann stresses when, in "Germany and the Germans," he relates the dangerous elements in the German soul to musicality. He proceeds to describe music as the typically German art form:

Music is calculated order and chaos-breeding irrationality at once, rich in conjuring, incantatory gestures, in magic of numbers, the most unrealistic and yet the most impassioned of arts, mystical and abstract. If Faust is to be the representative of the German soul, he would have to be musical, for the relation of the German to the world is abstract and mystical, that is, musical, — the relation of a professor with a touch of demonism, awkward and at the same time filled with arrogant knowledge that he surpasses the world in "depth."
What constitutes this depth? Simply the musicality of the German soul, that which we call its inwardness, its subjectivity, the divorce of the speculative from the socio-political element of human energy, and the complete predominance of the former over the latter. Europe always felt it and understood its monstrous and unfortunate aspects.[52]

Thus even the gift whereby Germany so greatly enriched Western culture, musicality, proves to contain seeds of the German

51. "Germany and the Germans," p. 51.
52. *Ibid.*, pp. 51–52.

catastrophe. On this point we see how uncompromisingly Mann settles his accounts with the tradition of German culture. We can also guess what it must have cost Mann to cast suspicion on the cultural and intellectual values that underlay his entire life and work. *Doctor Faustus* is not merely an indictment of Germany's destiny. It is the artist's indictment of himself.

Doctor Faustus and Mann's political and historical writings of the 1930's and 1940's represent Germany's development in the preceding five centuries as a process of decay, in the course of which admirable qualities succumb to exaggeration and unfortunate combinations and acquire a demonic character that smoothes the way for Nazism. Mann distinguishes several facets in the nation's catastrophic situation: politico-historical, psychological, moral, and religious or metaphysical, and he tries to track down the specific source of evil in each of these fields.

Having cited a few examples to show how Mann traces the course of the degeneration process, we must still face up to a question touched on earlier: What forces control history? Do events have a meaning and a goal, or is everything pure chance? As we saw, Mann uses at least two explanatory principles, that of causal determinism and that of the "recurrence of identical cases." Those principals run parallel; Thomas Mann does not commit himself one way or the other. Yet neither of these explanatory principles answers our question. Merely describing the laws or mechanisms that seem to rule events will never reveal their meaning. Meaning can only be determined within a religious or metaphysical context. It seems undeniable that in *Doctor Faustus* Mann tries to interpret history from a religious and metaphysical point of view. To support this intuition, we must seek the key to the symbolism of music and especially of Adrian's last composition, *The Lamentation of Dr. Faustus*.

5

The Lamentation of Dr. Faustus

MUSIC AS A SYMBOL-LANGUAGE

In our analysis of the paradigmatic role of music in *Doctor Faustus*, we concentrated on its intellectual and political implications. But Mann's description of the issues central to music theory applies equally to literature, in fact to the very questions with which Mann wrestled in the writing of the novel. It is possible to demonstrate that the discussions of "strict style" can be read as a commentary on the novel itself. That Mann chose a strict form of composition for his novel became clear when we examined the comprehensive outline of history he offers; it provides an extremely rigid scheme, which radically limits the scope allowed to free invention. But Mann sets further limitations on himself, and he seems to enjoy portraying and interpreting his own method in more or less disguised terms.

Since *Doctor Faustus* belongs to what Mann calls the "stage of critique," we are not surprised to find considerable space devoted to commentary and analysis. Scholars and critics who approach the novel are always struck by the fact that the novel seems to explain itself. Erich Heller puts this pointedly:

There is no critical thought which the book does not think *about itself*. With its theme that "art has become too difficult," it has made criticism either too easy or impossible, and maneuvered the critic into a position where he is bound to plagiarize the object of his critique.[1]

This passage criticizes by implication those scholars who never get beyond quoting and paraphrasing what the book says about itself; usually these critics do not realize that their comments are simply derivative. It should be possible, however, to utilize fully the hints and guidelines in the novel without allowing the work to dictate its own terms. The first step to a critical use of the novel's self-commentary is breaking the code in which Mann recounts the problems of literary creation.

What is said in *Doctor Faustus* about composing music and

1. Heller, *The Ironic German*, p. 277.

about musical form can, in most instances, be directly applied to literary contexts. Indeed, literature is Mann's primary concern, and musical terminology serves as a cipher concealing the element of personal confession in the novel, as a symbol-language whereby he gains perspective on his own preoccupations and manages to work them into the biography of his fictitious musician. As *The Story of a Novel* indicates, Mann considers music a paradigm — the purest and most appropriate expression of what all art is about.

Once we perceive that Mann's musical terminology is a code, we understand why his discussions of music and compositions remain fairly unspecific. The reader is never confronted with an example in musical notation; technical details such as exact keys are mentioned but account for a very small part of the lengthy expositions. Mann admits in *The Story of a Novel* that he was obliged to perform a very delicate balancing act: he had to invest the passages on music with an air of concreteness and expertise in order to create the necessary illusion of reality; yet he also had to preserve enough generality to do justice to his literary intentions and concerns.[3] As a layman, Thomas Mann naturally had difficulty with the strictly technical explanations; that he succeeds with them is due to his mentor Adorno. Since many of the technical details in Adrian Leverkühn's compositions originated with Adorno, we must be careful not to read too much symbolic meaning into them. But the comments by Mann on the intellectual import of the compositions are his own and certainly apply to the novel itself.

Because the two tendencies in Mann's musical analyses sometimes work at cross-purposes, several critics speak patronizingly of false interpretations and misunderstandings. But this criticism grows out of lack of insight into Mann's intentions.[4]

Mann scholars have long been aware that Mann employs something analagous to musical structure in his works; there has been considerable discussion of his use of such form elements as the leitmotif, and Mann himself makes no secret of his predilection for them. As early as 1918 he exclaims in the *Betrachtungen eines Unpolitischen*, "you may judge my products, my attempts in art, as you wish and as you feel you must, but they were always good scores, every one of them."[5] In a

2. *The Story of a Novel*, p. 41.
3. *Ibid.*, p. 40.
4. See above, p. 74–75.
5. P. 310.

speech on *The Magic Mountain* in 1939 he points out that he used leitmotifs in the novel as "symbolic and allusive formulas" that preserved the unity of the work.[6] And in *The Story of a Novel* Mann states a more radical position than ever before: he declares that "my book itself would have to become the thing it dealt with: namely constructivistic music."[7] And elsewhere he says that the book is not only *about* music, but "also practices it."[8]

Mann's pronouncements provide the assurance that we may safely interpret the musical elements in *Doctor Faustus* as referring to problems of literary composition and principles of form. Such an approach turns out to have unexpected benefits.

The numerous generalizations about the situation and tasks facing contemporary music lend themselves most readily of all to interpretation in terms of literature. A quotation like the following quite obviously applies to the novelist Thomas Mann:

> To remain on the height of intellect; to resolve into the matter-of-course the most exclusive productions of European musical development, so that everybody could grasp the new; to make themselves its master, applying it unconcernedly as free building material and making tradition felt, recoined into the opposite of the epigonal; to make technique, however high it had climbed, entirely unimportant, and all the arts of counterpoint and instrumentation to disappear and melt together to an effect of simplicity very far from simplicity, an intellectually winged simplicity — that seemed to be the object and the craving of art. [321]

If one substitutes "literary development" for "musical" and replaces "all the arts of counterpoint and instrumentation" by "the technical devices used by the novelist Mann," the whole argument relates directly to *Doctor Faustus*. Earlier the author confirms our idea that music and literature are interchangeable when he adds after the word "music," "and she stood for them all" (320), meaning all the arts.

The reader follows some of Adrian's major compositions from the time he begins collecting material, through the actual composing, to the finished work of art, and at each stage he can find allusions to Mann's own method of composition. One characteristic of the novel is that a great deal of work — collecting and sorting a large body of material — preceded the

6. "The Making of The Magic Mountain," p. 44.
7. P. 64 [translation amended].
8. *Ibid.,* p. 41.

writing. When Adrian is laying the groundwork for the oratorio *Apocalypsis cum figuris*, Zeitblom notes that "he wrote, sketched, collected, studied, combined" (355). It is noteworthy that most of Adrian's preliminary studies are purely literary; in fact he reads the same apocalyptic and visionary writings dating from ancient times and the Middle Ages, that Mann mentions in *The Story of a Novel* as part of his preparations for *Doctor Faustus*. Before Adrian composes his setting of the *Gesta Romanorum*, he studies not only the work itself but also anything else that seems pertinent and inspires him to compose, Kleist's essay on marionettes, for example (305). Similarly, Mann, as he was working on *Doctor Faustus*, read numerous works superficially unrelated to the subject matter of the novel, which nevertheless stimulated his work at a deeper level.

This "scientific" procedure results in the majority of the work's being finished before the composer sets pen to paper. Mann says of Adrian's last composition, the *Lamentation*, "In a more concrete and physical sense the work is done, indeed, before the composition even begins" (488). Another passage in *Doctor Faustus* gives an even clearer picture of the uniqueness of the method: "The whole disposition and organization of the material would have to be ready when the actual work should begin, and all one asks is: which is the actual work?" (193) Since the work of art grows out of a predetermined body of material, the relation of the finished work to its source material becomes an important aesthetic issue. We usually find that Adrian's work parodies its material, and the parallel to Thomas Mann is so obvious that no commentary is necessary. Dependence on written sources tends to reveal itself in direct quotations, and Mann does not fail to mention that Adrian has "in general a definite liking to quote, to make word-plays on something or someone" (137).

Another aspect of Adrian's and Mann's method is its intellectualism, its liking for sober, careful disposition of material. Once, as Adrian looks at a half-covered sheet of music, Zeitblom compares him to a chess player who "measures on the checkered field the progress of a game, to which musical composition bears so suggestive a resemblance" (304). It is certainly a feat of cool combination worthy of a skilled chess player for an artist to link his life and that of Nietzsche with Germany's history and simultaneously adapt it to the pattern of the old Faust chapbook. Writing such a work does indeed constitute the solution of a task or a problem. Adrian feels precisely this way about composing the *Apocalypsis*: Mann says that "the flashing up and stating of a problem, the task of composition (over which he had heretofore always lingered), was one with its lightninglike solution" (359). The parallel between Mann and Adrian would be incomplete if Mann had not, as he does in the above quotation, designated inspiration as the opposite and complement of cerebral calculation.

One reason for the special method Mann uses in *Doctor Faustus* is that he felt the crisis in art had shown the need for new methods that would have more bearing on reality than was possible within the self-sufficient world of illusion provided by the art forms of the past. Adrian has similar reasons for developing his particular style. A work of art, he says,

is work: art-work for appearance's sake — and now the question is whether at the present stage of our consciousness, our knowledge, our sense of truth, this little game is still permissible, still intellectually possible, still to be taken seriously; whether the work as such, the construction, sef-sufficing, harmonically complete in itself, still stands in any legitimate relation to the complete insecurity, problematic conditions, and lack of harmony of our social situation; whether all seeming, even the most beautiful, even precisely the beautiful, has not today become a lie." [180]

Mann relates the crisis in music directly to the social evolution of Europe in the twentieth century; he found this thought confirmed in Adorno's sociological approach to music, and it agreed with his own conviction that the decline of the novel was part of the decline of the bourgeois world.

If what the novel tells us of Adrian's preparations for his compositions is also true of *Doctor Faustus*, at the next stage, too, when the material is arranged and unified, Mann ascribes his own principles to Adrian. At this stage the musical terminology is not quite so transparent, but a truly probing analysis of the novel's formal structure occurs in Adrian's description of "strict style."

"STRICT STYLE"

Adrian describes "strict style" in a conversation with Zeitblom that takes place in Chapter 10: "I will tell you what I understand by 'strict style.' I mean the complete integration of all musical dimensions, their neutrality towards each other due to complete organization" (191). Adrian illustrates this highly abstract definition by explaining the sample of strict style in his song, "O lieb Mädel," from the Brentano cycle. This composition is based on the five-note figure h-e-a-e-e-flat, which is simultaneously a letter code for the name Hetaera esmeralda.[9] "It is like a word, a key word, stamped on everything in the song, which it would like to determine entirely" (191). By analogy one can see the Hetaera motif, symbol of the fateful infection, as a key to the whole novel, to a certain extent even determining the course of the action.

Adrian finds, however, that the five notes of the Hetaera motif give him too little leeway, and he works out what he thinks would be the ideal of strict style:

"One would have to go on from here and make larger words out of the twelve letters, as it were, of the tempered semitone alphabet. Words of twelve letters, certain combinations and interrelations of the twelve semitones, series of notes from which a piece and all the movements of a work must strictly derive. Every note of the whole composition, both melody and harmony, would have to show its relation to this fixed fundamental series. Not one might recur until the other notes have sounded. Not one might appear which did not fulfill its function in the whole structure. There would no longer be a free note. That is what I would call 'strict composition.' " [191]

As already indicated, this passage owes much to Adorno, including several word-for-word quotations. For this reason we cannot translate the musical theory it enunciates directly into literary categories. Adrian's choice of a twelve-tone row obviously derives from Schönberg. Yet the basic concept of strict style does apply to Doctor Faustus. Zeitblom uses the concept of "rational organization through and through" (191) to sum up his friend's explanations, and although the phrase comes from Adorno,[10] it expresses an essential feature of the structure of Doctor Faustus. If one replaces the idea of twelve tones by the idea of a series of basic motifs, our quotation becomes an accurate description of Doctor Faustus. Although Mann's previous novels use the leitmotif, in this novel the motifs have taken on such dimensions that almost everything in the novel can be assigned to one of them. The pattern of motifs thus provides an instance of Zeitblom's "organization." This pattern

9. J. M. Stein compares this first step of Adrian's toward a twelve-tone system to Schönberg's early experiments with short motifs that had the same function as the later twelve-tone sequences. He mentions in particular Schönberg's piano compositions, Op. 11. See "Adrian Leverkühn as a Composer," p. 258, n.4.
10. T. W. Adorno, Philosophie der neuen Musik, p. 55.

has quite frequently been studied,[11] but a few specific examples may prove of interest.

The chapter on Jonathan Leverkühn and his experiments introduces several major motifs. Jonathan's study of the Luther Bible (13) establishes Protestant theology as a significant force in the events to come. In addition we have Jonathan's scientific interest, referred to as "speculating the elements" (13). Such seemingly innocuous reading matter as the illustrated work on butterflies brings in the most important motif of the whole novel, the Hetaera. Every reader knows that this extraordinary butterfly undergoes metamorphosis and becomes the woman who leads Adrian into perdition, but it is easy to overlook the exact repetition that characterizes each reappearance of the motif; in this case we are entitled to speak of a true leitmotif. Zeitblom describes the butterfly's flight "in transparent nudity, loving the duskiness of heavy leafage," "like a petal blown by the wind" (14). Adrian sees in the Leipzig brothel "clear-wings, esmeraldas, et cetera, clad or unclad" (142). These very words appear again in Adrian's farewell speech, when he tells how he followed his Hetaera "into the twilit shadowy foliage that her transparent nakedness loveth, and where I caught her, who in flight is like a wind-blown petal" (498).

Mann puts Jonathan Leverkühn's studies of shells and snails (15) and his interest in osmotic plants and the "devouring drop" (18–19) through a series of ingenious and complicated variations. This group of motifs merges in the devil scene with the theme of disease, represented by Adrian's hereditary disposition toward migraine and by the effects of syphilis on the brain (235). The motif of the "devouring drop" reappears when

11. K. Heim gives thorough and detailed evidence of how carefully *Doctor Faustus* (hereafter cited as *DF*) is worked out as a score; he is convinced that "just as every chord must be justified polyphonically, every event and almost every sentence in the novel has its place in the consistent texture of motifs and themes that make up the work" ("Thomas Mann und die Musik," pp. 285–86). Olschewski also analyzes the web of leitmotifs, without however using the musical analogy as does Heim (H. Olschewski, " 'Doktor Faustus' von Thomas Mann"). H. Grandi ("Die Musik in Roman Thomas Manns") and J. Lesser ("Thomas Mann in der Epoche seiner Vollendung") likewise discuss the major leitmotifs, the latter working on the premise that all the smaller motifs are variations of the central devil motif. Aspects of this question are discussed by J. Krey in "Die gesellschaftliche Bedeutung der Musik im Werk von Thomas Mann" and by J. C. de Buisonjé in "Bemerkungen über TMs Werk." Among those who treat the motif of disease are E. Fromm ("Symphonia pathologica,") and E. Hofmann (*Thomas Mann: Patholog — Therapeut? Eine Zusammenschau seiner Thematik*).

Adrian composes a setting to Klopstock's ode *Spring Festival* with its theme of the "drop to the bucket." Mann himself points out the recurrence of the leitmotif by recalling Father Lever-kühn's passion for "speculating the elements" (266) and he prepares for its reappearance by having Zeitblom anticipate Adrian's account of his voyage into the ocean depths (266). The motif of the ocean reiterates the mollusk and snail motif and introduces a further symbol for Adrian's demonic infection, Andersen's little mermaid (235, 500). To discuss all the variations of these motifs would exceed the scope of our investigation. But it should be emphasized that all these minor motifs can be grouped under the major heading of the devil motif.[12] Thomas Mann hints that Jonathan Leverkühn's experiments and speculation are "the work of the 'Tempter'" (17), and one aspect of the demonic in *Doctor Faustus* is ambiguity. This ambiguity is first suggested symbolically in the fact that the snail and mollusk shells Jonathan examines were earlier used at times as "vessels for poisons" and at times as "shrines and reliquaries" during the Mass (16).

Before concluding our discussion of a small selection from the overwhelming wealth of leitmotifs, we should like to trace one motif more carefully: the motif of "mygrims." Heim gives a rough outline, pointing out that Adrian's inherited migraine gradually intensifies as a result of syphilis until the development of the motif reaches its almost unbearable climax in the description of Echo's meningitis.[13] The motif occurs innumerable other times, and always at important moments. Thus Adrian's migraine first makes its appearance at his puberty (44) — as medical experience would lead one to expect — and his interest in music manifests itself almost simultaneously. The headaches come in reaction to his heavy load of schoolwork compounded by extracurricular study of the classics, philosophy and medieval music (71). During his university years the headaches persist (112), and now Adrian begins to ponder the more deep-seated causes of his suffering. In his letter to Kretschmar he rejects the idea that external factors such as overwork might be responsible: the migraine comes rather "from satiety, from cold boredom" (130). After Adrian's encounter with the Hetaera the headaches inaugurate their more virulent form with an attack of dizziness during Adrian's music

12. Lesser, *Thomas Mann*, p. 386.
13. Heim, "Thomas Mann," p. 290.

lesson followed by a "two days' migraine" (158). At his sister Ursula's wedding, "this sacrificial feast of a maidenhead" (186), Adrian suffers from migraine, apparently in protest against this concession to sensuality. It is significant that Adrian's and Zeitblom's subsequent discussion of marriage and the lust of the flesh should lead to exposition of the "strict style" concept; the conversation peters out because Adrian is too much in pain (194).

Like all the major themes of the book, the migraine motif undergoes a kind of modulation in the interview with the devil. Adrian has a headache when the devil first makes his appearance, and the visitor explain the true nature of the affliction:

"Oh, thy father is not so ill-placed in my mouth. He was a shrewd one, always wanting to speculate the elements. The mygrim, the point of attack for the knife-pains of the little sea-maid — after all, you have them from him. . . . Moreover, I have spoken quite correctly: osmosis, fluid diffusion, the proliferation process — the whole magic intreats of these. You have there the spinal sac with the pulsating column of fluid therein, reaching to the cerebrum, to the meninges, in whose tissues the furtive venereal meningitis is at its soundless stealthy work." [235]

Several times the mermaid motif's connection with the migraine motif is suggested when the headaches are compared to seasickness (314, 342); the mermaid thus joins the symbolic complex to which belongs such a motif as the Hetaera, the symbol of infection.[14] At the end of his visit, the devil makes the connection even more explicit: "The coldness in you is perhaps not prefigured, as well as the paternal head paynes out of which the pangs of the little sea-maid are to come?" (249)

When Adrian moves to Pfeiffering he explains to his future landlady, Frau Schweigestill, that he might prove a difficult lodger because of the headaches. She explains that she is well acquainted with this illness because her husband — Jonathan Leverkühn's double — also suffers from it (257). During Adrian's years in Pfeiffering the migraine worsens steadily, and he experiences several acute crises, usually when he is conceiving one of his major compositions; while composing he enjoys complete though deceptive freedom from pain, but beforehand and afterward he undergoes tortures. During Echo's short stay in

14. The motif of the little mermaid is discussed by V. A. Oswald, "Thomas Mann and the Mermaid." Cf. D. J. Enright, "The Anti-Diabolic Faith: Thomas Mann's *Doctor Faustus*," *The Apothecary's Shop: Essays on Literature*, p. 135.

Pfeiffering Adrian is plagued by headaches, and when Echo becomes ill, Adrian is firmly convinced that he has infected the child. In his farewell speech he refers to Echo as his son (501), thus invoking the earlier theme of heredity.

Mann's consistent adherence to the leitmotif technique certainly deserves to be called "rational organization through and through" (191); such an extremely complicated texture of motifs presupposes that the novel was carefully plotted with definite goals in mind. What is new in *Doctor Faustus* is not the use of the leitmotif but, as with the montage, the extent and uncompromising coherence of its use. All of Mann's works can be regarded as "good scores," but only *Doctor Faustus* realizes the ideal of "strict style."

Mann's comparison of the strict style in composition to the magic square (192) reveals the rationalistic or intellectualistic aspect of the new technique. Adrian's reproduction of the magic square from Dürer's "Melencolia" becomes a sort of leitmotif, suggesting on the one hand Adrian's preference for mathematical calculation and on the other his Faustian inclination toward magic. The square has the magical property that whether one adds up its numbers horizontally, vertically or diagonally, the sum is always 34 (92). This symmetry represents a total order and is at the same time diabolically ambiguous.

One phenomenon early captures Adrian's attention: the fact that a note can be interpreted in different ways, according to whether one finds it in a horizontal, melodic context or in a vertical, harmonic one; Adrian sees herein the basic correlation between music and the magic square. In the discussion of strict style, the magic square acquires even greater significance. Zeitblom ponders Adrian's application of the concept of the constellation to a mingling of polyphonic and harmonic elements and eventually arrives at the subject of magic:

"Human reason! And besides, excuse me, 'constellation' is your every other word. But surely it belongs more to astrology. The rationalism you call for has a good deal of superstition about it — of a belief in the incomprehensibly and vaguely demonic, the kind of thing we have in games of chance, fortune-telling with cards, and shaking dice. Contrary to what you say, your system seems to me more calculated to dissolve human reason in magic." [193–94]

"Strict style" thus operates according to precise mathematical laws, but these pass over into number magic. The conjunction of twelve-tone technique and number magic strikes us as something Mann could well have invented, but in fact it already existed — in the person of Arnold Schönberg. Schönberg's fear of unlucky numbers expressed itself in peculiar ways. He tried, for instance, to avoid the number 13 at all costs, often numbering the bars in his compositions 11, 12, 12a, 14; and by chance or as a result of hysterical suggestion, he actually died on a Friday the 13th.[15] When one considers that in America Mann moved in the same social circles as Schönberg,[16] it seems surprising that Mann nowhere mentions hearing of this mania of Schönberg's or connects it with the twelve-tone method. Instead he seems to consider the relationship between strict style and magic his own invention:

. . . because, within the sphere of the book, within this world of a pact with the devil and of black magic, the idea of the twelve-tone technique assumes a coloration and a character which it does not possess in its own right and which — is this not so? — in a sense make it really my property, or, rather, the property of the book. Schönberg's idea and my ad hoc version of it differs so widely that, aside from the stylistic fault, it would have seemed almost insulting, to my mind, to have mentioned his name in the text.[17]

As we indicated earlier, Schönberg was of a different opinion. The debate that arose between him and Mann dealt on the surface with the rights to the twelve-tone technique, but part of Schönberg's violent indignation may have come from seeing his own superstitiousness made to denote diabolical influence.[18]

We cannot precisely determine whether Mann was wholly unaware of Schönberg's superstitions, but it is evident that the strict style in which *Doctor Faustus* is written has striking features of both mathematical construction and number magic. The book achieves mathematical symmetry by its division into equal halves. The first German edition is 772 pages long, and the end of the chapter containing the interview with the devil comes exactly in the middle, on page 386; there then begins a new epoch in Adrian's life. In *The Story of a Novel* Mann notes that he had written with the end of chapter 25 "half the book . . . exactly half by page count," and he adds the date: February 20, 1943.[19] This date is as close as possible to the middle of the entire period during which Mann worked on

15. W. H. Rubsamen, "Schoenberg in America," p. 488. See Krey, "Die gesellschaftliche Bedeutung . . . ," p. 329; he also refers to Rubsamen.
16. *Story of a Novel*, p. 29.
17. *Ibid.*, p. 36.
18. See above, p. 55.
19. *Story of a Novel*, p. 109.

Doctor Faustus: March 15, 1943–January 29, 1947.[20] Besides, the twenty-fifth chapter brings the action to the autumn of 1912, that is, to the exact middle of Adrian's life (252). At that time Adrian is 27½ years old, and he dies in 1940 at the age of 55 (509). The novel is thus intentionally arranged around the mathematical center.

Mann added a handwritten passage, later deleted, to the typed manuscript of *Doctor Faustus*, in which Zeitblom speaks of his "childish satisfaction" at setting the number 35 over the chapter he has just begun. This satisfaction undoubtedly has something to do with the division of the previous chapter into three parts; it has been pointed out that the threefold chapter bears the number of the magic square.[21] Mann seems to have written his insert to explain the curious division and then thought better of it.

The "childish" game with the chapter numbers grows out of Mann's pleasure in "numerical correspondences," many of which he discovered in his own life. The first sentence of *The Story of a Novel* alludes to this passage Mann had written in his *Sketch of My Life* in 1930:

Our wedding anniversary is near at hand, brought round by a year which is a round number, like all those that have been important in my life. It was midday when I came into the world; my fifty years lay in the middle of the decades, and in the middle of a decade, halfway through it, I was married. This pleases my sense of mathematical clarity, as does also the fact that my children come and go, as it were, in rhymed couples: girl, boy, boy, girl, girl, boy. I have a feeling that I shall die, at the same age as my mother, in 1945.[22]

In December, 1945 a journalist challenged Mann on this statement. Mann had to admit that by still being alive he was betraying his principles, but he did not relinquish the idea of an orderly pattern.[23]

It is easy to see that Mann's chapter divisions in *Doctor Faustus* may have been dictated by what he calls his "half-sportive belief in certain symmetries and numerical correspondences." All sorts of hypotheses have been put forward, none of them particularly convincing.[24] Krey goes through various mathematical contortions to prove that the number seven has

20. *Ibid.*, pp. 17, 231.
21. F. Kaufmann, "Dr. Fausti Weheklag," p. 26.
22. *A Sketch of My Life*, p. 78.
23. *Story of a Novel*, p. 4.
24. H. Mayer ponders the significance of the number 25 and its possible connection with the devil motif (*Thomas Mann*, p. 341).

special significance for the novel.[25] According to his theory, one can divide the novel into seven "books," each of which comprises seven chapters. But this theory contradicts Mann's statement in *The Story of a Novel* that he considered dividing the book into six chapters.[26] He never carried out this intention, but the potential demarcation lines can easily be recognized. The novel contains several digressions about events of the war during the 1940's. These five passages neatly divide the novel into six sections. Furthermore, each of these passages is set off by asterisks from the rest of the chapter in which it occurs (175, 253, 482), and a figure is mentioned who appears nowhere else in the book, Monsignor Hinterpförtner (172, 251, 336).

Since these three criteria coincide, we can use them to work out the division Mann was probably thinking of: Book 1: Chapters 1–4 (Adrian's family and childhood); Book 2: Chapters 5–20 (Adrian's youth and years as a student); Book 3: Chapters 21–25 (musical breakthrough and the interview with the devil); Book 4: Chapters 26–32 (move to Pfeiffering, period up to the First World War); Book 5: Chapters 33–45 (anticipation of catastrophe in the Kridwiss discussions and in Adrian's apocalyptic oratorio; catastrophe in individual lives: Clarissa, Ines, Rudi, Echo); Book 6: Chapters 46–47 (The *Lamentation*, farewell speech, finale).

Some of the numerical mysteries remain unsolved. Why did Mann divide Chapter 34 in three? Did he have a particular reason for ending the book with Chapter 47, or did he wish to avoid the natural number 49? These questions cannot yet be answered. Perhaps Mann's diaries for the period will provide some information. But it is also possible that the number magic will prove to be a sort of private joke with no significance for the work as a whole.

One can thus see that *Doctor Faustus* fulfills Adrian's ideal of strict style by its consistent leitmotif and theme treatment and its use of mathematical and magical number configurations. Since the novel corresponds to this stylistic ideal for music, we are entitled to apply Mann's pronouncements on musical theory to literature as well.

Doctor Faustus meets a further standard first formulated by Adrian and later repeated at important junctures in the novel. Adrian says of the notes in the predetermined row upon

25. Krey, "Die gesellschaftliche Bedeutung . . . ," p. 329.
26. *Story of a Novel*, p. 232.

which a twelve-tone composition should be based, "Not one note might appear which did not fulfil its function. . . . There would no longer be a free note" (191). In his analysis of the oratorio *Apocalypsis cum figuris* Zeitblom remarks upon the curious correspondences between various parts of the work: "but in the searing, susurrant tones of spheres and angels there is not one note which does not occur, with rigid correspondence, in the hellish laughter" (379). And he says of Adrian's last composition, the *Lamentation*: "This style, this technique, he [Adrian] said, admitted no note, not one, which did not fulfil its thematic function in the whole structure — there was no longer any free note" (486). This phrase, consciously repeated by Zeitblom, appears once more in reference to the same work: "just because there is no longer any free note" (488).

The idea that every note should be "bound" presents no difficulties, but how does it work in a literary context and how can it be applied to Mann's novel? To see the material of *Doctor Faustus* as "bound," one must think in terms of larger units than the single words and sentences that might seem the logical equivalent of single notes. If we take larger linguistic units, we can derive from the sentence "there is no longer any free note" two possible descriptions of *Doctor Faustus*, neither of which excludes the other. In a concrete sense, much of the novel's material is unfree because it is quoted verbatim from sources outside the novel. If we accept this interpretation, the statement about the "bound" notes simply expresses the theory behind the quotation technique. Support for this interpretation may be gathered from Mann's pointed reminders that the technique calls for preselected material. The *Faustus* material is preselected insofar as it was available to Mann before he began the actual writing. Mann appropriately mentions this type of groundwork immediately after using the phrase "there is not a single free note" (488).

Yet this interpretation cannot satisfy us completely. Whereas Adrian's entire work is characterized by "bound" notes, the lack of freedom stipulated by our quotation properly applies only to a limited portion of Thomas Mann's novel. His insistence that every bit of the musical material must be bound only makes sense if we can interpret bondage in another way: as a symbol for the concept of total, rational structuring. In this case a "bound" work would have its basic layout and its individual sections determined absolutely by a series of themes or leitmotifs, the equivalent of the tone row. *Doctor Faustus* certainly contains such a series of motifs, although they may not number exactly twelve. It is a matter of taste how generally or narrowly one defines these motifs. Demonic inspiration through disease, the aristocratic inclination of art to isolation, Faustian man's overweaning curiosity: these motifs appear, with variations and ramifications, in almost every episode of the novel and determine its course. Here, too, predetermination or preselection takes place: Mann sets himself a certain task to fulfill and chooses several different time levels and complexes of ideas which he is to fuse into an artistic unity.

If Adrian Leverkühn's and Thomas Mann's preliminaries and their principles of composition coincide, may one not suspect that the conditions under which their works came into being would reveal certain similarities? In other words, might it not be possible to read the descriptions of Adrian's compositions as descriptions of the novel? Perhaps one cannot prove conclusively that each of Adrian's works corresponds to one of Mann's,[27] but parallels between Adrian's and Mann's late works abound. In fact, the evocation of Adrian's cantata, *The Lamentation of Dr. Faustus,* can be read in every point as a description of the novel *Doctor Faustus.* A few critics have seen this possibility, but they mention only vague similarities.[28]

Before we analyze the *Lamentation* from this point of view, we should note that Mann lets Zeitblom draw parallels between this work and an earlier work of Leverkühn's, the *Apocalypsis cum Figuris.* Many of the methods that lend the *Lamentation* its particular flavor are anticipated in the earlier oratorio (487). This means that the description of the *Apocalypsis* provides

27. B. A. Sørensen ("Thomas Manns 'Doktor Faustus,'" p. 87) suggests that Adrian's compositions represent a "transfiguration performed on the musical level of Thomas Mann's works," but he does not give any concrete evidence in support of his contention. Without drawing a general parallel, H. M. Wolff (*Thomas Mann,* p. 116) compares *Buddenbrooks* to Adrian's *Meerleuchten.* Both works are written within the framework of tradition that their authors have already outgrown.

28. W. D. Williams ("Thomas Mann's Doctor Faustus," p. 277) proceeds from the statement in *DF* that all of Adrian's works except the *Lamentation* are parodistic and suggests that this fact indicates Mann's intention to stress that his novel is serious despite the obvious elements of parody. Olschewski ("'Doktor Faustus,'" p. 137) points out that Mann's and Goethe's Faust works are clearly parallel in that they conclude by overcoming despair through the hope of grace. Krey ("Die gesellschaftliche Bedeutung . . . ," p. 330) points out that both are works of maturity dealing with a man's tragic downfall; both are constructed according to calculated formal principles.

valuable hints and clarifications, while the *Lamentation* itself describes the novel as a whole.

THE LAMENTATION OF DR. FAUSTUS

The outward similarity between Adrian's *Lamentation* and Mann's novel is so apparent that it need not be discussed: both are based on the old folk legend. In both cases the chapbook serves as a direct source; the emphasis falls on the final phase of Faustus' life. Both artists use exact quotations, Adrian primarily in his "Oratio Fausti ad Studiosos," Mann in the corresponding section, the scene of Adrian's farewell speech and in the passages we have already indicated. An interesting sidelight is that Zeitblom repeatedly refers to the *Lamentation* as *Faustus* (178, 487), the name Mann adopts for his book through out *The Story of a Novel.*

The *Lamentation* is Adrian's last composition, his final work. Mann thought *Doctor Faustus* his last while he was writing it. In *The Story of a Novel* he calls it his "Parsifal," a "book of doom."[29] The fact that both are final works sheds light on their apocalyptic character. In both works the downfall of the central figure becomes symbolic for a general catastrophe. The novel's basic mood parallels the sustained lament of the oratorio. The sense of doom, expressed as mourning in the *Lamentation,* has a more clearly apocalyptic cast in Adrian's earlier oratorio, appropriately entitled *Apocalypsis cum figuris.* In a letter about *Doctor Faustus* Mann stresses the apocalyptic aspect of the novel: "The book, as art, is something late, final, extreme, and its very boldness and honor consist in being extreme."[30]

If the character and general mood of the *Lamentation* mirror the novel, the details are even more pertinent. Zeitblom's analysis of this work is much more detailed than his earlier discussions of Adrian's work, taking up a good seven pages (485–91). We shall follow this analysis point for point and interpret it wherever possible as a description of the novel *Doctor Faustus.* We adhere to Zeitblom's order for the most part, but when he repeats himself, we combine all his comments on a given subject and treat them in the most appropriate context.

29. Pp. 20, 27 [translation amended].
30. E. Fischer, "Zu zwei Briefen von TM," *Sinn und Form,* pp. 78–79. See Mann's letter of March 23, 1949 to G. Lukács: "Briefwechsel mit Thomas Mann," p. 669 and E. Hilscher, "Ein Künstler als Abenteurer," p. 139.

At the beginning of his analysis Zeitblom points out the curious dual nature of the work:

Woe, woe! A *De Profundis*, which in my zeal and love I am bound to call matchless. Yet has it not — from the point of view of creative art and musical history as well as that of individual fulfilment — a jubilant, a highly triumphant bearing upon this awe-inspiring faculty of compensation and redress? Does it not mean the "break-through" [485]

These words strike through to the very heart of the novel: lamentation, sense of doom, the national catastrophe, the humiliation and defeat of the individual characters — all these terrible things are transformed into an aesthetic and moral triumph for the poet. One must conclude from this passage that Mann thought highly of the artistic value of his novel, and there is nothing to contradict such an assumption. But he valued the personal achievement as highly as the artistic success of the work; *The Story of a Novel* testifies to the fact that Mann considered bringing *Doctor Faustus* to a conclusion a real test of strength: "At least it is a moral accomplishment."[31] When Mann speaks here of accomplishment he is plainly referring not so much to the tremendous amount of work involved in the book as to the courage and the endurance demanded by such a self-examination and confession.

Zeitblom chooses the word "break-through" to characterize this triumph of artistic form over the material; his quotation marks [in the German text only] indicate that he is alluding to the discussion of the concept earlier in the book. Breakthrough in the *Lamentation* consists in the "reconstitution of expressivism" and in "a reversal of . . . calculated coldness . . . into a voice expressive of the soul" (485). That means that "strict style" becomes capable of direct human expression. Precisely this paradox makes the novel unique: despite the montage and all the quotations, *Doctor Faustus* remains unquestionably Mann's own creation and reaches a climax of meaningfulness and personal commitment not found in any of his previous works. The Thomas Mann so often accused of being cerebral and lacking in creative imagination has written, with *Doctor Faustus*, a deeply affecting and expressive novel. He demonstrates that free invention is certainly no prerequisite of great art.

The second part of Zeitblom's analysis begins with a generalization on his foregoing exposition: The *Lamentation* is not

31. P. 231.

the only work in which expressiveness becomes lamentation, for "one may state boldly that all expressivism is really lament" (485). For corroboration Zeitblom goes back to Monteverdi. Does this digression simply serve the purpose of giving Zeitblom's musical analysis a factual basis? If we disregard the details that are obviously chosen to maintain the illusion of musical concreteness, this passage unquestionably applies to *Doctor Faustus*. Zeitblom's historical retrospect concentrates on a particular phenomenon, the echo effect:

It does not lack significance that the *Faust* cantata is stylistically so strongly and unmistakably linked with the seventeenth century and Monteverdi, whose music — again not without significance — favored the echo-effect, sometimes to the point of being a mannerism. The echo, the giving back of the human voice as a nature-sound, and the revelation of it *as* nature-sound, is essentially a lament: Nature's melancholy "Alas!" in view of man, her effort to utter his solitary state. Conversely, the lament of the nymphs on its side is related to the echo. In Leverkühn's last and loftiest creation, echo, favorite device of the baroque, is employed with unspeakably mournful effect. [486]

There are two possible interpretations of this passage on the echo. The formal devices of leitmotif and literal repetition function in the novel as a sort of echo. But in addition, one of the most important characters is called Echo, a nickname derived by the child himself from his real name, Nepomuk. It might at first seem far-fetched to link this character with the technical concept of the echo, but if one observes the role of little Nepomuk in the novel, the reference comes to make very good sense. Zeitblom uses the terms "echo" and "lamentation" almost synonymously; the chapter on Echo's death is, in effect, a searing song of lament. The child comes to symbolize the mourning of every living being. Zeitblom speaks of Echo's "heartrending moans" (475), thus himself echoing Monteverdi's "Lamento" as well as Adrian's (and Mann's) *Lamentation*. When Zeitblom evokes "the giving back of the human voice as a nature-sound," that is, the transformation of man's lamentation into a lamentation by the whole universe, one is involuntarily reminded of the connection between Adrian and the dying child. Both suffer, both lament, and Echo's lamentation, less self-conscious than Adrian's, also has more immediacy of expressiveness. If one keeps Nepomuk in mind when reading Zeitblom's evocation of passages in the *Lamentation* where expressiveness becomes pure lament, many phrases acquire greater concreteness. For example, Zeitblom links the "voice expressive of the soul" with "sincerity of creature confidence" (485): this description of the music conveys perfectly Adrian's relation to Nepomuk. The words "echo . . . employed with unspeakably mournful effect" acquire a very real meaning when one interprets the echo as an allusion to Nepomuk.

But Nepomuk does more than echo Adrian's human lament. Within the series of developing leitmotifs, the chapters devoted to him provide a sort of echo of earlier sections in the novel, especially of a passage on which Mann lavished great care: the description of the Arietta movement in Beethoven's piano sonata Opus 111. Heim sees Kretschmar's lecture at the piano as a motif that reappears in Adrian's unfinished lecture to his friends on the *Lamentation*; on the basis of this recurrence Heim draws a parallel between Adrian and Beethoven. He also notes that the description of the Arietta applies to *Doctor Faustus*. Heim interprets the lovely melodic passages which Kretschmar sings falsetto as an anticipation of the passages dealing with Echo.[32]

But the Echo passages span such a wide register of feeling that they can hardly be summed up in the Beethoven melodies alone. In fact, one can interpret the entire analysis of the Arietta movement as a detailed anticipation of the chapters on Echo. Even the general characterization of the Arietta theme suggests the child and his innocent suffering: "destined to vicissitudes for which in its idyllic innocence it would seem not to be born," the theme is compared to "a brief soul-cry" (54) — this might well be an allusion to the role Echo plays in the novel. The words with which Kretschmar scans the musical theme contain clear references to Nepomuk; "heaven's blue" — the child's heavenly blue eyes are mentioned repeatedly; — "lover's pain" — the phrase captures Adrian's feeling for Nepomuk and also introduces the idea of self-sacrificing love in a broader sense, so that we are prepared for the innocent child who prays for the entire world (472) and finally becomes a sacrifice. "Fare-thee well" — these words of parting foreshadow Adrian's parting from Echo and from everything human, and by suggesting that Beethoven's sonata is a work of leave-taking, they link this work to all the other motifs of leave-taking in the novel. The phrase "on a time" suggests that all these words

32. Heim, "Thomas Mann," p. 304.

and expressions point to something yet to come, that these motifs will reach their full development later in the novel.

Kretschmar's analysis of the sonata movement next passes to the development of the Arietta theme. Kretschmar points out the tremendous contrast between the bass and the treble; the "poor" motif hovers abandoned over a dizzying abyss — in the same "utterly extreme situation" (55) that Adrian must experience as he watches heaven and hell fighting over the child. After this stormy section something completely unexpected occurs toward the end of the sonata: the theme reappears, slightly modified. Instead of d-g-g it has c-c♯-d-g-g; this transformation is interpreted in purely human terms:

. . . this added C sharp is the most moving, consolatory, pathetically reconciling thing in the world. It is like having one's hair or cheek stroked, lovingly, understandingly, like a deep and silent farewell look. It blesses the object, the frightfully harried formulation, with overpowering humanity, lies in parting so gently on the hearer's lips in eternal farewell that the eyes run over. [55]

The words with which Kretschmar scans this "melodic expansion" also indicate a change of mood. "Heaven's blue" becomes "Oh thou heaven's blue"; what was previously just a statement, referring among other things to the color of Echo's eyes, becomes here almost a prayer. The emphasis seems to shift from "blue" to "heavens." The parting cry similarly requires a new dimension: "Fare thee well for aye." This phrase applies to the Beethoven sonata, to the Echo episode and to the novel *Doctor Faustus* as a whole. The adventurous lot of the little motif comes to an end, Echo's suffering ceases, and the novel on Germany's plight reaches completion after many an inner struggle for the author. The other scanning phrases express the same attitude: "Now forget the pain," " 'Twas all — but a dream," "Great was God in us," "Friendly be to me."

We should like to submit that all these phrases, as well as the whole interpretation of the Arietta movement, refer to Echo. He at first appears simply as an unusually angelic child, but gradually he becomes symbolic of *the* child and of all the innocent suffering in the world. A small, seemingly insignificant detail supports our contention that the Arietta theme foreshadows Echo. When telling how Kretschmar's little audience scatters after the lecture, Zeitblom says, "for a long time we heard it like an echo from the remoter streets into which the audience dispersed, the quiet night streets of the little town:

'Fare — thee well,' 'fare thee well for aye,' 'Great was God in us'" (56). The word "echo" fits in here quite naturally, but we may be sure that Thomas Mann would never use such a symbolic word casually.

We have dwelt on the role of Echo as a leitmotif because it is pertinent to the passage in which Zeitblom couples the *Lamentation* with Monteverdi's use of the echo. Monteverdi's music has other characteristics that make it akin to Adrian's oratorio:

A lament of such gigantic dimensions is, I say, of necessity an expressive work, a work of expression, and therewith it is a work of liberation; just as the earlier music, to which it links itself across the centuries, sought to be a liberation of expression. Only that the dialectic process — by which, at the stage of development that this work occupies, is consummated by the change from the strictest constraint to the free language of feeling, the birth of freedom from bondage — the dialectic process appears as endlessly more complicated in its logic, endlessly more miraculous and amazing than at the time of the madrigalists. [486]

From the point of view of musical history it is not illogical to equate Monteverdi's and Adrian's achievements, assuming that Adrian actually practices Schönberg's twelve-tone method. The connection between the two composers may have been suggested to Mann by Křenek's *Music Here and Now*, which we have already shown to have provided significant material for *Doctor Faustus*. Křenek says of Monteverdi:

In his historical importance, relevant to medieval polyphony and modern tonality, Monteverdi occupies a position analogous to the place held today by Arnold Schoenberg with respect to tonality in decay and the new language of atonality.[33]

Monteverdi's situation is more complicated than Schönberg's, however. Křenek finds it noteworthy

that Monteverdi's success in achieving powerful expression was in proportion to the degree in which he passed the boundary lines of the new tonality already visible at that time, rather than when he realized tonality within its own bounds. Thus the first composer to bring the new theory to its climax injected into it the poison that was to cause its death almost before he had attained his purpose.[34]

Leverkühn, too, constructs the Schönbergian ideal of strict style as a way of achieving subjective expression; paradoxically,

33. E. Křenek, *Music Here and Now*, p. 119.
34. *Ibid.*, p. 120.

self-expression breaks through the restraining rules of the new technique.

Musical history thus provides a good pretext for relating the *Lamentation* to Monteverdi's *Lamento*; but is it also possible to read this part of Zeitblom's analysis as a description of the novel *Doctor Faustus*? Can we discover an author or a work of which *Doctor Faustus* could be a "reconstruction," as the *Lamentation* is a "reconstruction" of Monteverdi? Indeed, this presents no problem: Mann's *Doctor Faustus* in its entirety and in its details imitates the old Faust chapbook. This interpretation is historically quite plausible: when the chapbook was printed for the first time in 1587, Monteverdi was twenty years old. To be sure, his creative life falls in the early years of the seventeenth century — the *Lamento d'Arianna* was written in 1608 — but we need not worry at such a minor chronological inconsistency; what is astonishing is that Mann was able to fit a historically correct musical fact so neatly into his symbolic scheme.

The musical equivalent of the chapbook is not Monteverdi alone; several times Zeitblom mentions that the *Lamentation* reaches back to the "time of the Madrigalists" (486), and a later passage admits that the madrigal stands for the chapbook: "There are a hundred references to the tone and spirit of the madrigal, and a whole movement, the exhortation to his friends at the meal on the last night, is written in strict madrigal form" (488). The concept of a "strict madrigal form" is musically not quite permissible, but the phrase makes immediate sense if one paraphrases it as "written in the form of the old chapbook." Adrian's farewell speech, the "movement" which is referred to, is indeed a correct imitation of the farewell scene in the chapbook and contains, as we have demonstrated, several exact quotations from it. And the novel as a whole contains "a hundred references to the tone and spirit of the chapbook."

The idea of a reconstruction of Monteverdi or of the chapbook expresses itself not only in an imitation of the old prototypes but also in use of their principles on a higher level. In order to understand this properly, we must recall that Mann read in Křenek that Monteverdi and Schönberg (read: Leverkühn) figured as boundary markers on either side of the tonal era. In terms of this historical position, "reconstruction" means a return to expression unrestricted by the principles of tonality. Transferring these conditions to the literary plane will necessarily involve speculation, but it is not impossible. First we must find the literary period that corresponds to the age of tonal-harmonic music, that is, to the period of classical and romantic music. Thomas Mann usually refers to this literary equivalent as the "bourgeois" epoch, and the chapbook and *Doctor Faustus* do indeed stand at either end of the period. In music the interim was presided over by the tonal system, which stifled free articulation and had to be overcome or eliminated before music could acquire new powers of expression. The analogue to the tonal period within the bourgeois epoch in literature, or, to limit our scope, within the history of the Faust motif, finds its best exponent in Goethe, whose decidedly bourgeois Faust represents a considerable change from the chapbook, to which Mann was to revert as his point of departure.

We are not trying to suggest that either classical music or Goethe's *Faust* lack expressive power — if one gives "expressive" its usual sense. But we have seen that in the analysis of the *Lamentation* "expression" and "lament" are used synonomously. The *De profundis* lament of the universe expressed in the *Lamentation* and in *Doctor Faustus* would be incongruous in a literary world where man finds salvation by means of moral exertions, just as it is incongruous in a musical world where all available means were invoked to express in notes Schiller's hymn to joy. Thus it is also logical that Adrian's reconstruction of Monteverdi's *Lamento* should retract Beethoven's Ninth Symphony and that Mann's reconstruction should in effect retract Goethe's *Faust*.

It is safe to assume that the Ninth Symphony and Goethe's *Faust* were two of a kind to Thomas Mann. The fact that both works date from the same period is probably less important than that they share a fundamental attitude toward man and his possibilities. Both are trustfully optimistic, filled with belief in man's nobility. Goethe's *Faust* is saved because of his constant exertions to perfect the nobility inherent in man. And Beethoven's chorus proclaims with Schiller's words its faith in the coming kingdom of joy and brotherly love.

Although the attitude expressed by Goethe and by Beethoven in his use of Schiller, is largely the same, Schiller's idealistic message is more unambiguous and emotionally more consistent than Goethe's *Faust*, a work full of dramatic conflict, variety, and contradiction. The relationship between the *Lamentation* of *Doctor Faustus* and the novel *Doctor Faustus* could be described the same way; in general both works express a belief in the destructive powers of the demonic, both are wholly lament, since the lament alone adequately expresses the human situation. But there is an important difference between them. The *Lamentation* is unambiguously and solely lament, whereas the more complicated world of the novel has room for the very opposite. *Doctor Faustus*, like Goethe's *Faust*, is a contradictory and often obscure work, but its general character represents a retraction of the Goethean work. No matter how one interprets individual sections of both works, the fact cannot be denied that Faust is saved, whereas Adrian Leverkühn is damned. One can read many passages as negative allusions to Goethe's *Faust*;[35] this confirms our present interpretation: the *Lamentation* likewise alludes negatively to the Ninth Symphony. One of the negative allusions to Beethoven is contained in the motto of the *Lamentation*, of which Zeitblom says, " 'Alas, it is not to be!' How the words stand, almost like a musical direction, above the choral and orchestral movements of '*Dr. Fausti Wehe-klag*' " (490).[36] If we insert in place of the works of Beethoven and Adrian the works of Goethe and Mann, we find that these, too, have mottoes that negate each other. The novel *Doctor Faustus* has a motto in the usual sense, nine lines from the second Canto of Dante's *Inferno*, and there are good reasons for thinking that Mann intended his motto as an equivalent to the "Dedication" with which Goethe introduces his *Faust*. This dedication describes how the poet Goethe sinks down into the world of memory. A throng of figures rises from the cloudy past and conjures up "images of happy days." Thomas Mann's Dante quotation also speaks of the poet's remembering the past:

> Day was departing and the dusky air
>> Loosing the living things on earth that dwell
>> From their fatigues; and I alone was there
> Preparing to sustain the war, as well
>> Of the long way as also of the pain,
>> Which now unerring memory will tell.
> O Muses! O high genius, now sustain!
>> O Memory who wrote down what I did see,
>> Here thy nobility will be made plain.[37]

35. See above, p. 48–49.
36. See above, p. 91.
37. *The Divine Comedy of Dante Alighieri*, tr. M. B. Anderson, p. 7.

187

Like Dante, Mann prepares himself for battle and prays for aid and strength in completing the difficult task ahead; like Dante he is about to traverse an inferno. In the "Dedication" Goethe remains passive and receptive; he gives himself up to memories that bring tears to his eyes. The similarity between the Dante quotation and the "Dedication" is great enough for one to assume that Mann intended an allusion; the differences only emphasize the negative connection — Mann's retraction of Goethe.

Zeitblom's discussion of the *Lamentation*'s kinship to Monteverdi leads directly into a reiteration of Adrian's theory of strict style. Next Zeitblom comments on a particular aspect of the formal strictness of the *Lamentation*: the curious question of identity.

Now, have I not, when I attempted to give some idea of Leverkühn's apocalyptic oratorio, referred to the substantial identity of the most blest with the most accurst, the inner unity of the chorus of child angels and the hellish laughter of the damned? There, to the mystic horror of one sensitive to it, is realized a Utopia in form, of terrifying ingenuity, which in the *Faust* cantata becomes universal, seizes upon the whole work and, if I may so put it, causes it to be completely swallowed up by thematic thinking. This giant "lamento" (it lasts an hour and a quarter) is very certainly non-dynamic, lacking in development, without drama, in the same way that concentric rings made by a stone thrown into water spread ever farther, without drama and always the same. [486–87]

If we exclude the reference to the time required to play the oratorium (a detail copied from Beethoven's Ninth Symphony), this passage, too, reads as a description of *Doctor Faustus*. It might seem misleading to call a novel filled with such shattering events "undynamic" and "without drama." But seen from the outside, the life of the main character is undramatic, and the different stages of his life can easily be compared to concentric circles or, as Mann expresses it in the sentence following our quotation, to a "mammoth variation-piece" on one and the same theme. The repetitions of the parent figures, the dog, the brother and sister, the old tree and the pond with ice cold water are variations verging on identity. The same is true of the different intellectual milieus with which Adrian comes in contact. The Winfried Society's nationalism recurs in the Kridwiss circle, and the combination of the demonic with medieval hysteria follows Adrian from Kaisersaschern to Halle, is interpreted in the interview with the devil, and finally manifests itself in the pre-Nazi circles in the Munich of the 1920's. Variation or identity: the definition may be left up to individual taste; at all events, this compositional principle forms the basis of Mann's version of history as recurrence. In an external sense as well the novel displays variations and concentric circles, for what else are some of the leitmotifs? In the true leitmotif, after all, the same succession of notes or the same turn of phrase reappears unchanged in different contexts, and Mann follows this practice in his earlier works. In *Doctor Faustus*, however, most of the leitmotifs undergo an often highly significant metamorphosis. The development of the Hetaera motif fits the metaphor of the concentric circles. Spreading out from the center — Jonathan Leverkühn's illustrated work on tropical butterflies — the variations pass through wider and wider circles, through the prostitute and the infection to demonic inspiration, and finally to syphilitic paralysis and apocalyptic doom.

The different variational movements in the *Lamentation* "correspond to the textual units of chapters of a book" (487).* The "book" is, of course, the old chapbook, and here Zeitblom's analysis need not be decoded, for it applies directly to the novel.[38] One sentence from the "Oratio Fausti ad Studiosos" in the chapbook forms the thematic core of the *Lamentation*: "These words: 'For I die as a good and as a bad Christian,' form the general theme of the variations" (487). Mann allows Zeitblom to point out that this sentence has exactly twelve syllables, corresponding to the twelve tones that form the musical basis of the composition. Mann borrowed this scheme from Schönberg, and it cannot be transferred literally to the novel, but symbolically it is as appropriate to the novel as to the oratorio. Of the theme Zeitblom says: "It is the basis of all the music — or rather, it lies almost as key behind everything and is responsible for the identity of the most varied forms — that identity which exists between the crystalline angelic choir and the hellish yelling in the *Apocalypse*." (487)

This identity manifests itself on a different level from the identity discussed above. We are no longer dealing with questions of form but with the identity of two moral and metaphysical poles — of good and evil, heaven and hell. There can

---

* Translator's note: Mann actually says, "of the book."
38. The table on p. 47 indicates how closely the events of the chapbook coincide in their sequence with those of *DF*.

be no doubt that this identity is present in *Doctor Faustus,* but Mann's convoluted manner of expression surrounds this fact with deepest secrecy. When tracking it down, we can begin with the conversations in which identity is treated as an abstract problem. Another aspect of the problem appears under the heading of "ambiguity," a recurrent motif in the novel. For example, in his early experiments with modulations Adrian is already enthralled by the ambiguity of the different notes: they take on different functions according to the harmonic context. Adrian comments cogently: "Music turns the equivocal into a system" (47). This idea recurs when Mann says of the *Apocalypse* oratorio that it reveals "the profoundest mystery of this music, which is a mystery of identity" (378).

Such statements provide hints similar to those in the analysis of the *Lamentation.* But the issue of identity is not really discussed in the novel; it is rather to be found in the novel's very structure. Here, as in the *Lamentation,* we are dealing with the identity of opposites. We have already used the terms "good and evil, heaven and hell," but these oppositions also occur in a more concrete form. While working on his novel Mann was not so much concerned with the philosophical and religious problem of good and evil as with the relationship between the good and the bad Germany and with the hold his two-faced country had on him. He saw himself forced to admit the dreadful truth that the bad Germany could not be dissociated from the good Germany: the two were identical, and he had to accept and cope with both these sides of Germany. We have already discussed the inner struggle that preceded this realization. In the novel his thoughts and experiences find their most direct expression in the figure of Adrian Leverkühn, who unites within himself both poles. But Adrian is not the only instance of identity; Zeitblom is another, and he and Adrian possess in addition a secret identity with each other. Mann speaks in *The Story of a Novel* of the "two protagonists who had too much to conceal, namely, the secret of their being identical with each other." [39] This is not the place to ask whether the words "For I die as a good and as a bad Christian" imply a Christian attitude on Mann's part, but both Adrian Leverkühn and Thomas Mann could say, "I die as a bad and as a good German."

Zeitblom remarks of the motif of identity in the *Lamentation,* "It already occurs and makes itself felt long before it is reintroduced with the text, in its place as a choral group —

39. P. 90.

there is no true solo in the *Faustus* — rising up until the middle, then descending, in the spirit and inflexion of the Monteverdi *Lamento*" (487). As we have just seen, examples of identity and ambiguity appear as motifs and as a principle of structure from the very beginning of the novel, but an explicit formulation of this principle does not come until the interview with the devil, where it is "reintroduced with the text." Thus for instance the ambiguity of music, which early in the novel reveals itself on a simple technical level as the variation in the identity of a given note according to its context, takes on in Adrian's discussion with the devil the dimensions of an intellectual problem that embraces all the issues in the novel:

A highly theological business, music — the way sin is, the way I am. The passion of that Christian for music is true passion, and as such knowledge and corruption in one. For there is true passion only in the ambiguous and ironic. The highest passion concerns the absolutely questionable. [242]

This twofold attitude toward music is in fact one characteristic of Adrian, who combines hot intensity with cold irony. At the core of Adrian's nature is an ambiguity or biopolarity that dissolves into an all inclusive identity on the moral and metaphysical plane. We see it most clearly in the interview with the devil, when the external split into two voices becomes a symbol of inner schism. And since the discussion occupies the exact center of the novel, one can easily connect Zeitblom's words "rising up until the middle" with the novel itself.

We must also elucidate the interpolation that "there is no true solo" in the *Lamentation*. We might be inclined to think that Mann would include such a detail for the sake of musical accuracy if it were not that the statement is so emphatic as to imply a broader applicability.

If we visualize a novel as a major piece of music with vocal and instrumental passages, the solo passages would be represented by the single voices, that is, the individual characters and their plights. In this sense *Doctor Faustus* would contain numerous solos; however, our earlier examination showed that many of the individual characters are composites of various sources. This is true first and foremost of the central character, whom one might compare to a chorus — a chorus of voices from German intellectual history. The same might be said for many other characters, although to a lesser degree; as individuals they live in the Halle or Munich of the twentieth century, but their names reveal them to be echoes from the past.

191

Some characters in the novel are unequivocal insofar as they are modeled after a real person; this is the case with Ines and Clarissa Rodde, portraits of Mann's sisters Julia and Carla. Yet even here, the characters' fates are so typical for their times that they come to stand for an entire generation, losing their claim to being solo voices. These dissolute daughters of a decadent bourgeoisie represent a type that we repeatedly encounter in the literature of the early twentieth century, Mann's early works included. Ines' creeping spiritual malady, her experiments with drugs, and Clarissa's macabre games with death are typical examples of the phenomena to which the decadents devoted themselves. Once we realize what these characters personify, Mann's use of such intimate and personal details becomes more comprehensible.

We have already mentioned the metaphysical issues raised by Zeitblom's long passage on the twelve-syllable sentence, "For I die as a good and as a bad Christian." But we find in addition that Zeitblom's remarks on the technicalities of the composition help interpret the novel. He offers one of the most trenchant descriptions of the "strict style" principle:

. . . a formal treatment strict to the last degree, which no longer knows anything unthematic, in which the order of the basic material becomes total, and within which the idea of a fugue rather declines into an absurdity, just because there is no longer any free note. But it now serves a higher purpose; for — oh, marvel, oh, deep diabolic jest! — just by virtue of the absoluteness of the form the music is, as language, freed. [488]

Here we again encounter the concept of "break-through" in art. Previously it was an ideal, something to strive for; in the *Lamentation* it is realized, just as the novel realizes a similar paradox: the objective — historical reality and a concrete body of material — becomes the vehicle of extreme subjective expressiveness.

From the idea of subjective expressiveness Zeitblom reverts to the idea of lament. The next part of his analysis begins as follows:

But precisely in the sense of résumé there are offered musical moments of the greatest conceivable possibility of expression: not as mechanical imitation or regression, of course; no, it is like a perfectly conscious control over all the "characters" of expressiveness which have ever been precipitated in the history of music, and which here, in a sort of alchemical process of distillation, have been refined to fundamental types of emotional significance, and crystallized. [488]

192

It is tempting to quote here what Mann said at his Frankfurt address in 1949 for the two hundredth celebration of Goethe's birth. He gives a detailed account of his own life and work during the years of exile and confesses that his literary activity "tended precisely in these years more and more toward a conscious linguistic construct, toward experimental pleasure in pulling all the stops of our language's wonderful organ, toward an effort at once to recapitulate and to advance the state of the German language and of the expressive possibilities of German prose." [40] The "wonderful organ" probably refers to the range of styles and periods in the German tradition. As we have shown, *Doctor Faustus* contains reminiscences of several different periods in the history of the German language. Some of Echo's speech patterns and prayers revive the Middle High German of the thirteenth century, and the allusions to Hartmann von Aue suggest approximately the same period.[41] Large sections of the novel take their tone from the language of the Reformation period, sometimes via direct quotations from Luther's writings or from the Faust chapbook. The seventeenth century is represented by quotations from *Simplicissimus*.[42] It is harder to discover stylistic and linguistic features that belong definitely to the eighteenth or nineteenth century, but there are occasional direct quotations, as well as stylistic parodies, Mann's version of the murky abstractions of philosophical dialectics, for example.[43]

Later in his analysis Zeitblom speaks of "suspensions," of "chromatic melody," "falling intervals," and "dying-away declamations" (488–89). In a very general sense these expres-

40. "Frankfurter Ansprache im Goethe-Jahr," *Altes und Neues* (hereafter cited as *AN*), p. 417.

41. This is pointed out by Erika Wirtz, "Zitat und Leitmotiv bei Thomas Mann," p. 127. Cf. what Mann says about Nepomuk's function of "invoking a form of language even earlier than the Lutheran, i.e., Middle High German" (*Briefwechsel Thomas Mann / Robert Faesi*, p. 110, letter dated May 11, 1955).

42. See G. Orton, "The Archaic Language in Thomas Mann's 'Doctor Faustus,'" p. 71.

43. It would be interesting to interpret *DF* as a conscious "recapitulation" of different types of novel from romanticism on, including the realistic novel, the naturalistic novel, the symbolistic novel and the experimental novel of our own times. However, Mann nowhere suggests anything to support such a proceeding; on the contrary he is skeptical of any rigid "schematic" distinctions between literary forms and genres ("Die Kunst des Romans," [1939], *AN*, pp. 387–88). The preliminary steps to such an interpretation can be found in Mayer (*Von Lessing bis Thomas Mann*, p. 403), who sees *DF* as "a retraction of *Wilhelm Meister*."

sions belong to the theme of lament, but the concepts seem to owe more to Adorno than to Mann's thematic intentions.[44]

More fruitful than trying to account for each of Zeitblom's descriptive phrases is to examine correspondences between sections of the novel and the movements of the cantata. Instead of giving a blow-by-blow account of the *Lamentation*, Zeitblom concentrates his detailed analysis on the high points. One of the early movements is the "cynical choral scherzo, wherein 'the evil spirit sets to at the gloomy Faustus with strange mocking jests and saying'— that frightful 'then silence, suffer, keepe faith, abstain; of thy ill lot to none complayne; it is too late, of Gode despair, thy ill luck runneth everywhere' " (489). This description reminds us primarily of Chapter 25, Adrian's conversation with the devil, a conversation at once cynical and full of macabre humor. This chapter is extremely "choral" in the sense suggested above: out of Adrian speaks a chorus of voices: the chapbook, Hugo Wolf, Nietzsche.[45] Evidence that the Scherzo may legitimately be equated with Chapter 25 is the little verse that provides the text for the Scherzo: "Then silence, suffer. . . ." This verse was found by Mann in Scheible's edition of the chapbook, and it begins with the words "Whist!, mum's the word," the very words with which Adrian begins his account of the conversation with the devil (222).[46]

We never learn precisely where the Scherzo occurs in the *Lamentation*, but for the last three movements Zeitblom gives full particulars. After "an orchestral piece in the form of grand ballet-music" comes a "tragic chorus, *a capella*," which gradually gives way to a purely orchestral adagio (489). The first of these three movements is described as a "gallop of fantastic rhythmic variety," an "orgy of infernal jollity" (489). This description indicates a long section in which several figures execute their dances to different rhythms. The ballet music recalls "the spirit of the *Apocalypsis*" (489); all these details

44. Cf., however, "Goethe and Tolstoy," (1922): "But the really fruitful, the productive, and hence the artistic principle is that which we call reserve. In the sphere of music we love it as the painful pleasure of the prolonged note. . . . In the intellectual sphere we love it as irony." (*Essays of Three Decades*, p. 173). Without mentioning this passage from the analysis of the *Lamentation*, Mayer (*Thomas Mann*, p. 345–46) uses the musical analogy: he sees Adrian's study of theology as a sort of "prolonged note" building up to the predetermined "key," i.e., Adrian's vocation to be a composer. M. Gregor (*Wagner und kein Ende*, p. 54) likewise sees the irony in Mann's prose style as the equivalent of the Wagnerian prolongation.

45. See above, pp. 48, 68–69, 61–62.

46. J. Scheible, *Das Kloster*, p. 641.

point to the section of the novel in which one character after another seems to step before the footlights and perform his dance of despair. In the second half of the novel Mann devotes several chapters to destinies that touch the central figure only in passing: Ines and Clarissa Rodde's and Rudi Schwerdtfeger's, for example. They all perish, thus becoming actors in the novel's great apocalypse. The music that seems to suggest this portion of the novel is also described as the "wild conception of the carrying-off" (489).

After the orchestral movement in the cantata comes a burst of lamentation by the tragic chorus. We have seen that the direct expression of lament is the echo; perhaps this part of the composition corresponds to the section of the novel that recounts Echo's tragic death. For the chorus gives way to the final movement, a symphonic Adagio undoubtedly equivalent to the end of the novel. Since Zeitblom returns later to this last movement, we shall withhold our interpretation for a while.

In a somewhat perplexing phrase, Zeitblom states that the *Lamentation* is a work "without parody" (489). *Doctor Faustus* is widely considered the culmination of Mann's parodistic art of narrative, and one critic who considers reading the *Lamentation* and the novel as parallels feels that this phrase makes the whole undertaking questionable. His only way to avoid such a conclusion is to submit that *Doctor Faustus* is "plainly parodistic in style" but utterly earnest in its basic attitude.[47] This interpretation strikes us as plausible; it is confirmed by Zeitblom's remark that the *Lamentation* is "as a whole" "darker in tone" than Adrian's earlier works, which were plainly parodistic (489).

Following his remark that the various lesser voices are dependent on the main part — a formulation directly relevant to the novel — Zeitblom points out a symbolic leitmotif:

Long ago I said in these pages that in *Faustus* too that letter symbol, the Hetaera-Esmeralda figure, first perceived by me, very often governs melody and harmony: that is to say, everywhere where there is reference to the bond and the vow, the promise and the blood pact. [489]

In the novel, too, the Hetaera motif occurs in connection with the pact. The contract is concluded in the brothel episode, and the Hetaera is mentioned both in the conversation with the devil (248) and in Adrian's farewell speech (498); at both times "there is reference to . . . the promise and the blood pact."

47. Williams, "Thomas Mann's 'Doctor Faustus,'" p. 277.

The next stage of Zeitblom's analysis deals with the relation of chorus and orchestra in the *Lamentation*:

Above all the *Faust* cantata is distinguished from the *Apocalypse* by its great orchestral interludes, which sometimes only express in general the attitude of the work to its subject, a statement, "Thus it is." But sometimes, like the awful ballet-music of the descent to hell, they also stand for parts of the plot. [489]

We might be tempted to equate the orchestral parts of the *Lamentation* with the descriptions of music in the novel, construing the *Lamentation* chapter as a "Thus it is" with respect to the whole novel. But far too many factors interfere with such an interpretation. The orchestral parts stand, rather, for sections of the action, as the ballet music stands for the series of personal catastrophes in the second half of the book.

One might alternatively interpret the choral passages of the oratorio as equivalent to the individual, personal level of the novel, while the orchestral parts stand for the symbol level. The following passage on the *Apocalypsis cum figuris*, which anticipates the *Lamentation* in many respects, suggests that such an interpretation is valid:

Chorus and orchestra are here not clearly separated from each other as symbols of the human and the material world; they merge into each other, the chorus is "instrumentalized," the orchestra as it were "vocalized," to that degree and to that end that the boundary between man and thing seems shifted. [375]

Mann added this passage after the manuscript was already typed, which indicates that he was especially anxious to clarify this relationship between chorus and orchestra. When applied to the novel, this description suggests that the distinctions between the individual, personal and the representative or symbolic become blurred; this, indeed, proves the case with most of the figures in the novel. For the *Apocalypse*, Zeitblom's example of this blurring is the part of the whore of Babylon, sung by a coloratura soprano whose flutelike notes occasionally blend completely into the orchestra. This precisely conveys the role of the Hetaera esmeralda in the novel. Her individual personality merges more and more with the symbolic, "orchestral" aspect of the novel. On the other hand, the "singing of the devils" is accompanied by a small orchestra in which the saxophone and trumpet "suggest a grotesque vox humana" (375). In *Doctor Faustus* the devil, who belongs primarily to the symbolic, that is, orchestral level, speaks in a strikingly human voice during his grotesque conversation with Adrian.

The difference between chorus and orchestra affects far more than the technical aspects of composition. It becomes part of the chain of antitheses that belongs to Adrian's very essence and thereby to the essence of the novel: the chorus, the real vox humana, usually stands for human warmth; in the *Lamentation* it is destroyed:

> Purely orchestral is the end: a symphonic adagio, into which the chorus of lament, opening powerfully after the infernal gallop, gradually passes over — it is, as it were, the reverse of the "Ode to Joy," the negative, equally a work of genius, of that transition of the symphony into vocal jubilation. It is the revocation. [489–90]

When Zeitblom examines the relation of the *Lamentation* to the Ninth Symphony, he leaves all technical considerations aside and dwells instead on the ethical and metaphysical implications of the cantata. He recalls what Adrian said at Echo's death — "Alas, it is not to be" — detecting in it a negative form of religious feeling (490). We have already discussed the meaning of the motto, and the rest of this part of the analysis applies directly to the novel. In metaphysical or religious matters Mann had no reason to preserve a distinction between music and literature; he could dispense with musical terminology.

In the *Lamentation* the "negative form of religious feeling" takes on flesh and blood in the negative image of Christ presented by Faustus. The legendary Faust's leave-taking from his friends is described as "another Last Supper" (490), and we are supposed to see Adrian's leave-taking in the same light. Toward the end of the book Adrian's Christlike features are much stressed. One episode in the *Lamentation* is a reversed allusion to Christ in the Garden of Gethsemane:

> What I mean is a conversion, a proud and bitter change of heart, as I, at least, read it in the "friendly plea" of Dr. Faustus to the companions of his last hour, that they should betake themselves to bed, *sleep in peace*, and let naught trouble them. In the frame of the cantata one can scarcely help recognizing this instruction as the conscious and deliberate reversal of the "Watch with me" of Gethsemane. [490]

This passage suggests, along with the biblical reference, a motif from one of Kretschmar's lectures on Beethoven in Chapter 8; after describing Beethoven's struggles with the fugue in the Credo of the *Missa Solemnis*, he tells the anecdote of how Beethoven leaves his room in the middle of the night after hours of intensive work and asks for something to eat. When he finds the maids asleep, he bursts out, "Could you not watch one hour with me?" (58) This episode points up Adrian's negative relation to Beethoven. Adrian and Beethoven both allude to Jesus' words in Gethsemane, but Adrian's allusion is bitterly satiric, in the spirit of the chapbook.

Although Adrian considers himself a fiendish spirit of negation, Zeitblom searches to the last for signs of a more human attitude. At the beginning of the last chapter Zeitblom reverts to the Gethsemane motif. He accepts the fact that Adrian's work represents the reversal of Jesus' words, but he interprets Adrian's desire to gather his friends around him once more as an expression of his deeply human fear of solitude. "But the human remains, after all: the instinctive longing, if not for aid, then certainly for the presence of human sympathy, the plea: 'Forsake me not! Be with me at my hour!' " (492).

Zeitblom subsequently draws a parallel between the historical Dr. Faustus and Christ. Like Christ, Faustus is subjected to temptation, but in his case it is

an inversion of the temptation idea, in such a way that Faust rejects as temptation the thought of being saved: not only out of formal loyalty to the pact and because it is "too late," but because with his whole soul he despises the positivism of the world for which one would save him, the lie of its godliness. [490]

Within the novel we have an example of this type of salvation attempt: Rudi Schwerdtfeger's request that Adrian should write a violin concerto for him; the result would be that Adrian's music would reach a broad public, thus bringing Adrian into positive contact with the world. Zeitblom considers this proposal an effort at seduction, although he immediately modifies the expression and speaks of "an impudent intrusion of familiarity upon solitude" (351). Seduction is implicit in the scene at an artist's gala in Munich when the violin concerto is first mentioned. Rudi takes Adrian's arm in what Zeitblom considers a forward manner and strolls around the hall with him. Adrian is perfectly aware of Rudi's intentions: " 'What he wants,' he responded, 'is that I should write a violin concerto for him with which he can be heard in the provinces.' " (203)*
Adrian, with his aristocratic arrogance, takes offense at the idea of his becoming widely known, and he reassures Clarissa, who fears that he might accede to Rudi's wish: " 'You have too high an opinion of my flexibility,' he retorted, and had Baptist Spengler's bleating laugh on his side" (204). Spengler's

* Translator's note: "make a name for himself in the provinces" is closer to the original.

goatlike laughter foreshadows our later discovery that he is one of the devil's chosen ones (232).

The idea of reversed temptation emerges more clearly later on in the *Lamentation* "in the scene with the good old doctor and neighbor who invites Faust to come to see him, in order to make a pious effort to convert him. In the cantata he is clearly drawn in the character of a tempter (490)." In the novel the impresario Saul Fitelberg fills the description of a tempter who energetically tries to lure Adrian out of his solitude and into contact with the world; he has unmistakably satanic features: the Hetaera's almond-shaped eyes (399, cf. 142) and the devil's tortoiseshell rimmed glasses (399, cf. 238). Zeitblom remarks of the old neighbor: "the tempting of Jesus by Satan is unmistakably suggested" (490). If it is permissible to read the *Lamentation* as a description of *Doctor Faustus*, Fitelberg's visit to Adrian should certainly contain an allusion to Satan's visit to Jesus, and that proves in fact to be the case. Fitelberg announces frankly that he has come to tempt Adrian, "to bear you on my mantle through the air and show you the kingdoms of the earth and the glory of them." (400). The biblical allusion is obvious: "Again, the devil taketh him up into an exceeding high mountain, and sheweth him all the kingdoms of the world, and the glory of them" (Matt. 4:8). Here the parallel between the *Lamentation* and *Doctor Faustus* becomes unmistakable.

The last part of Zeitblom's analysis of the *Lamentation* ignores technicalities and dwells on the spiritual or metaphysical connotations of the final movement. Again we think we are reading a description of the novel:

But another and last, truly the last change of mind must be thought on, and that profoundly. At the end of this work of endless lamentation, softly, above the reason and with the speaking unspokenness given to music alone, it touches the feelings. [490]

Thomas Mann here suggests that some things can be expressed by "music alone," and are thus closed to interpretation. But since Mann has constructed *Doctor Faustus* according to musical principles, we may conclude that he hoped to endow the end of the novel with something of that "speaking unspokenness" usually reserved for music. And indeed, this formulation seems to do justice to the final pages of the novel. To the very end Mann leaves the door open to varying interpretations; there has been great controversy over whether the novel ends on a note of hope or despair. We shall say more about the religious implications of the novel in our last chapter; here we must point out a few more details in the last movement that correspond to features of the novel.

By suppressing the human voice, Adrian makes the purely instrumental final movement of the *Lamentation* retract the Ninth Symphony. But not only the human voice is silenced: gradually the orchestra falls silent: "one group of instruments after another retires, and what remains, as the work fades on the air, is the high G of a cello, the last word, the last fainting sound, dying in a pianissimo-fermata" (491). It is not difficult to find an equivalent in the novel. In the last section all the voices but one have been silenced; the only one left is the lonely man whose last words die away like a musical note. The solitary cello note is called "the last *word.*" The meaning is plainly figurative, since there is no vocal part at the end of the cantata. If the last note can be called a word, the cantata and the novel clearly become interchangeable.[48] Finally, we have a word-for-word correspondence between the end of the oratorio and the end of the novel. Zeitblom says in concluding his analysis: "It would be but a hope beyond hopelessness, the transcendence of despair . . . the miracle that passes belief" (491). And in the last paragraph of the novel Zeitblom asks: "When, out of uttermost hopelessness — a miracle beyond the power of belief — will the light of hope dawn?" (510). Both passages link the idea of hope with light; the last note of the *Lamentation* is likened to a "light in the night" (491).[49]

48. Heim ("Thomas Mann," p. 309) interprets the last G as a symbol of the word "grace."

49. R. Engländer ("Thomas Manns Faustusroman som musikalisk spegelbild," p. 24) sees the end of the *Lamentation* as an allusion to the last bars of Mahler's *Lied von der Erde.* Kretschmar's analysis of Beethoven's Op. 111 seems to anticipate an important element in the analysis of the *Lamentation.* Heim ("Thomas Mann," p. 309) sees a connection between the last high cello note of the *Lamentation* and the meaning-laden C-sharp that Beethoven adds to the Arietta theme at the end of the last movement. Certainly the metaphysical significance attributed to each of the two notes corresponds in many ways, although the C-sharp is not the last note of the sonata. In Kretschmar's interpretation this C-sharp acquires broad spiritual implications: he calls it the "most moving, consolatory, pathetically reconciling thing in the world" (55). This note raises the composition to a higher, almost religious level, which is also reflected in the words with which Kretschmar scans the theme; "Friendly be to me" (55) for example would be a prayer by the composer which Beethoven would be justified in uttering after all he had inflicted, according to Mann's interpretation, on the theme. Zeitblom likewise says of the last movement of the *Lamentation* that it "sounds like the lament of God over the lost state of His world, like the Creator's rueful 'I have not willed it'" (491).

6

Religious Implications of Doctor Faustus

PSYCHOLOGY OR METAPHYSICS?

If we assume that Zeitblom's commentary on the end of *The Lamentation of Dr. Faustus* can be carried over to the novel *Doctor Faustus*, then the novel ends with a religious question: is Adrian condemned eternally to darkness and damnation, or will the light of mercy and reconciliation fall upon him and all that he stands for? The critics and scholars vary so widely in their answers to these questions that one sometimes wonders whether they are discussing the same book. The reason for this divergence of opinion undoubtedly lies in the deep and intentional ambiguity of the novel; the reader can easily impose his own convictions and opinions on *Doctor Faustus*.

Critical discussion of the religious issue in *Doctor Faustus* was spearheaded by Hans Egon Holthusen's study "Die Welt ohne Transzendenz" ["World without Transcendence"] of 1949.[1] As the title indicates, Holthusen denies Mann's works a religious dimension. He contends that all religious terms have lost their true significance for Mann and become secularized. Metaphysical yearning is completely alien to Mann. Holthusen argues that no one can really believe in sin once he has suspended the polarity between God and the devil; Holthusen considers the devil in *Doctor Faustus* a simple psychological projection and not a metaphysical reality; words like "Tempter," "damnation," and so on are either meaningless or

1. H. E. Holthusen, "Die Welt ohne Transzendenz," *Merkur* 3 (1949), 38–58, 161–80. Also published in book form with the same title. We find the same attitude in W. Muschg, who sees Mann as a complete nihilist (*Tragische Literaturgeschichte*, p. 425–26), and in A. White, who holds that the religious terminology occasionally used by Mann — "evil," "the sinful," "grace," etc. — is an empty shell that "contains no pearls when opened" ("Die Verfluchten und die Gesegneten: eine Studie über die Helden Thomas Manns als Betreter des Verbotenen und Vertreter des Bösen," p. 154). Of the many essays and notes that deal with Holthusen's argument we mention only A. Bauer's "Thomas Mann und seine Widersacher," and B. Blume's "Perspektiven des Widerspruchs: zur Kritik an Thomas Mann."

good only for creating atmosphere. Holthusen calls it theologically absurd that a whole people should literally go to the devil; he even refuses to admit that Mann's book is in any way moving or convincing.

Holthusen owes much to Erich Kahler's excellent study, "Die Säkularisierung des Teufels" ["The Secularization of the Devil"] of 1948, the title of which has become a slogan in Mann criticism. Kahler's position is by no means so extreme as Holthusen's, and in fact he later condemned Holthusen's one-sided interpretation of *Doctor Faustus*. In his commemorative address for Thomas Mann [2] (1956) Kahler explains that Mann's work is characterized by an "immanent transcendence, transcendence born of the intellectual view." [3] There are many similar interpretations of *Doctor Faustus*. [4] Walter Berendsohn speaks of a marked religiousness free of denominationalism, [5] and E. C. Regula comes to the conclusion that disease is presented in *Doctor Faustus* in terms of purely religious concepts. [6] Olschewski, Hilscher, Yourcenar, and many others offer vaguely religious interpretations. [7]

Other critics, however, are not satisfied with picking out a generally religious tone; they want to establish that Mann's work has definitely Christian features. Thus Anna Hellersberg-Wendriner mentions the "basically Christian orientation of Mann," [8] and Helmuth Burgert speaks of his "concealed Christianity." [9] Sagave interprets the end of *Doctor Faustus* in a similar sense as "une espérance chrétienne" ["Christian expectation of salvation"]. [10]

2. E. Kahler, "Säkularisierung des Teufels: Thomas Manns Faust."

3. E. Kahler, "Gedenkrede auf Thomas Mann," p. 547.

4. See for example L. Leibrich, "Expérience et philosophie de la vie chez Thomas Mann," pp. 303–4; G. W. Field, "Music and Morality in Thomas Mann and Hermann Hesse," p. 178; W. Prinzing, *Stil der Schwebe im "Doktor Faustus*," pp. 59, 67–67. Cf. W. Grenzmann, *Dichtung und Glaube* pp. 64–65.

5 Berendsohn, "Faustsage und Faustdichtung," p. 378.

6. Regula, "Die Darstellung und Problematik der Krankheit im Werke Thomas Manns," p. 286, 300.

7. H. Olschewski, " 'Doktor Faustus' von Thomas Mann," pp. 135, 140; E. Hilscher, "Thomas Manns Religiosität," pp. 289–90; M. Yourcenar, "Humanism in Thomas Mann, p. 162.

8. Hellersberg-Wendriner, *Mystik der Gottesferne*, p. 5. She argues that Mann appears only superficially a naturalist: she wants him counted one of the "dynasty of the German mystics" (p. 6).

9. Burgert, "Verborgene Christlichkeit," p. 340.

10. P.-P. Sagave, *Réalité sociale et idéologie religieuse dans les romans de Thomas Mann*, p. 127.

If the novel is really so ambiguous as these contrary interpretations seem to indicate, the attempt to achieve final clarity may be hopeless. However, certain pointers both in the novel and in Mann's statements about it have not been sufficiently taken to heart; they justify a fresh investigation of the religious meaning of the novel. But first we shall examine briefly the obvious religious motifs and concepts in *Doctor Faustus* upon which most previous attempts to interpret the novel according to religious categories are based.

The Faust motif is at home in a realm that deserves to be designated as religious: the realm of the devil and the demonic. Throughout the novel we encounter appropriate motifs. When the devil appears and concludes the pact, he simply puts the seal of inevitability on a progression that begins with Jonathan Leverkühn's experiments, continues with Schleppfuss and his lectures, with Adrian's visit to the brothel, with the descent into the ocean and the journey to the stars and reaches its tragic end in Adrian's phantasizing as his mind gives way. But all these manifestations of the demonic are laid before us by the skeptical humanist Zeitblom, who would love to dismiss the possibility that Adrian's hallucination might be a reality (221), but who also speaks quite matter-of-factly of the "powers of darkness" (4) and the "nether world" (4). He wavers between the skeptical theory that the devil is a psychic projection of Adrian's and a secret fear that evil exists as a real figure and a destructive power.[11] By giving the novel two protagonists and projecting himself into two contrasting figures, Mann is able to remain faithful to his aesthetic canon of irony and to illuminate all the important issues in the novel from two sides; this explains why critics in search of Mann's "true" opinion are usually baffled. While the humanist Zeitblom skeptically notes the psychological phenomena connected with the demonic and comments upon them, Adrian reveals a passionate commitment to the issue of guilt and retribution.

Adrian broods over religious questions all his life, revealing what Mann considers a German characteristic, the theological

11. Compare Zeitblom's words, "I shudder at the admission which lies in the very words, seeming even conditionally and as a possibility to entertain his actuality . . ." (p. 221) with Mann's own statement (quoted by de Buisonjé in "Bemerkungen über Thomas Manns Werk: Doktor Faustus," p. 196): "From the very beginning the devil makes his presence felt in the novel, but appears personally to arrange the pact in the middle. Zeitblom tries not to believe in his reality. So do I."

bent. Adrian's childhood environment, which represents historically the transitional Reformation period, harbors the three faiths that have shaped Germany's intellectual and social development: Catholicism, personified by Zeitblom and his family, Protestantism, the faith of the Leverkühn family, and Judaism, embodied in the rabbi Dr. Carlebach (7). The Jewish element later emerges as a definite force in the figures of Fitelberg and Dr. Chaim Breisacher; as we saw earlier, Mann felt that the Jews' fate as the chosen and guilty people formed a parallel to the Germans.[12] But *Doctor Faustus* is not only a book about Germany; it is also a personal confession. Mann himself was raised as a Protestant, gained entrance to a Jewish family by his marriage to Katia Pringsheim, and lived in Catholic Munich during most of his adult life before the emigration.

We saw that Mann alludes in the chapters on Halle to some of the more important phases of Germany's religious and theological development. Adrian seldom takes part in the theological discussions, but when he speaks, it is with a decided bias toward orthodoxy and restraint (for example, 119). Zeitblom, on the other hand, explains that, although he is not indifferent to religion, he thinks it a dubious undertaking to construct scientific systems on the basis of religious feeling (88). In the novel Mann portrays music and theology as related disciplines with a parallel evolution; thus Adrian's shift from theology to music by no means indicates a break with his earlier religious preoccupations. On the contrary, as time goes by his religious brooding deepens, and he now chooses the Bible and the legends of the saints as sources of texts for the *Apocalypsis cum Figuris* and the *Gesta* Suite. In the last phase of his creative life Adrian seems obsessed with the idea of sin and retribution. In the interview with the devil he already suggests the audacious but genuinely Lutheran idea that the greater the sinner, the closer he is to divine grace. " 'A capacity for sin so healless that it makes its man despair from his heart of redemption — that is the true theological way to salvation' " (247). But gradually this defiant speculating with divine grace, familiar to us from Schleppfuss's lectures, gives way to the conviction that precisely this attitude constitutes the unforgivable sin (502). Still, Adrian's last composition, the *Lamentation*, enshrines the thought that good and evil are profoundly akin; the whole

12. See above, p. 126–27.

work is after all based on the sentence, "For I die as a good and as a bad Christian" (487).

On the other hand, it is the skeptical Zeitblom who interprets the end of the oratorio as a suggestion of grace. While Adrian feels himself at the end to be irredeemable, he becomes in Zeitblom's eyes a martyr and almost a savior. Zeitblom stresses his likeness to Christ (for example, 483), and Adrian's farewell from his friends becomes, in the spirit of the chapbook, a sort of Last Supper.[13] But the expression "Ecce-homo countenance" (509) calls up twofold associations; Adrian is not only a suffering martyr but also, like Nietzsche, the victim of megalomania. Thus Mann simultaneously provides a psychological explanation, as if he were intentionally avoiding anything that would permit an unequivocal interpretation of the book as religious. Sometimes he seems deliberately to draw on religious associations in order to increase the pathos of his narrative. Echo's fate, for example, strikes us as all the more terrible, precisely because the boy's prayers emphasize his angelic nature.

But Zeitblom allows certain details to pass without comment, and these most critics have overlooked. In the discussion of breakthrough in Chapter 30 Zeitblom offers a definition of Germanness that touches Adrian to the quick: " 'threatened with envelopment, the poison of isolation, provincial boorishness, neurosis, implicit Satanism . . .' " (308). Here Zeitblom is brought up short in his tirade by Adrian's expression, "the look, the familiar one," which Zeitblom always finds distant and insulting and which is always followed by a scornful smile. Adrian gets up, silent but shaken: "He moved away from the table, not toward Schildknapp, but to the window niche, where he had hung a saint's picture on the panelling" (308) * Such a precise description of Adrian's behavior strikes the reader as strange, and one wonders at its significance, since it occurs during an episode in which some of the central issues of the novel are touched upon. Adrian and Zeitblom have been discussing the idea of breakthrough, building on Kleist's idea that the artist must pass through the stage of reflection, "through an infinity," in order to achieve the gracefulness that is indigenous only to God and the marionette (308). Zeitblom defines the matter as more than a simple aesthetic problem. He sees broader

* Translator's note: Mann actually says, "straightened a picture of a saint."

13. Adrian's curious imitatio Christi is pointed out by W. Boehlich in his review of *Doctor Faustus* (hereafter cited as *DF*) in *Merkur*, 2 (1948), 595–96.

implications to the question of "release or lack of it"; in the last analysis it forms a part of the "craving to break through from bondage" that he considers uniquely German, in fact the definition of Germanness. Zeitblom's thoughts anticipate the questions raised by the end of the novel (485). In this context, Adrian's behavior becomes very meaningful when without any obvious motivation he goes over to the window and straightens a portrait of a saint. This seemingly involuntary act reveals that Adrian's concern is not aesthetic or national but religious; it is the question of his salvation.

In another, more agitated scene that takes place in the same room, Adrian lashes out at the devil for the suffering being imposed on Echo, and he begs the devil to put a quick end to the torture.

And he sprang up, stood against the wall, and leaned the back of his head against the paneling. "Take him, monster!" he cried, in a voice that pierced me to the marrow. "Take him, hell-hound, but make all the haste you can . . . Take him, scum, filth, excrement," he shrieked, and stepped away from me again as though back to the Cross. [477]

The last few words sound like a metaphor, a hasty comparison, but when one bears in mind that Adrian symbolizes Germany, one begins to suspect that Mann intends to suggest a connection between Germany's historical mission and the vicarious sacrifice of Christ. The idea seems rather audacious, and we have no unambiguous proof. Mann did, however, feel that Germany occupied an exceptional position among the nations, that the Germans were a chosen people with a particular "will to suffering." [14] In this case one should not force the analogy between Adrian and Germany, but it is quite obvious that Adrian's mission as an artist does amount to a sort of vicarious sacrifice. Several times Mann stresses Adrian's role as the savior of an art trapped in an insufferable situation. The devil promises Adrian in biblical tones:

You will lead the way, you will strike up the march of the future, the lads will swear by your name, who thanks to your madness will no longer need to be mad. On your madness they will feed in health, and in them you will become healthy. [243]

Adrian himself is aware that his great sin was committed not for its own sake but for the sake of the breakthrough for which contemporary art cries:

14. *Leiden an Deutschland*, p. 55.

But an one invite the divil as guest, to pass beyond all this and get to the break-through, he chargeth his soul and taketh the guilt of the time upon his shoulders, so that he is damned. [499]

Doctor Faustus is thus permeated with religious, not to say Christian, motifs, concepts and symbols. But so far we can draw no conclusions about Mann's own point of view. He undeniably had a profound interest in religious matters — his ten-year preoccupation with motifs from the Old Testament provides ample evidence. But did Mann have a personal concern with religion or was he simply interested in its significance for the German people? A few personal statements from the period when Mann was working on *Doctor Faustus* will cast some light on the question.

Mann's lectures and essays of the early 1940's frequently employ such concepts as "Christian," "God," and "grace," but it is difficult to determine precisely what they meant to him. When we discussed Mann's concept of democracy we discovered that it was so broad that it occasionally seemed to merge with his humanistic belief in the dignity and nobility of man. In a magazine article of 1942, "How to Win the Peace," Mann speaks first of mankind's need for universal norms and then continues:

We may call this ultimate tie "God" or "truth" or "freedom" or "right" — it is all the same. We may simply call it "democracy," a word whose religious overtones, if our ears were ever indifferent to them, are more audible today than ever.[15]

Here Mann's liberal humanistic attitude reveals a clear inclination to pass over into the religious. In another essay of the same period Mann describes the hoped-for new humanism:

It will not disavow its religious traits, for in the idea of human dignity, of the value of the individual soul, humanism transcends into the religious. Concepts like freedom, truth, justice, belong to a trans-biological sphere, the sphere of the Absolute, to the religious sphere.[16]

But Mann is not satisfied with such vague general categories. A return to the fixed system of Christian norms forms the prerequisite for his new religious humanism and provides a means of correcting the chaotic uncertainty that characterizes the present situation. In the same essay he explains:

What needs to be re-established more than anything else are the commandments of religion, of Christianity. . . . From these commandments must be derived the fundamental law under which the peoples

15. "How to Win the Peace," pp. 176–77.
16. "What is German?" p. 85.

of the future will live together and to which all will have to pay reverence.[17]

Many of Mann's statements from this period reiterate the desire or the need for this sort of durable religious bond. Mann points to the disastrous results of excessive freedom and considers that only religious ties provide the necessary balance. His stress on the etymological kinship of "obligation" and "religio" is highly significant in the context of *Doctor Faustus*.

OBLIGATION AND FREEDOM

Mann discusses, in "How to Win the Peace," "those universal ties for which we have the word *religio*, 'religion.' "[18] The tie or bond is thus for Mann an essential component of all religion — and the bond offers an excellent descriptive key to the composition of *Doctor Faustus*. Insofar as we can prove that Mann saw a relationship between the two kinds of bond, considered them somehow two sides of one and the same thing, we can discover an important motive for the aspiration toward "strict style." The principle of strict style according to which both Adrian's *Lamentation* and Mann's own novel are constructed grows out of an inner need that parallels the yearning of modern man to be bound by a fixed spiritual and metaphysical order. Furthermore, if the two kinds of bond are parallel or analogous phenomena, one type — strict artistic form — can serve as a symbol for the other. Thus the aesthetic aspect of the novel can be seen as expressing the intellectual, cultural, and social crisis in Germany that forms the book's theme.[19]

17. *Ibid.* Mann's positive attitude toward Christianity manifests itself quite a bit earlier. See for example the introduction to *Mass und Wert* (*Order of the Day*, tr. H. T. Lowe-Porter, E. Meyer, E. Sutton, pp. 88–104). E. Hilscher, who examines Mann's attitude to Christianity at various times in his career, sees the mid-1920's as a turning point; from then on Mann's interest in religious problems intensifies steadily, culminating in the discussion of purely theological matters in *DF* and *The Holy Sinner*. E. Hilscher also remarks, however, that Mann was always rather reserved toward Christ and the idea of immortality, also remaining critical of any over-dogmatic form of devotion ("Thomas Manns Religiosität").

18. "How to Win the Peace," p. 176.

19. Many scholars argue that when modern art engages in so many experiments in form, it is searching for some order in the chaos that has resulted from life's being robbed of the dimension of eternity. This is E. Muir's premise in "The Decline of the Novel" (in *Essays on Literature and Society*). Muir contends that "there is perhaps only the problem caused

We have already discussed Mann's belief that romanticism and the growth of the bourgeoisie freed subjectivity from all objective systems of norms — cultural, social, political and artistic. According to Mann, the final results of this total subjectivity have not been felt until our century, in which anarchy prevails on all fronts.[20] Deliverance from this chaos can be found only in a new order, a new system of universal norms. The Nazis came to the same conclusion as Mann, and in fact totalitarian dictatorship does offer a system of bonds — but the system was a cruel distortion of Mann's vision. For bonds are not in themselves desirable; what matters is the binding principle. On the basis of this insight Mann steadfastly battled barbarism and dictatorship and urged the cause of bonds founded on a religious humanism. In the early 1940's Mann was sustained by his faith that the just cause would win out in the end, but he was also haunted by disturbing questions: Who could say that Germany had not submitted to dictatorship because of its longing for spiritual leadership and security; was it not a basically good and praiseworthy desire that had led Germany into the terrible error of National Socialism? And if this were the case, how had this transformation of the good Germany into an evil one come about? Who was to blame and what were the underlying causes? Mann tries to settle all these questions in *Doctor Faustus*. Adrian's most notable qualities, his chastity and spirituality, make him easy prey for the forces of temptation. Mann implacably traces Adrian's madness and obsession back to his purity and decency. According to this formula, the best qualities of the German people would also be the basis of the German catastrophe. As we have already discovered, Mann interprets the process as one of "demonization," analagous to the process whereby Adrian's noblest features make him a victim of the powers of darkness.

In *Doctor Faustus* the opposition of obligation and freedom is thus all-pervasive. It has been demonstrated that this pair of concepts forms a consistent motif in the novel,[21] but this

by the lack of a normal and complete order in which existence would have unity and meaning" (p. 145). E. Heller examines the formal strictness of *DF* from a similar standpoint and speaks of "a morality spontaneously resolved to preserve the continuity of form as the symbol and promise of something absolute and indestructible" (*The Ironic German*, p. 25).

20. See for example "Bekenntnis eines Siebzigjährigen: die Ansprache von Thomas Mann an die Zürcher Studentenschaft," p. 11.

21. J. Lesser, *Thomas Mann in der Epoche seiner Vollendung*, pp. 405–10.

motif has not yet been related to the central artistic and intellectual issues of the novel. The questions raised by this motif are extremely complicated, partly because Mann sometimes expresses himself diffusely and with excessive "profundity," partly, too, because the opinions on obligation and freedom are voiced now by Zeitblom, now by Adrian, and it is once more nearly impossible to determine Mann's own position. What we here attempt is simply a rough reconstruction of Mann's general ideas.

Like many others, the motif of obligation versus freedom is foreshadowed in Jonathan Leverkühn's experiments and speculations. The reader is introduced to the perfect geometrical structure of the ice flowers on the windowpanes and to the regular patterns of sand on the glass plate (18). This aspect of the motif reappears several times, for instance in Kretschmar's lecture "Music and the Eye" (60). Early in life Adrian shows an interest in various systems of order, an interest that he expresses as a schoolboy by experimenting with equations and logarithms, modulations and the circle of fifths (45 ff.). The motif acquires additional implications from Kretschmar's lecture on Beissel's composing system based on fixed tables of chords arranged according to the servant-master principle (65). Adrian's remark about Beissel is characteristic: "At least he had a sense of order, and even a silly order is better than none at all' " (68). One critic submits that this statement contains a clear political allusion; Adrian's argument can be invoked to defend any dictatorship, and Beissel is referred to as a "head shepherd" and "spiritual father," (63) and also as a "backwoods dictator" (67).[22]

The exposition of Beissel's theory anticipates Adrian's theory of strict style, which originates, as we have seen, in the inherent necessity for organization and system in music. In connection with strict style Adrian reminds Zeitblom of Beissel's system, and remarks that our times require something similar, "promising a remedy in an age of destroyed conventions and the relaxing of all objective obligations" (189). Adrian considers that only "law, rule, coercion, system" will save art from a subjective freedom that has already outlived itself. Zeitblom uses the political analogy to question Adrian's thesis that absolute obligation to art results in freedom: "But actually she is no longer freedom, as little as dictatorship born out of revolu-

22. *Ibid.*, p. 409.

tion is still freedom" (190). Adrian hastily brings the discussion back to art: "Organization is everything. Without it there is nothing, least of all art" (190). The function of this exchange is to suggest the political parallel to strict form in the arts. When the concept of strict style recurs in the discussion of the *Lamentation*, Mann can treat it as a strictly artistic matter; the reader already has the political implications in mind.

The political side of the motif also emerges clearly when the members of the Winfried Society establish that subjection to a strict social or national system represents an obvious substitute for religion (121–22). This idea evolves further within the Kridwiss circle, whose members advocate might, dictatorship and "despotic tyranny" (366). This ideology, inspired by Sorel's *Réflexions sur la violence*, contains such obvious features of the surrogate for religion as the idea that the masses should be "provided with mythic fictions" (366). In 1947, the year *Doctor Faustus* was published, Mann discusses in a lecture the yearning for a totalitarian system. He explains that with the spiritual vacuum created when the Renaissance and the Enlightenment liberated the Western world from the authority of the Church, "the attractiveness of political totalitarianism" becomes a phenomenon one can well understand. He continues:

And in fact even today one can quite well picture a future race that would no longer understand the concept of freedom that prevailed during the nineteenth century, would no longer yearn for it, and would be perfectly content to move within the given limits and bonds of the total state, with its dictatorial and indisputable principles.[23]

There is no doubt that Mann considers this a terrifying prospect, although he would prefer to subject the individual to such a total state rather than maintain the present "rudderlessness and disorientation." (The question of Mann's attitude toward communism only becomes vital for the last part of his life and cannot be discussed here.[24])

One should beware of interpreting the contrast between obligation and freedom as a strict either-or proposition. On the artistic level the contrast appears as a dialectical antithesis. Adrian accepts the iron discipline of strict style in the belief that total obligation will lead to a new and higher freedom, to intense subjective expression. This thought forms the basis

23. "Bekenntnis eines Siebzigjährigen," pp. 11–12.
24. See K. Sontheimer, *Thomas Mann und die Deutschen*, pp. 154–61.

of the breakthrough concept, realized in Adrian's *Lamentation*, where the twelve-tone method conveys a shattering personal confession. Zeitblom experiences deep and grateful astonishment at this aesthetic paradox; he senses that he is in the presence of the sacred mystery of all great art.

Since the need for artistic ties corresponds to the human need for religious norms, we can expect to find an equivalent to artistic breakthrough on the human, religious level. And in fact the concept of breakthrough is repeatedly linked to more general human and political concerns (307–8, 321–2). In his analysis of the *Lamentation*, Zeitblom creates a direct parallel, although he presents it as a question:

> But take our artist paradox: grant that expressiveness — expression as lament — is the issue of the whole construction: then may we not parallel with it another, a religious one, and say too (though only in the lowest whisper) that out of the sheerly irremediable hope might germinate? [491]

This would be the "miracle that passes belief" (491). Mann thus seems to suggest the thought — or the hope — that beyond the laws of aesthetics dwells a higher freedom, corresponding to the divine grace that transcends human law and culpability. In the last analysis divine grace would provide the only deliverance from the bloody and fiendish dictatorship to which Germany had condemned itself. Mann deals directly with this question in an article written during the work on *Doctor Faustus*, in late August and early September, 1945:

> The pact with the devil is a venerable old German temptation, and a German novel inspired by the sufferings of the past few years would probably have to take this dreadful bargain as its theme. But in our greatest poem the devil is even cheated out of the individual soul of Faust, and far be it from us to suggest that Germany has gone to the devil once and for all. Divine grace surpasses any signature in blood. I believe in it and I believe in Germany's future, no matter how desperate the present may seem, no matter how hopeless all the destruction.[25]

Of course one must consider that Mann is suiting his words to the situation: the article was intended as edification and solace for the German people. Mann's commentary on this article in

25. "Warum ich nicht nach Deutschland zurückgehe," p. 364. The article is an answer to W. von Molo's open letter to Mann in the *Hessische Post* appealing to Mann to return to Germany. See *The Story of a Novel*, tr. R. and C. Winston, p. 133. The letter of reply was first published in *Aufbau* on September 28, 1945.

The Story of a Novel reveals that his attitude wavered far more than the article indicates. He says he completed the article "in a spirit of conciliation and, at the end, of heartening encouragement. Or so I tried to tell myself." [26] But even with this reservation, the article still gives a clear picture of the general tendency of Mann's thoughts.

Mann's statements on his novel attest to his deep involvement in the religious issue; notable is his correspondence with Karl Kerényi in June, 1949. Kerényi speaks of the "manifestly Christian theme" of *The Holy Sinner*, which he sees as the "unfolding of a seed that was already present thematically and organically in 'Doctor Faustus.'" [27] Mann replies:

What you wrote about the religious, Christian character of the 'Faustus' affected me very much and filled me with the satisfaction that one receives from hearing the truth. It *is* true and almost self-evident: how could such a radical book not extend into the religious sphere. And yet it has been called "godless." That shows you the caliber of those who professionally write on "belles lettres." That is why I exclaim: *"You* should write about it!" [28]

Mann responds in much the same vein to Sagave's monograph on him. His letter of May 25, 1954 says, "Si j'ai lu votre livre avec tant de joie . . . c'est que vous y parlez d'une idéologie religieuse qui forme le fondement de toute mon œuvre, de toute mon existence, une notion par laquelle votre pensée est 'fixée' et guidée." ["I read your book with great pleasure because in it you speak of a religious ideology that forms the basis of my entire work, of my entire existence; you orient your thoughts by this concept and let them be guided by it."] [29] To be sure, Sagave assigns this religious base to Mann's entire work, but as we have seen, Sagave specifically considers that the end of *Doctor Faustus* expresses a "Christian expectation of salvation."

26. Pp. 137–38.
27. *Gespräch in Briefen*, p. 164.
28. *Ibid.*, p. 167.
29. "Huit lettres inédites à P.-P. Sagave," p. 385. In a speech delivered in 1950 Mann rejects the thought that his work has an anti-Christian character. On the contrary, he holds that his work as an artist expresses a religious "drive for rectification." And he continues, using an idea familiar to us from *DF*: "And thus will it continue to the end, when I will say with the words of Prospero, 'And my ending is despair.' And there will be for me, as there was for Shakespeare's magician, only one comforting thought: the thought of grace, that supremely sovereign power whose proximity one has already sensed with astonishment upon occasion and which alone has the right to cross off all debts as paid" (*Meine Zeit* [Amsterdam, 1950], pp. 8–9.

213

An artist's view of his own intentions several years after completing a work may, of course, be open to question. But we are not dealing here with large stretches of time, only two to seven years, and we have every reason to assume that Mann's statements to Kerényi and Sagave represent his state of mind during his work on *Doctor Faustus*. Our grounds for this assumption stem from an examination of a final group of symbols in the novel.

THE HOPE BEYOND HOPELESSNESS

One passage often cited in religious interpretations of *Doctor Faustus* is the final paragraph of Zeitblom's discussion of the *Lamentation*, where he designates artistic and religious breakthrough as the "hope beyond hopelessness" (491).

Critics have seen a vague connection between this passage and the novel as a whole, interpreting it as Mann's formulation of what he sought to achieve with his book. We have already shown that Zeitblom's analysis describes not only the novel in general but the end of the novel in particular. If we accept this interpretation of the symbolic function of the *Lamentation* within the novel, there can be no doubt that the end of *Doctor Faustus* raises the issue of divine grace.[30]

Although the religious perspective that opens out in the final pages seems to appear almost out of the blue, closer examination will show that the idea of grace is foreshadowed symbolically in an earlier section and thus forms an integral part of the novel. Like the idea of strict style, Mann first presents the theme of grace in purely musical terms. As the full implications of this theme are far from obvious, a fairly probing commentary seems justified.[31]

The episode we have in mind is Adrian's visit to the Leipzig brothel. He reports in his letter to Zeitblom that he was seized with confusion when he realized where he had been brought:

30. In his commentary on the end of the *Lamentation* in *Story of a Novel*, Mann uses the word "grace" (222). He says of Adorno's share in the shaping of the end: "He had no objections to make on musical matters, but took issue with the end, the last forty lines, in which, after all the darkness, a ray of hope, the possibility of grace, appears. Those lines did not then stand as they stand now; they had gone wrong. I had been too optimistic, too kindly, too pat, had kindled too much light, had been too lavish with the consolation."

31. H. Mayer gives an extremely short commentary on the allusion to the *Freischütz. (Von Lessing bis Thomas Mann*, p. 389).

" 'I stood, not showing what I was feeling, and there opposite me I see an open piano, a friend, I rush up to it across the carpet and strike a chord or twain . . .' " (142). Adrian's behavior derives, as we have shown, from an episode in Nietzsche's life. But Mann has made a significant addition: Nietzsche's letter to Deussen mentions only that he struck a few chords; in *Doctor Faustus* we learn exactly *which* chords Adrian strikes:

> I wot still what it was, because the harmonic problem was just in my mind, modulation from B major to C major, the brightening semitone step, as in the hermit's prayer in the finale of the *Freischütz*, at the entry of timpani, trumpets and oboes on the six-four chord on G. [142] * 32

What induced Mann to give such a precise description of the chords? For this is such a central episode that we may assume the reference to *Der Freischütz* has a definite function. Besides, this opera turns up several times, used as a symbol or to intensify the mood; it, too, deals with a diabolic pact. These chords from the finale of the last act, however, have nothing demonic about them; their significance becomes clear from a brief summary of the plot.

In order to win Agatha, the daughter of the forester Kuno, the young hunter Max lets himself be drawn by his demonic rival, Kaspar, into dealings with the devil. When Agatha is to be given to the victor in a shooting contest, Max hopes to win by using a magic bullet. But the deception is uncovered, and the prince condemns Max to give up Agatha and flee the land. Like Adrian, Max has sinned by selling himself to the devil, and the drama seems about to end with his punishment and damnation. But in the last scene a reversal occurs, marked by the entrance of a new character. Speaking for divine grace, the hermit persuades the prince to soften his harsh sentence. After a long ensemble in B major giving thanks for Max's pardon, the hermit's deep voice emerges alone; he urges faith in God, and the orchestra modulates from B to C major:

Doch jetzt erhebt noch eure Blicke
zu dem, der Schutz der Unschuld war.33
[But now your eyes raise up to Him, who
Forever helps the blameless ones.]

* Translator's note: "C" in the original.
32. Waltershausen's little book on *Der Freischütz* is a direct source for Adrian's theoretical remarks on this passage; see above, p. 86.
33. *C. M. Weber's sämtliche Compositionen*, ed. H. W. Stolze, 1:83–84.

215

Adrian's first reaction when he finds himself misled is to strike the chords of Weber's prayer to the Protector of the innocent. Here, as so often when Adrian is involved, the action acquires an ironic twist: in the milieu of a brothel such a prayer takes on a mocking tone. The irony deepens when we realize that although this modulation was considered audacious in Weber's time and later became a favorite of Wagner's, to Adrian it would seem rather banal.

But the irony conceals something more serious. Why does Adrian choose this chord progression, rather than one from the demonic passages of the opera? In Palestrina he alludes clearly enough to the pact in *Der Freischütz*, to the decisive scene in the Wolf's Glen:

Samiel. It giveth a man to laugh. Where then is your C-minor fortissimo of stringed tremoli, wood and trombones, ingenious bug to fright children, the romantic public, coming out of the F-sharp minor of the Glen as you out of your abyss — I wonder I hear it not! [227]

Adrian's interview with the devil only confirms the pact already concluded with the Hetaera esmeralda. Thus one would logically expect that the brothel scene would contain a reference to the demonic aspect of the opera. Instead Adrian strikes chords that are described as a step from darkness into light, the "brightening semitone step" (142). This paraphrases Waltershausen, who describes the "modulation to a glowing C major" and continues, "a mighty light floods the darkened stage."[34] He sees the half-tone rise in tone as "perhaps the greatest intensification of which music is capable."[35] It can hardly be accidental that Mann chooses this particular musical effect to foreshadow the transformation from darkness to light at the end of the *Lamentation* — and of *Doctor Faustus*. Despite his pact, Adrian maintains all his life an inner purity, as Zeitblom often insists; Mann suggests that Adrian and all he embodies will be saved.

We may summarize the symbolic meaning of the *Freischütz* reference as follows: the visit to the brothel represents a decisive step in the direction of the pact, with its accompaniment of guilt and damnation. Nonetheless there is hope that grace may bring liberation from the demonic and the art inspired by it. The extent of Adrian's awareness of this connection remains

34. *Der Freischütz*, H. W. Walterhausen, p. 113.
35. *Ibid.*, p. 114.

uncertain. In his letter to Zeitblom he says of the chords. " 'I wot it now, afterwards, but then I wist not, I but fell upon it' " (142). But there can be no doubt that Mann in this early episode intentionally anticipates the end of the novel.

We can see another connection between *Der Freischütz* and *Doctor Faustus*. Adrian considers his *Lamentation* the retraction of Beethoven's Ninth Symphony, but the lingering cello note at the end of the cantata makes this retraction not altogether unambiguous; indeed, Zeitblom interprets it as the "hope beyond hopelessness" (491). Applied to the novel, this interpretation would indicate that in spite of the mood of desperation and mourning in *Doctor Faustus*, there remains a faint suggestion of the confidence expressed in the final chorus of the Ninth Symphony. The symbolic anticipation invoked with the finale of *Der Freischütz* would support this expectation. The words immediately following those quoted above bear a strong resemblance to certain ideas in Schiller's "Ode to Joy." They both express the same pious, if somewhat naïve trust in a merciful Father:

> Ja, lasst uns die Blicke erheben
> Und fest auf die Lenkung des Ewigen baun,
> Fest der Milde des Vaters vertraun!
> [Yes, let us now raise up our eyes
> And trust in the guidance of God our Lord,
> Bless the mercy upon us outpour'd.]

The original version of Schiller's ode says of grace and the forgiveness of sins:

> Rettung von Tyrannenketten,
> Grossmut auch dem Bösewicht,
> Hoffnung auf den Sterbebetten,
> Gnade auf dem Hochgericht!
> Auch die Toten sollen leben!
> Brüder, trinkt und stimmet ein,
> Allen Sündern soll vergeben
> Und die Hölle nicht mehr sein.[36]
> [Deliv'rance from the chains of tyrants,
> Mercy for our enemies,
> Hope before the gates of death,
> Pardon at the Judgment Seat!
> And the dead shall live once more!
> Brothers, drink and raise your voices,
> Sinners all will be forgiven
> This will be an end to hell.]

36. Schiller, *Sämtliche Werke* [Säkulär-Ausgabe] 1:289.

And the oft-quoted chorus says:

> Brüder — überm Sternenzelt
> Muss ein Lieber Vater wohnen.[37]
> [Brothers, o'er the firmament
> A dear Father must be dwelling.]

This interpretation of the relation of the *Lamentation* to the Ninth Symphony shows that in *Doctor Faustus* Mann gives a more complex, more varied picture of his religious opinions than in the letters, essays, and lectures. This coincides with what Mann says in *The Story of a Novel* about the book's character as a personal confession.[38] He discovered that such a confession was feasible only with a strictly objective and impersonal form, with the "anti-self-important mockery" made possible by the biographical form.[39] Yet he calls the work one "that took the form of the most disciplined art and at the same time stepped out of art and became reality."[40] With the novel form as covering, Mann could express thoughts and feelings that stirred him to the depths.

This idea of protective masks proves essential to an interpretation of the final words of the novel. A prayer addressed directly to God is placed in the mouth of the fictitious biographer Zeitblom; it is, as we saw, a piece of montage from the literature on Nietzsche.[41] At the same time, the prayer expresses Mann's own deepest concern. In analogy to the *Lamentation*, these last words might be said to break through the strictness of form and arrive at purely personal expression. It can hardly be a coincidence that Mann has smuggled his own name into the sentence with which he concludes his account of his country's tragic plight. These final words refer to the aging and lonely author himself:

A lonely man [German: *Mann*] folds his hands and speaks: "God be merciful to thy poor soul, my friend, my Fatherland!"

37. This quotation includes some lines of the ode not used by Beethoven, but I feel justified in using them because they express one of the central ideas of the poem.
38. *Story of a Novel*, pp. 31, 32, 87, 154.
39. *Ibid.*, p. 38.
40. *Ibid.*, p. 87.
41. See above, p. 60.

Appendix

Summary of the Contents of *Doctor Faustus* and List of the Quotations in the Different Chapters

Since *Doctor Faustus* lacks chapter headings and a table of contents, it may prove difficult for the reader to orient himself quickly or to recall certain passages when he needs them. For this reason the following brief sketch of the contents is offered. Since the distribution of the quotations was not indicated earlier, it will be given here. Only the works that Mann copied directly are mentioned. This list of sources will probably be supplemented in the years to come. The page numbers refer to the Lowe-Porter translation of 1948.

1. Introduction (3–6). Zeitblom undertakes his task. Genius and the demonic. Adrian and love. His coldness.

2. Zeitblom (7–10). Ancestry and youth of the biographer. Studies and travels 8. Marriage and professional life 10.

Bekker, *Musikgeschichte*

3. Jonathan Leverkühn and his experiments (11–20). Buchel. Adrian's birth 11. Jonathan 12. His Bible studies 13. Butterflies and sea creatures 13. Visible music, ice flowers, 17–18. The devouring drop 18. Osmotic growths 19.

Portmann, *Falterschönheit*
Masarey, *Kunstgebilde des Meeres*

4. The mother and the childhood milieu (21–29). The mother 21. People on the farm 23. Suso 23. The surroundings 24. Comparison with Pfeiffering 25. Singing canons with Hanne 27.

5. Childhood years in the parental house (30–34). Zeitblom

219

on the present war situation. Adrian's first impressions of music 31. Adrian at school and being tutored 32.

6. Kaisersaschern (35–38). The town and its history. Its atmosphere: hysteria of the waning Middle Ages 36. Its eccentrics 37.

Mann, *Germany and the Germans*

7. Nikolaus Leverkühn and Adrian's years at the Gymnasium (39–48). The uncle and his household. The musical instrument collection 40. Adrian as a *Gymnasium* pupil 44. Modulation exercises 46. The uncle discovers his interest in music 47.

8. Kretschmar's lectures (49–69). Kretschmar. First lecture, Beethoven's Opus 111, 51. Second lecture, Beethoven and the fugue 56. Comments on this lecture 59. Third lecture, "Music and the Eye" 60. Fourth lecture, "The Elemental in Music" 62. Beissel 63. Comments on the lecture about Beissel 67.

David, essay on Beissel

Bekker, *Musikgeschichte*

9. Adrian as Kretschmar's pupil (70–79). Zeitblom's excuse for length of previous chapter 70. Adrian's literary studies 71. Piano lessons 72. Harmony, chords, polyphony 73. Orientation in the history of music 75. The *Lied* 77. The *Leonora* overture 78.

Bekker, *Musikgeschichte*

10. End of school and choice of profession (80–85). Decision to study theology — out of arrogance 80. Theology and music 82. Discussion at Buchel after graduation 84. Adrian's laughter 84.

11. Halle's theological traditions (86–91). The Reformation period 87. Pietism 88. Liberal theology 89. The Winfried Society 91.

Tillich, Letter to Mann

12. Study of theology. Prof. Kumpf (92–98). Adrian's lodgings 92. Preliminary study of philosophy 93. The theological

Tillich, Letter
Luther, *Letters*
Grimmelshausen, *Simplicissimus*

and music 163. *Love's Labour's Lost* 164. The club in the Café Central 166. Schildknapp and his activities 166.

21. Foreign travel and various compositions (172–84). Long digression on the political situation. Reflections on narrative technique 176. Trips: to Graz 177, to Switzerland 178. Fraud and banality 181. The Brentano songs 182.

Die Weltwoche, Nov. 12, 1943

22. Strict style (185–94). Wedding of Adrian's sister. Discussion on marriage 186. The Shakespeare opera 189. Freedom and sterility in art 190. Strict style 191. Migraine, cold 194.

Adorno, *Philosophie*

23. Move to Munich (195–210). Adrian's lodgings in the Rambergstrasse 195. The Rodde ladies 196. Their circle 198. Schwerdtfeger 198. The rest of Adrian's circle 200. First visit to Pfeiffering 204.

24. Adrian in Palestrina (211–20). The Manardi house 211. The family 212. Work on the Shakespeare opera 215. More on the life and contacts in Palestrina 218.

Harris, *Shakespeare*

25. The interview with the devil (221–50). "Whist, mum's the word" 222. Frame of the visit 222. First guise of the devil 223. Identifies himself 225. Dürer, *Freischütz* 227. Time offered for sale 229. Silence, Schweigestill 231. Medieval flagellants — syphilis. Spengler an Esmeraldus 231. Medical details on syphilis 233. Inspiration 235. The devil changes shape 237. Modern music 238. Convention and freedom 239. Kierkegaard, music and theology 242. Disease and genius 242. The devil changes shape again 243. The devil on hell 244. Attritio and contritio 246. Devil changes shape again 247. The

Waltershausen, *Der Freischütz*
Hugo Wolf, *Letters*
Nietzsche, *Ecce Homo*
Bahle, *Eingebung und Tat*
Adorno, *Philosophie*
Faust chapbook
Mann, "Dostoevsky"

pact 248. The devil foretells Adrian's life 249.

26. Adrian settles in Pfeiffering (251–61). The present situation and the double time-reckoning 251. Telephone discussion with Frau Schweigestill 253. Adrian comes to Pfeiffering. The dog 255. Adrian's daily schedule and living quarters 256. Early part of the stay in Pfeiffering 258. Zeitblom comes to Freising 261.

27. Cosmic Phantasies (262–75). *Love's Labour's Lost.* Settings of Blake, Keats, Klopstock 262. Descent into the ocean 266. Astronomical fantasies 270. *Marvels of the Universe* 274.

"Wunder der Meerestiefe"
Potter, "We Live Inside a Globe"
Descovich, "Dehnt sich das Weltall aus?"
"Science," *Time*

28. Munich 1913–14 (276–84). Social life and music-making 276. Breisacher 279. Progress and barbarism 280. Breisacher and the Jews 281.

Bekker, *Musikgeschichte*

29. The Rodde sisters and Rudi Schwerdtfeger (285–98). Clarissa 285. Ines and Institoris 287. Rivalry between Rudi and Institoris 289. Rudi's life style 293. Ines' awakening love for Rudi 293.

30. War breaks out (299–309). War enthusiasm 299. Munich under mobilization 302. Zeitblom takes leave of Adrian 303. Adrian's work 305. Discussion of breakthrough 306. Kleist 308.

Kleist, *Über das Marionettentheater*

31. Adrian's life during the war. *Gesta* (310–323). The first phase of the war. Zeitblom returns to civilian life 310. Nackedey, Rosenstiel 312. *Gesta* 315. The idea of breakthrough 320.

Gesta Romanorum

32. Ines Institoris (324–35). The wedding. Frau Rodde moves to Pfeiffering 324. Ines' social life and apartment 327. Her children 329. Growing love for Rudi 330. She confides in Zeitblom 332.

33. Adrian's illness (336–51). The collapse of 1918 and the situation in 1944, 336. Adrian ill 341. The

little mermaid 343. Adrian receives various visits 345. Rudi
comes 347. He asks Adrian to
write him a violin concerto 350.
34. Apocalypsis cum figuris (352–
61). Adrian well again. End of
the war 352. Dürer 354. Conception of the oratorio 355. Preliminary studies 355. Working it out
357.

Vogler, "Die Jenseitsvorstellugen
vor Dante"

34. (continued) Kridwiss and his
circle (362–70). The circle's ideas
365. Might and dictatorship 366,
Zeitblom critical 368. Progress
and reaction 368. Symbol of the
"dead tooth" 370.

Mann, *At the Prophet's*

34. (conclusion) More on the
Apocalypsis (371–79). Connection between the ideas of the
circle and the *Apocalypsis* 371.
Adrian's letter 372. Cultic music
373. Analysis of the oratorio 373.
Its performance 377. Infernal
laughter 377.

Bekker, *Musikgeschichte*

35. The end of Clarissa Rodde
(380–87). Her love affairs 381.
Her suicide 384. The funeral 385.
Ines' morphine addiction 386.

Mann, *A Sketch of My Life*

36. Frau von Tolna (388–96).
The inflation years. Some of
Adrian's compositions performed
388. Frau von Tolna 390. The
emerald ring 392. Performance
of the violin concerto in Vienna
395. Journey to Castle Tolna 396.
37. Fitelberg (397–408). His ar-
rival 397. Description of his appearance 398. Temptations of
the great world 402. Vain attempts at seduction 404. The
Germans and the Jews 406.
38. At the Bullingers' (409–16).
The violin concerto. Party at the
Bullingers' 409. Phonograph records 412. Delila's aria: the sensuous and idealism 414. Music and
the sensuous; Adrian and Rudi
414.
39. Marie Godeau (417–24). The
journey to Zurich. At the Reiffs'
417. Marie 418. Marie comes to

Bibliography

The bibliography has been updated and revised for the present translation by the author and the translator. In addition to works cited in the book, it includes a number of articles and books written since the German edition first appeared in 1961. English works or English translation of foreign works have been listed wherever possible.

ABBREVIATIONS

AN   *Altes und Neues: kleine Prosa aus fünf Jahrzehnten*
Briefe 1 Briefe 1889–1936
DVjs   *Deutsche Vierteljahresschrift für Literaturwissenschaft und Geistesgeschichte*
GLL   *German Life and Letters*
GR   *Germanic Review*
MLN   *Modern Language Notes*
Monatshefte   *Monatshefte für deutschen Unterricht*
NR   *Die Neue Rundschau*

WORKS BY THOMAS MANN

Adel des Geistes: Sechzehn Versuche zum Problem der Humanität. Stockholm, 1945.
Altes und Neues: kleine Prosa aus fünf Jahrzehnten. Frankfurt am Main, 1953.
"Bekenntnis eines Siebzigjährigen: die Ansprache von Thomas Mann an die Zürcher Studentenschaft." Göttinger Universitätszeitung 2 (1947): 22.
The Beloved Returns. Tr. H. T. Lowe-Porter. New York, 1940.
Betrachtungen eines Unpolitischen. Berlin [1918], 1919.
Briefe 1889–1936. Ed. E. Mann. Frankfurt am Main, 1961.
"Briefwechsel mit Thomas Mann." *Sinn und Form* 7 (1965): 669.
Briefwechsel Thomas Mann/Robert Faesi. Ed. R. Faesi. Zurich, 1962.
Buddenbrooks. Tr. H. T. Lowe-Porter. 2 vols. New York, 1924.
"A Communication." *Hudson Review* 2 (1949).
Confessions of Felix Krull, Confidence Man: The Early Years. Tr. D. Lindley. New York, 1955.
"Culture and Politics." *Survey Graphic* 28 (February, 1939): 149–51.
Deutsche Hörer! Fünfundfünfzig Radiosendungen nach Deutschland. 2d ed. Stockholm, 1945. Partial translation: *Listen Germany!* New York, 1943.

Doctor Faustus: The Life of the German Composer Adrian Lever-kühn as Told by a Friend. Tr. H. T. Lowe-Porter. New York, 1948.

"Dostoevsky — in Moderation." In *The Short Novels of Dostoevsky.* New York, 1945.

"From *Diaries 1933–1934*": see *Leiden an Deutschland.*

Essays of Three Decades. Tr. H. T. Lowe-Porter. New York, 1947.

Gespräch in Briefen. (Mann and K. Kerényi.) Zurich, 1960.

The Holy Sinner. Tr. H. T. Lowe-Porter. New York, 1951.

"How to Win the Peace." Tr. K. Katzenellenbogen. *Atlantic Monthly* 169 (1942), no. 2.

"Huit lettres inédites à P.-P. Sagave." *Cahiers du Sud* 43 (1956).

Joseph and His Brothers. Tr. H. T. Lowe-Porter. One-vol. ed., New York, 1948.

Last Essays. Tr. R. and C. Winston, T. and J. Stern. New York, 1958.

Leiden an Deutschland: Tagebuchblätter aus den Jahren 1933 und 1934. Los Angeles, 1946. Partial translation: "From: *Diaries 1933–1934.*" Tr. R. Winston. *Twice a Year* 14/15 (1946), pp. 39–50.

"Letter to E. Korrodi: Thomas Mann's View of Emigré Writers." *New York Times Book Review*, March 8, 1936, pp. 20–21.

Letters to Paul Amann 1915–1952. Tr. R. and C. Winston. Ed. H. Wegener. Middletown, Conn., 1960.

Listen Germany! See *Deutsche Hörer!*

The Magic Mountain. Tr. H. T. Lowe-Porter. New York, 1927.

"The Making of the Magic Mountain." Atlantic Monthly 191 (January, 1953): 41–45. Reprinted in *The Magic Mountain*, New York, 1953.

Meine Zeit. Amsterdam, 1950. Partial translation: "The Years of My Life," tr. H. and R. Norden. *Harper's* 201 (October, 1950): 250–64.

Nachlese: Prosa 1951–1955. Berlin/Frankfurt am Main, 1956.

Order of the Day: Political Essays and Speeches of Three Decades. Tr. H. T. Lowe-Porter, E. Meyer, E. Sutton. New York, 1942.

Pariser Rechenschaft. Berlin, 1926.

Past Masters and Other Papers. Tr. H. T. Lowe-Porter. New York, 1933.

Das Problem der Freiheit. Stockholm, 1939.

Royal Highness: A Novel of German Court Life. Tr. A. C. Curtis. New York, 1916.

A Sketch of My Life. Tr. H. T. Lowe-Porter. New York, 1960.

Stories of Three Decades. Tr. H. T. Lowe-Porter. New York, 1930.

The Story of a Novel: The Genesis of Doctor Faustus. Tr. R. and C. Winston. New York, 1961.

Thomas Mann's Addresses at the Library of Congress 1943–1949. Washington, D.C., 1963.

"Thomas Mann's Answer." *Saturday Review of Literature* 32 (January 1, 1949): 22–23.

Three Essays. Tr. H. T. Lowe-Porter. New York, 1929.

"Warum ich nicht nach Deutschland zurückgehe." *Neue Schweizer Rundschau*, Neue Folge, 13 (1945–46).

"What is German?" *Atlantic Monthly* 173 (1944), no. 5.

SECONDARY WORKS

Abendroth, W. *Hans Pfitzner*. Munich, 1935.

Adorno, T. W. *Kierkegaard: Konstruktion des Aesthetischen*. Beiträge zur Philosophie und ihrer Geschichte, vol. 2. Tübingen, 1933.

————. Philosophie der neuen Musik [1949]. 2d ed., Frankfurt am Main, 1958.

Allgemeine deutsche Biographie. Ed. R. v. Liliencron. Leipzig, 1881.

Altmann, L. "Our Great Symphonies Written by Lonely Men." *Opera and Concert*, November, 1941.

Andreas-Salomé, Lou. *Friedrich Nietzsche in seinen Werken*. 2d ed., Vienna, 1911.

Antheil, G. *Bad Boy of Music*. New York, 1945.

Bahle, J. *Eingebung und Tat im musikalischen Schaffen: ein Beitrag zur Psychologie der Entwicklungs- und Schaffensgesetze schöpferischer Menschen*. Leipzig, 1939.

Bates, H. W. *The Naturalist on the River Amazons*. London, 1863.

Batka, R. *Biographie Schumanns*. Musiker-Biographien, vol. 13, Reclams Universal-Bibliothek. Leipzig, n.d. [1891].

Bauer, A. "Thomas Mann und seine Widersacher." *Der Monat* 1, no. 6 (1949): 73 ff.

Becker-Frank, Sigrid W. "Untersuchungen zur Integration der Zitate in Thomas Manns *Doktor Faustus* mit Berücksichtigung der anderen späten Romane." Ph.D. dissertation, Tübingen, 1963.

Beebe, W. *Half Mile Down*. New York, 1934.

Bekker, P. *Beethoven*. 2d ed., Berlin, 1912.

————. *Musikgeschichte als Geschichte der musikalischen Formwandlungen*. Stuttgart / Berlin / Leipzig, 1926.

Bennet, E. A. *C. G. Jung*. London, 1961.

Berendsohn, W. A. "Faustsage und Faustdichtung." *Edda: Nordisk Tidsskrift for Litteraturforskning* 50 (1950): 371–82.

————. "Thomas Mann und das Dritte Reich." *Das Parlament* (Supplement: Aus Politik und Zeitgeschichte), 16 (1956).

————. "Thomas Manns Hinterlassenschaft." *Orbis Litterarum* 14 (1959).

Berger, E. *Randbemerkungen zu Nietzsche, George und Dante*. Wiesbaden, 1958.

Bergsten, G. "Musical Symbolism in Thomas Mann's 'Doctor Faustus.'" *Orbis Litterarum* 14 (1959).

Berlioz, H. *Memoirs of Hector Berlioz from 1803 to 1865: Comprising His Travels in Germany, Italy, Russia and England*. Tr. R. and E. Holmes. Ed. E. Newman. New York [1932], 1947.

Bertram, E. *Nietzsche: Versuch einer Mythologie*. Berlin, 1919.

Bianquis, G. "Thomas Mann et le 'Faustbuch' de 1587." *Etudes Germaniques* 5 (1950): 54–59.

Bibliographie zur deutschen Geschichte im Zeitalter der Glaubensspaltung 1517–1585. Ed. K. Schottenloher, II. Leipzig, 1935.

Blankenagel, J. C. "A Nietzsche Episode in Thomas Mann's *Doktor Faustus*." *MLN* 63 (1948).

Blissett, W. "Thomas Mann: The Last Wagnerite." *GR* 35 (1960): 50–76.

Blomster, W. V. "Textual Variations in 'Doktor Faustus.'" *GR* 39 (1964).

Blume, B. "Perspektiven des Widerspruchs: zur Kritik an Thomas Mann." *GR* 31 (1956): 181 ff.

———. *Thomas Mann und Goethe*. Bern, 1949.

Blunck, R. *Friedrich Nietzsche: Kindheit und Jugend*. Munich, 1953.

Boehlich, W. "Thomas Manns 'Doktor Faustus.'" Merkur 2 (1948).

Boeninger, H. R. "Zeitblom, Spiritual Descendant of Goethe's Wagner and Wagner's Beckmesser." *GLL* 13 (1959–60): 38–43.

Borcherdt, H. H. "Das Faustproblem bei Thomas Mann." *Jahrbuch des Wiener Goethe-Vereins*, N.F., 65 (1961).

Boss, W. *Einführung in den Roman 'Doktor Faustus' von Thomas Mann*. Bonn, 1948.

Boyer, J. "A propos du rôle de la musique dans le 'Doktor Faustus' de Thomas Mann." *Annales publiées par la faculté des lettres de Toulouse*, December, 1951.

Brandes, G. *Gesammelte Schriften*, vol. 3, pt. 2. Munich, 1902.

Brann, H. W. *Nietzsche und die Frauen*. Leipzig, 1931.

Briner, A. "Conrad Beissel and Thomas Mann." *American-German Review* 26 (1959–60), no. 2.

Brown, C. S. "The Entomological Source of Mann's Poisonous Butterfly." *GR* 37 (1962).

Buisonjé, J. C. de. "Bemerkungen über Thomas Manns Werk: Dr. Faustus (1947)." *Neophilologus* 41 (1957).

Burgert, H. "Verborgene Christlichkeit: eine Anmerkung zu Thomas Mann." *Zeichen der Zeit, Evangelische Monatsschrift* 7 (1953).

Bürgin, H. "Thomas Mann und die Musik." In *Der Musik-Almanach*, ed. V. Schwarz. Munich, 1948.

Butler, E. M. "The Traditional Elements in Thomas Mann's *Doktor Faustus*." *Publications of the English Goethe Society* 18 (1849): 1–33.

Carlsson, A. "Das Faustmotiv bei Thomas Mann." Deutsche Beiträge 3 (1949).

———. "Der Meeresgrund in der neueren Dichtung." *DVjs* 28 (1954): 221–33.

Cassirer, E. "Thomas Manns Goethe-Bild: eine Studie über Lotte in Weimar." *GR* 20 (1945).

Charney, H. and M. "'Doctor Faustus' and 'Mon Faust': An Excursion in Dualism." *Symposium* 16 (1962).

Childs, M. "Thomas Mann: Germany's Foremost Literary Exile Speaks Now for Freedom and Democracy in America." *Life*, April 17, 1939.

Colleville, M. "Nietzsche et le Doktor Faustus de Thomas Mann." *Etudes Germaniques* 3 (1948).

Dante Alighieri. *The Divine Comedy of Dante Alighieri*. Tr. M. B. Anderson. New York, 1944.

David, C. "Stefan George: Aesthetes or Terrorists?" In *The Third Reich*. London, 1955. (Published under the auspices of the International Council for Philosophy and Humanistic Studies and with the assistance of UNESCO.)

David, H. T. "Hymns and Music of the Pennsylvania Seventh-day Baptists." *American-German Review*, June, 1943.

Derleth, L. *Proklamationen*. [1904.] Munich, 1919.

Descovich, E. "Dehnt sich das Weltall aus?" *Neue Freie Presse*, June 27, 1934.

Deussen, P. *Erinnerungen an Friedrich Nietzsche*. Leipzig, 1901.

Devoto, D. "Deux musiciens russes dans le *Doktor Faustus* de Thomas Mann." *Revue de Littérature Comparée* 33 (1959): 104–6.

Diersen, I. *Untersuchungen zu Thomas Mann: die Bedeutung der Künstlerdarstellung für die Entwicklung des Realismus in seinem erzählerischen Werk*. Berlin, 1959.

Dippel, P. G. *Nietzsche und Wagner: Untersuchungen über die Grundlagen und Motive ihrer Trennung*. Bern, 1934.

————. "Thomas Mann und die Musik." *Wissenschaftliche Annalen*, ed. Deutsche Akademie der Wissenschaften, Berlin, 5 (1956).

Doerne, M. "Thomas Mann und das protestantische Christentum." *Die Sammlung* 11 (1956): 409 ff.

Doktor Johannes Faust's Magia naturalis et innaturalis, oder Dreifacher Höllenzwang, letztes Testament und Siegelkunst. Ed. J. Scheible. Stuttgart, 1849.

Dornheim, A. "Goethes 'Mignon' und Thomas Manns 'Echo': zwei Formen des 'göttlichen Kindes' im deutschen Roman." *Euphorion* 46 (1952).

Edschmid, K. *Ueber den Expressionismus in der Literatur und die neue Dichtung*. Tribüne der Kunst und Zeit, coll. K. Edschmid, I. Berlin, 1919.

Eiffert, E. "Das Erlebnis der Zeit im Werke Thomas Manns." Ph.D. dissertation, Frankfurt am Main, 1949.

Elema, J. "Thomas Mann, Dürer und 'Doktor Faustus.'" *Euphorion* 59 (1965).

Engelberg, E. "Thomas Mann's Faust and Beethoven." *Monatshefte* 47 (1955): 112–16.

Engländer, R. "Grundzüge der Beethoven-Literatur." *Dresdener Anzeiger*, March 26, 1927.

————. "Thomas Manns Faustroman: Ett verk om ett musikgeni." *Musikrevy: Nordisk tidskrift för musik och grammofon* 10 (1955).

————. "Thomas Manns Faustusroman som musikalisk spegelbild." Unpublished lecture series held at the University of Uppsala, winter semester, 1961.

Enright, D. F. *The Apothecary's Shop: Essays on Literature*. London, 1957.

Ewers, H. "Lübeck im Kunstwerk Thomas Manns." In *Der Wagen: ein lubeckisches Jahrbuch*. Lübeck, 1958.

Faesi, R. *Thomas Mann, ein Meister der Erzahlkunst*. Zurich, 1955.

Falterschönheit: exotische Schmetterlinge in farbigen Naturaufnahmen. Intro. A. Portmann; fwd. H. Hesse. Bern, 1935.

Feuchtwanger, L. "Thomas Mann im Exil." *NR*, special issue for Thomas Mann's 70th birthday, June 6, 1945.

Field, G. W. "Music and Morality in Thomas Mann and Hermann Hesse." *University of Toronto Quarterly* 24 (1955).

Fischer, E. *Kunst und Menschheit: Essays*. Vienna, 1949.

————. "Zu zwei Briefen von Thomas Mann." *Sinn und Form* 11 (1959).

Flake, O. *Nietzsche: Rückblick auf eine Philosophie*. Baden-Baden, 1947.

Flinker, M. *Thomas Manns politische Betrachtungen im Lichte der heutigen Zeit*. The Hague, 1959.

Förster-Nietzsche, E., and H. Lichtenberger. *Nietzsche und sein Werk*. Dresden, 1928.

Frank, J. "Reaction as Progress: or, The Devil's Domain." *Hudson Review* 2 (1949): 38–53.

Die Freideutsche Position. Rundbriefe der freideutschen Kameradschaft, no. 4 (Winter, 1931).

Fromm, E. "Symphonia pathologica: Thomas Mann." *Pharmazeutische Zeitung* 100 (1955).

Fuchs, G. *Sturm und Drang in München um die Jahrhundertwende*. Munich, 1936.

Gesta Romanorum, das älteste Mährchen- und Legendenbuch des christlichen Mittelalters zum ersten Male vollständig aus dem Lateinischen in's Deutsche übertragen, aus gedruckten und ungedruckten Quellen vermehrt, mit Ammerkungen und einer Abhandlung über den wahren Verfasser und die bisherigen Ausgaben und Uebersetzungen desselben versehen von Dr. Johann Theodor Grässe. 3d ed., Leipzig, 1905.

Glicksberg, C. I. "Twilight of the Novel." *Direction*, 1943.

Goethe, J. W. *Goethe's Faust*. Tr. L. MacNeice. New York, 1951.

Goldberg, O. *Die Wirklichkeit der Hebräer*. Berlin, 1925.

Grandi, H. "Die Musik im Roman Thomas Manns." Ph.D. dissertation, Berlin, 1952.

Gregor, M. *Wagner und kein Ende: Richard Wagner im Spiegel von Thomas Manns Prosawerk*. Bayreuth, 1958.

Grenzmann, W. *Dichtung und Glaube: Probleme und Gestalten der deutschen Gegenwartsliteratur*. 2d enl. ed., Bonn, 1952.

Grützmacher, R. H. "Spengler, Keyserlingk und Thomas Mann." *Deutsche Allgemeine Zeitung*, no. 264, 1925 (Sunday supplement).

Gumpert, M. "Für Thomas Mann." *NR*, special issue for Mann's 70th birthday, June 6, 1945.

Gundolf, F. *Stefan George in unserer Zeit*. [1913.] 3d ed., Heidelberg, 1918.

Gustafson, L. "Xenofon and *Der Tod in Venedig*." *GR* 21 (1946).

Harris, F. *The Man Shakespeare and His Tragic Life Story*. 2d rev. ed., London, 1911.

Hartmann, M. *Allgemeine Biologie: eine Einführung in die Lehre vom Leben*. Jena, 1927.

Hatfield, H. *Thomas Mann: An Introduction to His Fiction*. London, 1952.

Hécaen, H.-H.-O. "Manie et inspiration musicale: le cas Hugo Wolf." Ph.D. dissertation, Bordeaux, 1934.

Heim, K. "Thomas Mann und die Musik." Ph.D. dissertation, Freiburg im Breisgau, 1952.

Heimann, B. "Thomas Manns 'Doktor Faustus' und die Musikphilosophie Adornos." *DVjs* 38 (1964).

Heine, H. *Sämtliche Werke*. Ed. R. Frank, III. Munich/Leipzig, 1923.

Heller, E. *The Ironic German: A Study of Thomas Mann.* Boston/ Toronto, 1958.

Heller, P. "Thomas Mann's Conception of the Creative Writer." *PMLA* 69 (1954).

Hellersberg-Wendriner, A. *Mystik der Gottesferne: eine Interpretation Thomas Manns.* Bern/Munich, 1960.

Henning, M. *Die Ich-Form und ihre Funktion in Thomas Manns 'Doktor Faustus.'* Tübingen, 1966.

Hermlin, S., and H. Mayer. *Ansichten über einige neue Schriftsteller und Bücher.* Wiesbaden, 1947.

Hilscher, E. "Begegnung mit Thomas Mann." *Aufbau* 11 (1955).

———. "Ein Kunstler als Abenteurer." *Neue Deutsche Literatur,* no. 5 (1955).

———. "Thomas Manns Religiosität." *Die Sammlung* 10 (1955).

———. "Thomas Mann und Goethe." *Aufbau* 11 (1955).

Historia von D. Johann Fausten / dem weitbeschreyten Zauberer und Schwarzkünstler. Die deutschen Volksbucher, ed. R. Benz. Jena, 1924.

Hoffman, F. J. *Freudianism and the Literary Mind.* Baton Rouge, 1945.

Hoffmann, G. "Die Musik im Werk Thomas Manns." *Aufbau* 11 (1955).

Hofmann, E. *Thomas Mann: Patholog-Therapeut? Eine Zusammenschau seiner Thematik.* Graz, 1950.

Holmberg, O. *Thomas Mann och Det tredje riket.* Stockholm, 1942.

Holthusen, H. E. *Die Welt ohne Transzendenz: eine Studie zu Thomas Manns "Dr. Faustus" und seinen Nebenschriften.* Hamburg, 1949.

Holthusen, W., and A. Taubner. "Dürers 'Philipp Melanchton' und 'Bildnis einer jungen Frau' als visuelle Vorbilder für die Eltern von Adrian Leverkühn in Thomas Manns 'Doktor Faustus.'" *Die Waage* 3 (1963), no. 2.

Joël, K. *Nietzsche und die Romantik.* Jena/Leipzig, 1905.

Jonas, K. W. *Fifty Years of Thomas Mann Studies: A Bibliography of Criticism.* Minneapolis, 1955. Rev. ed., 1967.

Jung, C. G. *Essays on Contemporary Events.* Tr. E. Welsh, B. Hannah, M. Briner. London, 1947.

Kahler, E. "Gedenkrede auf Thomas Mann.' *NR* 67 (1956).

———. "Die Säkularisierung des Teufels: Thomas Manns Faust." *NR* 59 (1948).

Kantorowicz, A. *Heinrich und Thomas Mann: die persönlichen, literarischen und weltanschaulichen Beziehungen der Brüder.* Berlin, 1956.

Kaufmann, F. "An Address." In *The Stature of Thomas Mann,* ed. C. Neider. New York, 1947.

———. "Dr. Fausti Weheklag." *Archiv für Philosophie* 3 (1949).

———. "Imitatio Goethe: Thomas Mann and His French Confrères." *Monatshefte* 48 (1956).

———. *Thomas Mann: the World as Will and Representation.* Boston, 1957.

Kaufmann, W. A. *Nietzsche: Philosopher, Psychologist, Antichrist.* Princeton, 1950.

Kerényi, K. "Thomas Mann und der Teufel in Palastrina." *NR* 73 (1962): 328–46.

―――. See also in "Works of Thomas Mann," above.

Kesten, H. "Works and Deeds." In *The Stature of Thomas Mann,* ed. C. Neider. New York, 1947.

Kiremidjian, G. D. "A Study of Parody: James Joyce's *Ulysses* and Thomas Mann's *Doktor Faustus.*" Ph.D. dissertation, Yale University, 1964.

Kirsch, E. "Serenus Zeitblom — Beitrag zur Analyse des 'Doktor Faustus.'" *Wissenschaftliche Zeitschrift der Martin Luther-Universitat Halle-Wittenberg,* Gesellschafts-und sprachwissenschaftliche Reihe, vol. 7 (1957–58): 1103–9.

Klages, L. *Die psychologischen Errungenschaften Nietzsches.* Leipzig, 1926.

Kleist, H. von. *Sämtliche Werke und Briefe.* Ed. W. Herzog, vol. 5, part 2. Leipzig, 1911.

Koch-Emmery, E. "Thomas Mann in English Translation." *GLL* 6 (1952–53).

Kohlschmidt, W. "Musikalität, Reformation und Deutschtum: eine kritische Studie zu Thomas Manns 'Doktor Faustus,'" *Zeitwende,* 21 (1950): 541–50.

Kolb, A. *Franz Schubert: sein Leben.* Erlenbach/Zurich, 1947.

Koopmann, H. *Die Entwicklung des "Intellektualen Romans" bei Thomas Mann: Untersuchungen zur Struktur von "Buddenbrooks," "Königliche Hohheit" und "Der Zauberberg."* [Ph.D. dissertation, Bonn, 1960.] Bonner Arbeiten zur deutschen Literatur, ed. B. von Wiese, vol. 5. Bonn, 1962.

Křenek, E. *Music Here and Now.* Tr. B. Fles. New York, 1939.

Krey, J. "Die gesellschaftliche Bedeutung der Musik im Werk von Thomas Mann." *Wissenschaftliche Zeitschrift der Friedrich-Schiller-Universität Jena* 3 (1953–54). Gesellschafts- und sprachwissenschaftliche Reihe, 2–3.

Krökel, F. *Europas Selbstbesinnung durch Nietzsche: ihre Vorbereitung bei den französischen Moralisten.* Munich, 1929.

Kunitz, S. J. See *Twentieth-Century Authors.*

Kunstgebilde des Meeres: Muscheln und Schneckengehäuse. 15 color plates based on watercolors by Paul A. Robert. Intro. A. Masarey. Bern, 1936.

Landmann, G. P. *Stefan George und sein Kreis: eine Bibliographie.* Hamburg, 1960.

Lehnert, H. "Zur Theologie in Thomas Manns 'Doktor Faustus': zwei gestrichene Stellen aus der Handschrift." *DVjs* 40 (1966).

Leibrich, L. "Expérience et philosophie de la vie chez Thomas Mann." *Etudes Germaniques* 9 (1954).

Lesser, J. *Thomas Mann in der Epoche seiner Vollendung.* Munich, 1952.

Levin, H. *James Joyce: A Critical Introduction.* London, 1944.

Liebmann, K. *Nietzsches Kampf und Untergang in Turin.* Leipzig, 1934.

Life, April 16, 1937. "Famous German Champion: Dr. and Mrs. Mann Arrive in New York City on April 12."

Lindblom, J. "Inledande grundtankar i Martin Kählers teologi." *Bibelforskaren: Tidskrift för skrifttolkning och praktisk kristendom* 23 (1906): 441–68.

————. "Möten med Thomas Mann." *Sydsvenska Dagbladet snällposten,* August 12, 1960.

Lindsay, J. *Thomas Mann.* Oxford, 1954.

Lion, F. *Thomas Mann: Leben und Werk.* Zurich, 1947.

Lonsbach, R. M. *Friedrich Nietzsche und die Juden: ein Versuch.* Stockholm, 1939.

Lowe-Porter, H. T. "Doctor Faustus" (1948). In J. C. Thirlwall, *In Another Language: A Record of the Thirty-Year Relationship between Thomas Mann and His American Translator, Helen Tracy Lowe-Porter.* New York, 1966.

Lukács, Georg. *Thomas Mann.* Berlin, 1950.

Lukács, Gertrud. "Briefwechsel mit Thomas Mann." *Sinn und Form* 7 (1955).

Lundgren, G. *Thomas Mann.* Stockholm, 1940.

Luther, M. *Martin Luthers Briefe.* Sel. and ed. R. Buchwald. Vols. 1 and 2. 2d ed., Leipzig, 1909.

Maatje, F. G. "Die Duplikation der Zeit in Thomas Manns 'Doktor Faustus.'" In Maatje, *Der Doppelroman.* Groningen, 1964.

Magnussen, R. *Det saerlige Kors: Efterskrift til bogen: Soren Kierkegaard set udefra.* Copenhagen, 1942.

Mann, Erika. *The Last Year of Thomas Mann.* Tr. R. Graves. New York, 1958.

————. "Letter to My Father." In *The Stature of Thomas Mann,* ed. C. Neider. New York, 1947.

————. & Klaus Mann. *Escape to Life.* Boston, 1939.

————. & Klaus Mann. "Portrait of Our Father." In *The Stature of Thomas Mann,* ed. C. Neider. New York, 1947.

Mann, Heinrich. *Ein Zeitalter wird besichtigt.* Berlin, 1947.

Mann, Klaus. *Pathetic Symphony: a Novel about Tschaikowsky.* Tr. H. Oud. New York, 1948. (German ed., Amsterdam, 1935.)

————. *Vergittertes Fenster: Novelle um den Tod des Königs Ludwig II. von Bayern.* Amsterdam, 1937.

————. *Der Wendepunkt: ein Lebensbericht.* Berlin/Frankfurt am Mann, 1958. Partial translation: *The Turning Point: Thirty-five Years in this Century.* New York, 1942.

Mann, Michael. "Adrian Leverkühn — Repräsentant oder Antipode?" *NR* 76 (1965).

————. "The Musical Symbolism in Thomas Mann's *Doktor Faustus.*" *Music Review* 17 (1956).

Mann, Monika. *Vergangenes und Gegenwärtiges: Erinnerungen.* Munich, 1956. Translation: *Past and Present,* tr. Frances E. Reid and Ruth Hein. New York, 1960.

Mann, Viktor. *Wir waren fünf: Bildnis der Familie Mann.* Konstanz, 1949.

Mautner, F. H. "Die griechischen Anklänge in Thomas Manns 'Tod in Venedig.'" *Monatshefte* 44 (1952).

Mayer, H. "Ammerkungen zum 'Doktor Faustus' von Thomas Mann." *Sprache im Technischen Zeitalter*, no. 17–18 (1966).

———. *Thomas Mann: Werk und Entwicklung*. Berlin, 1950.

———. *Von Lessing bis Thomas Mann: Wandlungen der bürgerlichen Literatur in Deutschland*. Pfullingen, 1959.

———. *See* Hermlin, S.

Mersmann, H. *Die Kammermusik II: Beethoven*. Leipzig, 1930. (*Hermann Kretzschmar Führer durch den Konzertsaal*.)

Mette, H. J. "Doktor Faustus und Alexander: zur Geschichte des Descensus- und Ascensus-Motivs." *DVjs* 25 (1951).

Metzler, I. *Dämonie und Humanismus: Funktion und Bedeutung der Zeitblomgestalt in Thomas Manns "Doktor Faustus."* Ph.D. dissertation, Munich, 1960.

Meyer, Herman. *Das Zitat in der Erzählkunst: zur Geschichte und Poetik des europäischen Romans*. Stuttgart, 1961.

Michael, W. F. "Thomas Mann auf dem Wege zu Freud." *MLN* 65 (1950): 165–71.

Milch, W. "Thomas Manns 'Doktor Faustus.'" *Kleine Schriften zur Literatur- und Geistesgeschichte*. Ed. G. Burkhardt. Deutsche Akademie für Sprache und Dichtung, 10. Heidelberg/Darmstadt, 1957.

Mittasch, A. *Friedrich Nietzsche als Naturphilosoph*. Stuttgart, 1952.

Möbius, P. J. *Nietzsche: Ausgewählte Werke*, vol. 5. 3d ed. Leipzig, 1909.

Muckle, F. *Friedrich Nietzsche und der Zusammenbruch der Kultur*. Munich, 1921.

Muir, E. *Essays on Literature and Society*. London, 1949.

Müller, Joachim. "Faust und Faustus — Thomas Manns Roman und Goethes Tragödie." *Universitas: Zeitschrift für Wissenschaft, Kunst und Literatur* 16 (1961).

———. "Thomas Manns *Doktor Faustus*: Grundthematik und Motivgefüge." *Euphorion* 54 (1960): 731–43.

Müller-Blattau, J. M. "Die Musik in Thomas Manns 'Doktor Faustus' und Hermann Hesses 'Glasperlenspiel." *Annales Universitatis Saraviensis*, 2 (1953).

Muschg, W. *Tragische Literaturgeschichte*, 2d enl. ed. Bern, 1953.

Nadler, J. *Literaturgeschichte des Deutschen Volkes: Dichtung und Schrifttum der deutschen Stämme und Landschaften*, 4 vols. 4th completely rev. ed. Berlin, 1939–41.

Neider, C., ed. *The Stature of Thomas Mann*. New York, 1947.

Nemerov, H. "Thomas Mann's Faust Novel." In Nemerov, *Poetry and Fiction: Essays*. New Brunswick, N.J., 1963.

New Friends of Music: Program Book 1943–44, vol. 3. Carnegie Hall Series: Beethoven.

Newman, E. *Hugo Wolf*. London, 1907.

———. *The Unconscious Beethoven: An Essay in Musical Psychology*. Rev. ed., New York, 1930.

Nielsen, B. S. "Adrian Leverkühns Leben als bewusste mythische imitatio des Dr. Faustus." *Orbis Litterarum* 20 (1965).

Nietzsche, F. *The Complete Works*. Tr. A. Ludovici. Ed. O. Levy. Vols. 8, 15, 17. New York: 1911.

Oliver, K. "Two Unpublished Letters of Thomas Mann." Monatshefte 51 (1959).

Olschewski, H. " 'Doktor Faustus' von Thomas Mann: Struktur und Problematik eines modernen Romans." Ph.D. dissertation, Göttingen, 1954.

Orton, G. "The Archaic Language in Thomas Mann's 'Doktor Faustus.' " *Modern Language Review* 45 (1950).

Oswald, V. A. "Full Fathom Five: Notes on Some Devices in Thomas Mann's *Doktor Faustus.*" *GR* 24 (1949): 274–78.

———. "Thomas Mann and the Mermaid: a Note on Constructivistic Music," *MLN* 65 (1950): 171–75.

———. "Thomas Mann's *Doctor Faustus*: The Enigma of Frau von Tolna." *GR* 23 (1948): 249–53.

Petriconi, H. *Das Reich des Untergangs: Bemerkungen über ein mythologisches Thema.* Untersuchungen zur vergleichenden Literaturgeschichte, ed. R. Grossmann and H. Petriconi, I. Hamburg, 1958.

Pfitzner, H. *Die neue Aesthetik der musikalischen Impotenz: ein Verwesungssymptom?* Munich, 1920.

———. *Über musikalische Inspiration,* 2d enl. ed. Berlin/Grunewald, 1940.

Pickard, P. M. "Thomas Mann's *Dr. Faustus*: a Psychological Approach." GLL 4 (1950).

Pietsch, E.-M. "Thomas Mann und F. M. Dostojewski." Ph.D. dissertation, Leipzig, 1958.

Plöger, J. "Das Hermesmotiv in der Dichtung Thomas Manns." Ph.D. dissertation, Kiel, 1960.

Podach, E. F. *Gestalten um Nietzsche: mit unveröffentlichten Dokumenten zur Geschichte seines Lebens und seines Works.* Weimar, 1932.

———. *Nietzsches Zusammenbruch: Beiträge zu einer Biographie auf Grund unveröffentlichter Dokumente.* Heidelberg, 1930.

Politzer, H. "Of Time and Doctor Faustus." *Monatshefte* 51 (1959): 145–55.

Potter, R. D. "We Live Inside a Globe, Too." *American Weekly,* March 19, 1944, p. 4.

Prager Presse, [Aug., 1934?] "Die Wunder der Meerestiefe."

Prager Presse, Oct. 7, 1935, "Ecce Homo: Beethovens Gesprächsbücher erschienen."

Pringsheim, K. "Der Tonsetzer Adrian Leverkühn: ein Musiker über Thomas Manns Roman." *Der Monat* 1 (1949): 89.

Prinzhorn, H. *Nietzsche und das XX. Jahrhundert: zwei Reden.* Heidelberg, 1928.

Prinzing, W. *Stil der Schwebe im "Doktor Faustus."* Partial pub. of Ph.D. dissertation. Stuttgart, 1956.

Pütz, H. P. "Die teuflische Kunst des 'Doktor Faustus' bei Thomas Mann." *Zeitschrift für Deutsche Philologie* 82 (1963).

Redfield, J. *Music, a Science and an Art.* New York [1928], 1949.

Regula, E. C. "Die Darstellung und Problematik der Krankheit im Werke Thomas Manns." Ph.D. dissertation, Freiburg im Breisgau, 1952.

Reichert, H. W. "Goethe's *Faust* in Two Novels of Thomas Mann," *German Quarterly* 22 (1949): 213–14.

Reinhardt, K. *Nietzsches Klage der Ariadne.* Frankfurt am Main, 1936.

Reyburn, H. A. *Friedrich Nietzsche: ein Menschenleben und seine Philosophie.* Kempen-Niederrhein, 1947.

Rice, P. B. "The Merging Parallels: Mann's *Doctor Faustus,*" *Kenyon Review* 11 (1949).

Richter, B. *Thomas Manns Stellung zu Deutschlands Weg in die Katastrophe: ein Beitrag zum politischen Denken des Dichters.* Partial pub. of dissertation. Berlin, 1960.

Rochocz, H. "Thomas Manns 'Doktor Faustus' aus dem Geiste des Humors." *Deutsche Beiträge* 3 (1949).

Romanische Dichter. Tr. into German K. Vossler. 3rd ed., Munich, 1946.

Rubsamen, W. H. "Schoenberg in America." *Musical Quarterly* 37 (1951).

Rychner, M. "Thomas Mann und die Politik," *Hamburger Akademische Rundschau* 2 (1948).

Sagave, P.-P. *Réalité sociale et idéologie religieuse dans les romans de Thomas Mann: Les Buddenbrook, La montagne magique, Le Docteur Faustus.* Publications de la faculté des lettres de l'université de Strasbourg, Fasc. 124. Paris, 1954.

―――. "Zum Bild des Luthertums in Thomas Manns 'Doktor Faustus.'" *Sinn und Form,* 1965.

Schaper, E. "A Modern Faust: The Novel in the Ironic Key." *Orbis Litterarum* 20 (1965).

Scheible, J. *Das Kloster: weltlich und geistlich, meist aus der älteren deutschen Volks-, Wunder-, Curiositäten-, und vorzugsweise komischen Literatur. Zur Kultur- und Sittengeschichte in Wort und Bild,* vol. 5. Stuttgart, 1847.

―――. See also *Doktor Johannes Faust's Magia* . . .

Scherrer, P. "Thomas Mann und die Wirklichkeit." *Lübeckische Blätter* 120 (1960).

Schiller, F. *Gedichte. Sämtliche Werke* [Säkular-Ausgabe,] vol. 1. Stuttgart/Berlin, n.d.

Schindler, A. *Biographie von Ludwig van Beethoven.* Münster, 1840.

―――. *Anton Schindlers Beethoven-Biographie,* ed. A. C. Kalischer. Berlin, 1909.

Schneider, R. "Kurzer Nachruf auf Thomas Mann." *NR* 67 (1956).

Schönberg, A. See T. Mann, Works, "Thomas Mann's Answer."

Schopenhauer, A. *Two Essays by Arthur Schopenhauer.* Tr. Mme Karl Hillebrand. London, 1889.

Schubart, W. *Dostojewski und Nietzsche: Symbolik ihres Lebens.* Lucerne, 1939.

Schwerte, H. "Dürers 'Ritter, Tod und Teufel,' eine ideologische Parallele zum Faustischen." In Schwerte, *Faust und das Faustische: ein Kapitel deutscher Ideologie.* Stuttgart, 1962.

Seiferth, W. "Das deutsche Schicksal in Thomas Manns *Doktor Faustus.*" *Monatshefte* 41 (1949): 187–202.

Singer, S. *Sprichwörter des Mittelalters,* vols. 1 and 2. Bern, 1944–47.

Slochower, H. "The Devil of Many Faces: Man's Pact with the Evil One from the Volksbuch to Th. Mann." *Twelfth Street* 4 (1949): 196–204.

Sommer, J. *Dionysos: Friedrich Nietzsches Vermächtnis.* Vienna/Leipzig [1932], 1936.

Sontheimer, K. *Thomas Mann und die Deutschen.* Munich, 1961.

Sørensen, B. A. "Thomas Manns 'Doktor Faustus,' Mythos und Lebensbeichte." *Orbis Litterarum* 13 (1958).

Soergel, A. *Dichtung und Dichter der Zeit: eine Schilderung der deutschen Literatur der letzten Jahrzehnte.* Neue Folge. Vol. 2: *Im Banne des Expressionismus.* 6th ed., Leipzig, 1925.

Spengler, O. *The Decline of the West.* Tr. C. F. Atkinson, 2 vols. New York, 1926–28.

Sprichwörter des Mittelalters. See Singer, S.

Springer, B. *Die genialen Syphilitiker.* [1926] 2d–4th enl. ed., Berlin, 1933.

Stambauch, J. *Untersuchungen zum Problem der Zeit bei Nietzsche.* The Hague, 1959.

Stein, J. M. "Adrian Leverkühn as a Composer." *GR* 25 (1950).

Stewart, J. W. "On the Making of *Doctor Faustus.*" *Sewanee Review,* 59 (1951).

Stout, H. L. "Lessing's Riccaut and Thomas Mann's Fitelberg." *German Quarterly* 36 (1963).

Stravinsky, I. *Chronicle of My Life.* Tr. from the French. London, 1936.

Thieberger, R. *Der Begriff der Zeit bei Thomas Mann: vom Zauberberg zum Joseph.* Baden-Baden, 1952.

Thompson, D. "To Thomas Mann." In *The Stature of Thomas Mann,* ed. C. Neider. New York, 1947.

Tillich, P. "Aus den Materialien zum 'Doktor Faustus': Paul Tillichs Brief an Thomas Mann, 23. Mai 1943." *Blätter der Thomas Mann-Gesellschaft, Zurich,* no. 5 (1965).

Time, February 21, 1944. "Science."

Tuska, J. "The Vision of Doktor Faustus." *GR* 40 (1965).

Twentieth-Century Authors. First Supplement, ed. S. J. Kunitz. New York, 1955.

Venohr, L. *Thomas Manns Verhältnis zur russischen Literatur.* Frankfurter Abhandlungen zur Slavistik, vol. 1. Meisenheim am Glan, 1959.

Vierhundert Schwänke des sechzehnten Jahrhunderts. Ed. F. Bobertag. Deutsche National-Literatur, vol. 24. Berlin/Stuttgart, n.d.

Vogler, M. "Die Jenseitsvorstellungen vor Dante." *Neue Zürcher Zeitung,* December 1, 1945.

Volbach, F. *Das moderne Orchester: I. Die Instrumente des Orchesters: ihr Wesen und ihre Entwicklung.* 2d ed., Leipzig/Berlin, 1921.

Walter, B. *Theme and Variations: An Autobiography.* New York, 1946.

Waltershausen, H. W. von. *Der Freischütz: ein Versuch über die musikalische Romantik.* Munich, 1920.

Weber, C. M. von. *Der Freischütz: romantische Oper in drei Aufzügen.*

C. M. Weber's sämtliche Compositionen. Rev. and corrected H. W. Stolze. Wolfenbüttel, n.d.

Weigand, H. "Thomas Mann's Gregorius." *GR* 27 (1952).

Weigand, W. *Friedrich Nietzsche: ein psychologischer Versuch.* Munich, 1893.

Die Weltwoche, Nov. 12, 1943, article on Hindemith.

Die Weltwoche, n.d. "Neue Musik in Basel," signed "P. Mg."

Wescott, G. "Thomas Mann: Will Power and Fiction." In Wescott, *Images of Truth: Remembrances and Criticism.* New York, 1962.

White, A. "Die Verfluchten und die Gesegneten: eine Studie über die Helden Thomas Manns als Betreter des Verbotenen und Vertreter des Bösen." Ph.D. dissertation, Munich, 1960.

White, J. F. "Echo's Prayers in Thomas Mann's *Doctor Faustus.*" *Monatshefte* 42 (1950).

Williams, W. D. "Thomas Mann's Doctor Faustus." *GLL* 12 (1958–59).

Wirtz, E. "Zitat und Leitmotiv bei Thomas Mann." *GLL* 7 (1953–54): 126–36.

Wolf, H. *Hugo Wolfs Briefe an Oskar Grohe.* Ed. H. Werner. Berlin, 1905.

Wolff, H. M. *Thomas Mann: Werk und Bekenntnis.* Bern, 1957.

Wolffheim, H. "Das 'Interesse' als Geist der Erzählung: ein Beitrag zur Stilphysiognomie Thomas Manns." *Euphorion* 47 (1953).

Yourcenar, M. "Humanism in Thomas Mann." *Partisan Review* 23 (1956).

Zeuthen, L. *Soren Kierkegaards hemmelige Note.* Copenhagen, 1951.

UNPUBLISHED MATERIAL IN THE THOMAS MANN ARCHIVES, ZURICH

Adorno, T. Manuscript of the *Philosophie der neuen Musik,* typescript, 91 pp. (Corresponds to pp. 11–126 of the 1958 edition.)

Lesser, J. "Thomas Mann's 'Doktor Faustus' und Theodor Adorno's 'Philosophie der neuen Musik,' " typescript, 28 pp., dated London, 1951.

Letters to Thomas Mann from:
Michael Mann, dated July 6, 1943; May 22, 1945; May 29, 1945.
Paul Tillich, dated May 23, 1943.
Bruno Walter, dated May 31, 1943.

Mann, T. Manuscript of *Doktor Faustus,* typescript, 857 pp. Contains sections that were later deleted. Small handwritten revisions by Thomas Mann on the backs of the pages. Manuscript of the *Entstehung des Doktor Faustus (The Story of a Novel),* handwritten. Contains small passages later deleted.

"Musical articles from the Encyclopedia Britannica by Donald Francis Tovey." Typewritten list of titles of articles, made up by Michael Mann at the request of his father.

On Syphilis. Five handwritten pages in German describing the course of the disease. Written by an unknown hand (Martin Gumpert?) at Mann's request.

"Viola d'Amore Literature." Typewritten list with which Michael Mann provided his father.

Index of Names